NextGen Rights

The Ultimate Creator's Legal Playbook

by

Alander Pulliam

NextGen Rights

The Ultimate Creator's Legal Playbook, Volume 30

Alander Lee Pulliam Jr

Published by Alander Lee Pulliam Jr, 2025.

Table of Contents

Dedication

To Nosa — my brother, my fellow warrior, a gifted R&B singer, writer, and visionary entrepreneur.This journey is as much yours as it is mine. Your talent, resilience, and unwavering spirit continue to inspire me daily. You've shown me what it means to pursue your passion with relentless dedication, and I am forever grateful for your brotherhood, your faith, and your example.

To Peter Kessler — my brother in Christ, my confidant, my friend, my business partner, my right-hand man, and the most trusted person I know.Vibez — a brother, a friend, the hardest-working man I have ever met. Your loyalty, integrity, and tireless work ethic stand as a testament to the power of perseverance and brotherhood. You've been there through every challenge, every victory, and every moment of growth. Your unwavering support and genuine character have shaped me in ways words can't fully express.

To all of you — the warriors, the believers, the brothers in faith and purpose — this book is a reflection of the strength, endurance, and brotherhood we hold dear. It's dedicated to those who stand firm, work hard, and lift each other up, regardless of the obstacles we face.

This is a testament to the power of loyalty, faith, and brotherhood. I am honored to walk this path with you, and I dedicate this work to the legacy we are building together—one rooted in love, integrity, and relentless pursuit of excellence.

With all my heart,**Alander Pulliam**

Front Matter

This book is dedicated to every artist, athlete, and creator who dares to dream, to innovate, and to pour their heart and soul into their craft. It's for the musicians who pour their emotions into every note, the actors who embody characters with breathtaking vulnerability, and the athletes who push their physical and mental limits to achieve greatness. It's dedicated to those who relentlessly pursue their passions, often facing overwhelming odds and navigating a labyrinthine industry filled with complexities and potential pitfalls.

This work is also a tribute to the unsung heroes – the managers, agents, publicists, and, most importantly, the legal professionals who work tirelessly behind the scenes, often unnoticed, yet crucial to the success and protection of creative endeavors. They are the guardians of dreams, the navigators of legal waters, and the architects of successful careers. This book seeks to empower those who might not always have access to expensive legal counsel, providing a roadmap to navigate the intricate landscape of entertainment and sports law.

It's for the aspiring singer-songwriter in a small town, dreaming of a national tour; for the college athlete balancing academics with the pressure of potential endorsements; for the independent filmmaker shooting a masterpiece on a shoestring budget; for the podcast host building a community from their basement studio. This book is an investment in their futures, offering the knowledge and tools to protect their creative work, safeguard their financial well-being, and build sustainable, fulfilling careers.

This dedication is an acknowledgment of the hard work, dedication, and resilience required to thrive in these fiercely competitive industries. It is a testament to the importance of protecting one's intellectual property, securing fair compensation, and navigating the legal complexities that often overshadow the creative process. May this book serve as a beacon of knowledge, empowering creators and athletes to not only achieve their artistic goals but also to secure their rightful place in the world, and the lasting legacy of their achievements. Finally, this book is dedicated to the ongoing pursuit of justice and fairness within the entertainment and sports industries – a pursuit that remains a vital part of ensuring a thriving and equitable creative landscape for generations to come.

Chapter 1: The Entertainment and Sports Legal Landscape

The entertainment and sports industries, while seemingly glamorous and exciting, operate within a complex web of legal frameworks. Understanding this framework is crucial for anyone hoping to build a successful and sustainable career in these fields. Ignoring the legal aspects can lead to exploitation, lost revenue, and protracted legal battles that drain both time and resources. This section provides a foundational understanding of the key legal areas impacting creators and athletes, setting the stage for the more detailed explorations in subsequent chapters.

At the heart of protecting creative work lies

copyright law. This protects original works of authorship, including literary, dramatic, musical, and certain other intellectual works. For musicians, this means their songs, both the musical composition and the sound recording, are protected. For writers, it encompasses books, screenplays, and articles. Visual artists rely on copyright to protect their paintings, sculptures, and photographs. Copyright protection arises automatically upon creation of the work, but registration with the U.S. Copyright Office provides significant advantages, including the ability to sue for statutory damages and attorney's fees if your copyright is infringed. Understanding the nuances of copyright, such as fair use and derivative works, is essential for navigating the complexities of collaboration and licensing. A poorly understood copyright agreement can lead to significant financial losses or even the loss of control over your creative output.

Complementing copyright is

trademark law. Trademarks protect brand names, logos, and other source identifiers, distinguishing goods and services from one another in the marketplace. For athletes, this could mean protecting their name and logo associated with endorsements or personal brands. Musicians use trademarks to protect their stage names, album art, and unique branding elements. A strong trademark portfolio helps build brand recognition and prevents others from using similar marks that could confuse consumers or dilute the value of your brand. The process of registering a trademark involves careful research to ensure the mark is not already in use and compliance with various regulations, making expert legal guidance highly advisable.

Contract law forms the bedrock of most transactions in the entertainment and sports industries. From recording contracts to endorsement deals, licensing agreements to publishing contracts, nearly every professional undertaking involves a contract. Understanding the fundamental elements of a contract – offer, acceptance, consideration, and capacity – is crucial. A seemingly simple agreement can contain clauses with significant legal implications. For example, a poorly drafted recording contract might inadvertently grant a record label excessive control over an artist's creative output or unfairly restrict their financial compensation. Understanding clauses concerning ownership of master recordings, royalty structures, and termination rights is paramount. Many artists have found themselves locked into unfavorable contracts with little recourse, highlighting the critical need for legal review before signing anything. This extends beyond the initial agreement; the process of negotiating contract renewals, addenda, and riders requires a deep understanding of contract law and the ability to advocate for your rights.

The **regulatory landscape** adds another layer of complexity. Different regulatory bodies govern different aspects of the industry. For example, the Federal Communications Commission (FCC) regulates broadcasting, while the Federal Trade Commission (FTC) enforces advertising regulations, including those pertaining to endorsements. The National Collegiate Athletic Association (NCAA) imposes strict rules regarding student-athlete compensation, with recent changes in Name, Image, and Likeness (NIL) rules significantly altering the legal landscape for college athletes. International treaties and conventions also play a role in protecting intellectual property rights across borders. Keeping abreast of these evolving regulations requires staying informed about industry trends and legal updates. Ignoring regulatory compliance can lead to hefty fines or legal repercussions.

The intersection of these legal areas is where many challenges arise. For instance, a musician might need to navigate copyright issues related to sampling, trademark issues related to branding, and contract issues related to recording and publishing deals, all simultaneously. An athlete might face complexities surrounding their NIL rights, endorsement contracts, and image rights, requiring a nuanced understanding of the regulatory environment as well. The legal framework is not merely a set of rules to be followed but a dynamic system that demands awareness and adaptation.

The concept of **intellectual property (IP)** rights is pivotal to understanding the legal landscape. This encompasses copyright, trademarks, patents, and trade secrets. In the entertainment industry, IP represents the tangible and intangible assets that drive revenue and influence career trajectories. Music is an excellent example; it's not only the composition itself (protected by copyright) but also the sound recording (also protected by copyright) that creates value. The artist's brand and logo are safeguarded by trademark protection. Properly managing IP requires diligent registration and protection, preventing unauthorized use and ensuring maximum commercial exploitation of creative works. Failing to understand the nuances of IP could result in significant financial loss, legal battles, and loss of control over one's artistic creation.

Beyond the core legal areas, several other legal considerations impact creators and athletes. These include privacy rights, defamation, and rights of publicity, each presenting unique challenges in the public eye. Privacy rights protect individuals from the unauthorized disclosure of personal information. Defamation law deals with false statements that damage reputation. The rights of publicity protect an individual's right to control the commercial use of their name, image, and likeness. In today's digital age, navigating these issues is more critical than ever, especially given the pervasiveness of social media and online platforms.

The complexities of the legal framework necessitate professional legal counsel. Building a strong legal team, including a skilled entertainment lawyer and potentially a business manager, is an investment that pays significant dividends in the long run. The expertise of legal professionals offers crucial guidance in contract negotiation, intellectual property protection, and dispute resolution. A well-informed legal team is not just a reactive entity dealing with crises but also a proactive force guiding strategic decision-making throughout an individual's career. This proactive approach minimizes risk and maximizes opportunities, ensuring a sustainable and successful path in the dynamic worlds of entertainment and sports. Ultimately, a deep understanding of the legal landscape empowers creators and athletes to take control of their careers, protecting their creative work, securing their financial future, and building a legacy of success.

Contract law is the lifeblood of the entertainment and sports industries. Every deal, from a multi-million dollar endorsement to a seemingly insignificant gig, rests on a contract. Understanding its fundamentals is not merely advantageous; it's essential for survival in these fiercely competitive fields. This section will dissect the core principles of contract law, illustrating their practical applications through real-world examples and hypothetical scenarios.

The foundation of any valid contract rests on four pillars: offer, acceptance, consideration, and capacity. An

offer is a clear and definite proposal to enter into a contract. It must be specific enough to leave no room for ambiguity regarding the terms. A vague suggestion isn't an offer; a precise, detailed proposal is. Imagine a record label contacting a musician: a casual inquiry about their music is not an offer; a detailed proposal outlining specific terms like album release dates, royalty percentages, and promotional commitments constitutes a legally sound offer.

Acceptance is the unqualified agreement to the terms of the offer. A simple "yes" might suffice in some contexts, but typically, acceptance involves a formal signing of the contract or a written confirmation mirroring the offered terms precisely. Any changes, even seemingly minor ones, constitute a counter-offer, effectively nullifying the original offer and initiating a fresh negotiation cycle. Consider an athlete negotiating an endorsement deal; accepting the company's initial offer means agreeing to every detail, including the length of the contract, the payment schedule, and any restrictions on their public image.

Consideration is the exchange of value between the parties involved. This doesn't necessarily mean monetary value; it could be anything of legal value, such as a promise to perform a service, provide a good, or refrain from doing something. In a recording contract, the record label's consideration might be to invest in recording, producing, and marketing the artist's music, while the artist's consideration is their promise to deliver the recordings and participate in promotional activities. An athlete's consideration in an endorsement deal is their image and endorsement, while the company's consideration is the payment and other benefits.

Finally,

capacity refers to the legal ability of the parties to enter into a contract. Individuals must be of legal age and possess the mental capacity to understand the terms and consequences of their actions. Minors typically lack the capacity to enter binding contracts, while individuals deemed legally incompetent due to mental illness or incapacitation are also excluded. This is particularly important in the entertainment industry, where young artists may be pressured into signing contracts without fully grasping the implications. Their legal guardians or representatives must play a vital role in protecting their interests.

Beyond these fundamental elements, several other crucial aspects govern contract law.

Legality is paramount; contracts involving illegal activities are void. *Mutual assent*, or a "meeting of the minds," ensures both parties understand and agree on the terms. *Unconscionability* refers to contracts that are so unfair or one-sided as to be unenforceable. Courts will scrutinize contracts to ensure they are fair and reasonable, striking down those deemed exploitative. For instance, a contract forcing an artist to perpetually relinquish all rights to their work for a pittance would likely be deemed unconscionable.

Contract interpretation is another critical area. Ambiguity within a contract can lead to disputes. Courts generally favor interpretations that uphold the contract's validity and intent. Careful drafting and the use of precise language are vital in avoiding ambiguities. However, even meticulously drafted contracts can face challenges.

Breach of contract occurs when one party fails to fulfill their contractual obligations. The remedies for a breach can range from monetary damages to specific performance, depending on the circumstances and the severity of the breach. For instance, a record label breaching its contract by failing to promote an artist's album could be liable for significant monetary damages.

Negotiating contracts requires skill, knowledge, and often, legal representation. The initial negotiation phase is crucial; the better the negotiation, the stronger the contract. It's common for a negotiation to involve multiple drafts and extensive back-and-forth between the parties. A strong negotiator knows how to identify weaknesses in the opposing party's offer, while effectively advocating for their own interests. Having a lawyer involved can be invaluable during this stage, ensuring the terms protect the client's rights and maximize their potential benefits.

Let's look at some real-world examples. The recording industry has witnessed numerous instances of artists entering unfavorable contracts. In some cases, artists have signed away their master recording rights to their label, only to realize later they forfeit considerable long-term income streams. The rise of streaming services further highlights this issue, as artists' revenue often lags behind the service's significant profits. Negotiating a contract to retain master rights is crucial, allowing the artist to control their music's use and benefit financially from its ongoing success.

Another example concerns endorsement deals. Athletes may receive large upfront payments, but the contract may contain clauses restricting their ability to endorse competing products, thus limiting their future earning potential. A lawyer can review the contract to ensure the terms are fair, clear and protect against such limitations.

Conversely, there are examples of successful contract negotiations. The recent advancements in Name, Image, and Likeness (NIL) rights for college athletes have resulted in lucrative endorsement opportunities. These deals showcase the power of careful negotiation; well-advised athletes are securing beneficial terms that not only provide financial compensation but also protect their long-term image and brand value.

Navigating contract law isn't just about avoiding pitfalls; it's about maximizing opportunities. Understanding the nuances of contract law empowers individuals to secure favorable deals, protect their intellectual property, and build sustainable careers in entertainment and sports. It's about more than just signing on the dotted line; it's about shaping the future of your career through informed and strategic legal navigation. A proactive, well-informed approach is the key to unlocking success and ensuring a long-term, rewarding career in the dynamic world of entertainment and sports. The power is in your hands, but leveraging that power effectively requires a comprehensive understanding of contract law and its implications. And finally, remember, when in doubt, consult an experienced entertainment lawyer—a crucial step in securing your future.

Protecting your creative work is paramount in the entertainment and sports industries. Your ideas, your music, your performances, your brand – they are all valuable assets, and understanding how to protect them through intellectual property (IP) rights is crucial for long-term success. This isn't just about avoiding legal battles; it's about strategically leveraging your IP to maximize your earning potential and build a sustainable career. This section will delve into the three primary forms of IP protection: copyright, patents, and trademarks.

Copyright law safeguards original works of authorship, including literary, dramatic, musical, and artistic works, as well as motion pictures, sound recordings, and architectural works. The moment you create an original work and fix it in a tangible medium of expression (like writing a song, painting a picture, or filming a video), copyright protection generally attaches automatically. However, registering your copyright with the U.S. Copyright Office offers significant advantages. Registration provides legal proof of ownership, allowing you to pursue more substantial remedies in case of infringement. It also establishes a public record of your copyright claim, potentially deterring others from infringing on your work. Furthermore, registration is a prerequisite for bringing a copyright infringement lawsuit in many jurisdictions.

The scope of copyright protection is broad, encompassing the expression of an idea, not the idea itself. This means you can't copyright the concept of a superhero, for example, but you can copyright the specific portrayal of that superhero in your comic book or film. Copyright protection generally lasts for the life of the author plus 70 years, or, for corporate works, for 95 years from publication or 120 years from creation, whichever is shorter. During this period, you have exclusive rights to reproduce, distribute, display, perform, and create derivative works based on your copyrighted material. This means you control how your work is used and can license or sell those rights to others. Failing to register your copyright doesn't negate your rights, but it significantly limits your options in the event of infringement.

Consider a musician who composes a song. Their copyright protects the melody, lyrics, and overall arrangement of the song. This protection extends to recordings of the song as well, though sound recordings receive their own separate copyright protection. Unauthorized reproduction, distribution, or public performance of the song constitutes copyright infringement. This could include unauthorized downloads, streaming, or use in a film or television show. Similarly, a filmmaker's copyright protects their film's script, visuals, and soundtrack. Using scenes, dialogue, or even specific shots without permission can constitute infringement. An athlete's choreography created for a routine can also be copyrighted.

Let's explore a hypothetical scenario. Imagine a young artist creating a series of digital paintings. They decide to showcase their work on social media, and soon another artist begins producing highly similar paintings, profiting from their popularity. If the young artist has registered their copyright, they have a strong legal basis to demand the infringing artist cease and desist, seek monetary damages for lost profits, and potentially pursue legal action. However, without registration, their recourse is considerably limited. This underscores the critical importance of proactive copyright protection.

Patents, unlike copyrights, protect inventions. In the entertainment and sports industries, patents might apply to new technologies or equipment used in creating or delivering entertainment content. For instance, a new type of camera designed for high-speed filming in sports could be patentable. However, patents are generally more complex to obtain than copyrights. A patent application requires a detailed description of the invention, including its unique features and how it functions. The patent office rigorously examines the application to ensure the invention is novel, useful, and non-obvious. If approved, a patent grants exclusive rights to the inventor, allowing them to exclude others from making, using, or selling the invention for a specified period, usually 20 years from the date of application.

Trademarks, on the other hand, protect brand names, logos, and other branding elements that distinguish goods and services in the marketplace. In the entertainment world, this is crucial. Think of the recognizable logos of major studios or the names of popular television shows and characters. These are valuable trademarks that help consumers identify and connect with particular brands. Trademark registration provides significant benefits, including the exclusive right to use the trademark in connection with the specified goods and services, the ability to prevent others from using confusingly similar trademarks, and potential legal recourse against infringement.

Consider a professional athlete who develops a unique brand name and logo for their clothing line. Registering this trademark prevents others from using a similar name or logo, protecting their brand identity and preventing consumer confusion. Similarly, a musician may trademark their stage name or a distinctive logo associated with their music. This not only protects their brand, but it also increases its value and marketability. As with copyrights, registering your trademark is a proactive step toward protecting your brand identity. Without registration, you may find it significantly harder to protect yourself against potential infringements.

Beyond these core forms of IP protection, there are other relevant considerations. Moral rights, for example, grant creators certain rights related to the integrity of their work, such as the right to be attributed as the author and the right to prevent derogatory treatment of their work. The specific availability of moral rights varies across jurisdictions. Furthermore, the digital age presents unique challenges and opportunities in IP protection. Digital rights management (DRM) technologies help control the distribution and use of digital content, but these technologies are constantly evolving in response to technological advancements and legal challenges.

Understanding and leveraging your IP rights is a crucial part of building a successful career in entertainment and sports. It's not simply a matter of reacting to infringement; it's about proactively protecting your valuable creative assets. This requires strategic planning, comprehensive documentation, and, ideally, the guidance of an experienced entertainment lawyer. They can advise you on the best way to protect your specific works, navigate the intricacies of registration processes, and effectively enforce your rights in case of infringement. The proactive approach to intellectual property is not just about preventing legal issues; it's about building a strong foundation for your career, ensuring your creativity is rewarded, and maximizing your earning potential in a competitive and ever-evolving landscape. Remember, your creative work is your most valuable asset; safeguarding it effectively is not an optional extra, but an essential part of your overall business strategy. Invest in understanding the legal tools available to protect your work, and you'll be better equipped to build a sustainable and successful career.

The digital revolution has fundamentally reshaped the entertainment and sports industries, creating unprecedented opportunities for creators and athletes to reach global audiences. However, this shift has also introduced new complexities in managing and protecting intellectual property rights. Digital rights management (DRM) has become a critical aspect of navigating this new landscape, ensuring creators retain control over their work and receive appropriate compensation for its use.

The traditional methods of protecting intellectual property, while still relevant, are insufficient in the digital realm. Physical copies of music albums or films are easily duplicated; digital content, however, can be copied and distributed virtually effortlessly across the internet. This ease of replication necessitates robust digital rights management strategies to safeguard creators' interests. DRM encompasses a range of technologies and legal agreements designed to control access to and use of digital content. These technologies can range from simple password protection to sophisticated encryption methods, preventing unauthorized copying, distribution, and modification.

Streaming platforms like Spotify, Apple Music, Netflix, and Hulu represent a significant portion of content consumption. These platforms operate under complex licensing agreements with rights holders, dictating how their content can be accessed and utilized. Negotiating favorable terms in these agreements is crucial for creators, ensuring they receive a fair share of the revenue generated from streaming. These agreements typically specify the scope of the license (e.g., geographic restrictions, duration), the royalty rates, and the reporting mechanisms. Without careful consideration of these contractual terms, creators risk undercompensation and potential exploitation. A skilled entertainment lawyer can help artists navigate these complexities, ensuring they are not disadvantaged by complex contracts.

Social media platforms, such as YouTube, TikTok, Instagram, and Facebook, present another layer of complexity in digital rights management. While these platforms offer opportunities for creators to build their brands and reach vast audiences, they also present significant challenges in terms of unauthorized use and copyright infringement. Users frequently share, remix, and repurpose content without the creators' permission. Understanding the terms of service of each platform and proactively asserting copyright claims are crucial to protecting work in this context. Many platforms provide mechanisms for creators to claim ownership of their content and to report infringement. However, navigating these processes can be challenging, and legal advice is often recommended.

Consider the case of a musician who uploads their original song to YouTube. While the platform's copyright system helps identify and address unauthorized uses, the musician must actively monitor their content, report infringement, and potentially pursue legal action against persistent offenders. This necessitates a proactive approach, involving regular checks for copyright infringement and effective communication with the platform's support systems.

Beyond social media, the proliferation of peer-to-peer file-sharing networks and torrent sites presents a considerable threat to digital rights management. These platforms facilitate the unauthorized distribution of copyrighted material, undermining creators' ability to control and profit from their work. While legal efforts to combat these platforms are ongoing, they continue to pose a persistent challenge.

The use of digital watermarking technologies is also an important aspect of DRM. These technologies embed unique digital signatures into content, making it easier to trace unauthorized copies back to their source. This aids in identifying infringers and holding them accountable. However, the effectiveness of watermarking technologies varies depending on the sophistication of the technology and the efforts made to remove the watermarks. Therefore, a multi-faceted approach to DRM is necessary.

Another important aspect is the use of encryption technology to protect digital content from unauthorized access. Strong encryption methods can prevent unauthorized copying and distribution, but the effectiveness of encryption is constantly challenged by advances in decryption techniques. This constant arms race between creators seeking to protect their work and those seeking to bypass DRM measures highlights the ongoing need for vigilance and adaptation.

The legal framework surrounding digital rights management is constantly evolving, influenced by technological advancements and legal challenges. International copyright laws vary, creating complexities in managing rights across different jurisdictions. This necessitates a comprehensive understanding of both domestic and international laws to ensure adequate protection.

The importance of strong contracts in the digital age cannot be overstated. Digital contracts should clearly define the scope of rights granted, the permitted uses of the content, the royalty rates, the duration of the agreement, and the dispute resolution mechanism. These contracts must be carefully drafted and reviewed by legal professionals to protect the interests of creators. Ambiguous or poorly drafted contracts can lead to disputes and potentially substantial financial losses.

Furthermore, understanding and leveraging the protections offered under the Digital Millennium Copyright Act (DMCA) is critical for creators. The DMCA provides legal recourse against those who circumvent copyright protection measures or facilitate copyright infringement. However, effectively utilizing the DMCA requires a thorough understanding of its provisions and procedures. Misunderstanding the DMCA could compromise a creator's ability to protect their work.

For athletes, the digital landscape opens new avenues for endorsements, sponsorships, and building personal brands. However, these opportunities come with the responsibility of carefully managing their image and likeness rights in the digital sphere. Athletes must be vigilant about unauthorized use of their images and names in advertisements, social media posts, and other online content. This requires strong contracts with sponsors and agents, as well as a proactive approach to monitoring their online presence and addressing any unauthorized use. NIL (Name, Image, and Likeness) rights have become increasingly important for college athletes. Understanding these rights and establishing strong agreements with relevant parties are essential.

The future of digital rights management will likely involve the use of blockchain technology, artificial intelligence, and other advanced technologies to enhance security and streamline processes. These technologies hold the potential to simplify rights management, automate royalty payments, and improve enforcement against copyright infringement. However, these technological advancements also introduce new challenges, as the potential for abuse and unintended consequences must be carefully considered.

In conclusion, digital rights management is a complex and multifaceted field. Creators and athletes must adopt a proactive approach, developing comprehensive strategies that encompass robust contracts, technological safeguards, and a strong understanding of relevant legal frameworks. Seeking the advice of an experienced entertainment lawyer is essential to navigating this complex landscape, ensuring creators are able to protect their work, maximize their earnings, and build sustainable careers in the ever-evolving digital age. Ignoring the legal and technological aspects of DRM can have significant financial and reputational consequences. A thorough understanding of these principles is paramount to succeeding in the modern entertainment and sports landscape.

Building a strong legal foundation is not merely a matter of signing contracts; it's about cultivating a proactive and strategic approach to managing your career's legal aspects. This involves more than just reacting to problems as they arise; it's about anticipating potential challenges and building a robust defense against them. A key element of this proactive approach is assembling a skilled and reliable legal team.

Finding the right entertainment lawyer is crucial. Don't just settle for the first name you find; thoroughly research potential candidates. Look for lawyers with a proven track record in the specific area of entertainment or sports law relevant to your field. Specialization matters. A lawyer experienced in music contracts might not be the best fit for a professional athlete negotiating an endorsement deal. Consider their experience with similar clients, their success rate in negotiations and litigation, and their communication style. Do they respond promptly to your inquiries? Do they explain legal concepts in a clear and concise manner, making complex information accessible?

Beyond finding an exceptional lawyer, consider assembling a broader advisory team. This team might include a business manager, an accountant, and a publicist, all working in synergy to optimize your career's financial and public image. Your lawyer can offer advice on structuring your business affairs, ensuring you're operating in a legally sound and tax-efficient manner. A good accountant can help navigate the complexities of royalty payments, tax deductions, and investment strategies. A savvy business manager can provide guidance on financial planning, contract negotiation, and overall business strategy. The publicist can help manage your public image and media relations, preventing potential legal pitfalls that can arise from missteps in public statements or social media activity.

The synergistic nature of this team is crucial. Your lawyer, accountant, and business manager should communicate regularly to ensure consistency in legal, financial, and strategic planning. This collaborative approach provides a comprehensive safety net, minimizing the potential for conflicts of interest and maximizing the effectiveness of your overall strategy. For example, your business manager might identify a lucrative sponsorship opportunity, but your lawyer will help negotiate the contract, ensuring it protects your image and likeness rights and secures favorable financial terms. Simultaneously, your accountant will ensure the financial aspects of the deal are properly structured for tax optimization.

The value of this team extends beyond individual expertise; it provides a vital support system. The entertainment and sports industries are notoriously demanding, characterized by intense pressure, rapidly shifting trends, and complex legal challenges. Having a reliable and supportive team can provide a crucial buffer, allowing you to focus on your craft and performance without being overwhelmed by the logistical and legal intricacies of your career. This emotional and professional support is invaluable, especially during stressful periods such as contract negotiations or legal disputes.

Furthermore, building a strong legal foundation necessitates a deep understanding of your own rights and responsibilities. This involves familiarizing yourself with the fundamental principles of contract law, intellectual property rights, and the legal landscape specific to your industry. While your lawyer will handle the intricacies of legal documents, understanding the basic principles empowers you to participate actively in negotiations and decision-making. This knowledge fosters informed consent, ensuring you're not simply signing contracts blindly but making deliberate choices based on a solid understanding of their implications.

Don't underestimate the power of preventive measures. Proactively addressing potential legal risks can significantly minimize the chances of future disputes. This includes carefully reviewing all contracts before signing, ensuring you fully understand their terms and conditions. Seek clarification on any ambiguous clauses and don't hesitate to request revisions if necessary. Don't feel pressured to sign anything you don't fully comprehend. A well-crafted contract is a vital safeguard, protecting your rights and interests.

The same principle applies to intellectual property protection. Register your copyrights and trademarks proactively to prevent infringement and establish clear ownership of your creative works. This proactive approach can save you significant time, effort, and potential legal expenses in the long run. It's significantly easier and more cost-effective to address potential infringement early on than to engage in costly litigation later.

Another vital aspect of building a strong legal foundation is understanding your rights related to unions or guilds. Many creative industries have unions that protect the rights and interests of their members, providing collective bargaining power and advocating for fair compensation and working conditions. Joining a relevant union can provide substantial protection, especially when negotiating contracts with larger organizations.

Similarly, athletes may have union representation through their respective leagues or associations. Understanding the rights and protections offered by these organizations is crucial for negotiating favorable contracts and advocating for fair treatment. Negotiating contracts requires understanding not just your rights but also your leverage. The strength of your negotiating position is partly determined by your preparedness and your understanding of your worth. A strong legal team will be instrumental in helping you determine your market value and craft a contract that reflects it.

Finally, remember that building a strong legal foundation is an ongoing process, not a one-time event. Your legal needs will evolve as your career progresses. Regular consultations with your legal team are essential to address emerging challenges and adapt your strategies to the ever-changing landscape of the entertainment and sports industries. This proactive approach, coupled with a strong legal team and personal understanding of your legal rights, forms the bedrock of a successful and sustainable career. It's an investment in your future, protecting your creative work, securing your financial well-being, and allowing you to focus on what matters most: your craft and your passion. Neglecting this foundation can lead to costly mistakes, disputes, and potentially the derailment of your entire career. The proactive construction of a strong legal foundation is the cornerstone of long-term success in these demanding and competitive industries.

Chapter 2: Contract Negotiation and Deal Making

Understanding the intricacies of contract clauses is paramount to navigating the entertainment and sports industries successfully. These clauses, often buried within dense legal jargon, hold the keys to your financial security, creative control, and overall career trajectory. This section will dissect some of the most crucial contract clauses, providing you with the knowledge to negotiate favorable terms and protect your interests.

Let's begin with the

payment clause, arguably the most significant aspect of any contract. This clause details how and when you'll be compensated for your services. It's not simply about the total amount; it's about the structure of payments. Are you receiving an upfront payment, or are payments staggered over time? Are there milestones that need to be met before payments are released? What happens if the project is delayed or cancelled? Consider the case of a musician signing a recording contract. A poorly negotiated payment clause might result in minimal upfront payments, leaving the artist vulnerable if the album doesn't sell well. A strong payment clause would secure a substantial advance, ensuring financial stability regardless of the album's commercial success. Furthermore, the clause should clearly define the different types of royalties, such as mechanical royalties (for physical copies), digital royalties (for downloads and streams), and performance royalties (for public performances). Negotiating a favorable royalty rate is critical, as it represents a significant portion of your long-term earnings.

Next, we delve into the

term and termination clause. This clause outlines the duration of the contract and the conditions under which it can be terminated. For athletes, this often includes the length of their contract with a team or sponsor. In the entertainment world, it might define the period of exclusivity with a record label or talent agency. Critically, the clause must specify the circumstances under which either party can terminate the contract. It's essential to ensure that the termination process is fair and provides sufficient notice, preventing abrupt contract cancellations that could leave you in a precarious position. Consider a situation where an actor signs a multi-year film contract. The termination clause should clearly define what constitutes a breach of contract by either party, stipulating consequences such as compensation for lost opportunities. Furthermore, it should address the possibility of the project being canceled due to unforeseen circumstances, providing a clear mechanism for resolving such situations. A well-drafted termination clause will provide a safety net, minimizing potential disputes and ensuring a smooth resolution in case of unforeseen issues.

The

rights and ownership clause is another critical area. This clause outlines who owns the intellectual property rights associated with the work. For musicians, this could include the rights to their songs, recordings, and performances. For athletes, it might relate to their image and likeness rights. This section of the contract is a minefield of potential conflicts and needs meticulous attention. A poorly drafted clause could inadvertently transfer ownership of valuable intellectual property to a third party, limiting your control over your creative works. Imagine a situation where a screenwriter sells a script to a production company. The contract should explicitly define ownership of the script, including derivative works and future adaptations. Clarification on rights to sequels, remakes, merchandise, and any other possible exploitations of the intellectual property is essential. Ambiguity in this area can lead to costly litigation and significant financial losses. Thus, having a skilled entertainment lawyer review and negotiate this clause is paramount.

The

morality clause is becoming increasingly common in entertainment contracts. This clause allows the contracting party to terminate the agreement if the other party engages in conduct that damages their public image or reputation. This clause, however, requires careful consideration and precise drafting, ensuring it's not overly broad or vaguely defined. An overly broad morality clause can infringe on an individual's freedom of speech or expression, creating an unfair power imbalance. For example, a record label might use a morality clause to terminate an artist's contract for controversial social media posts, even if those posts are protected under free speech principles. Conversely, a well-defined morality clause, clearly outlining specific actions that constitute a breach of contract, provides a necessary level of protection for the contracting party without jeopardizing the artist's rights. The clause should be specific and unambiguous, listing specific behaviors that could justify termination.

Confidentiality clauses are vital in protecting sensitive information shared during contract negotiations. These clauses prevent the disclosure of confidential information, such as financial details, business strategies, or creative plans. Breaches of confidentiality can lead to significant legal repercussions, especially in the context of sensitive information like financial details or artistic ideas. Such clauses are particularly crucial in deals involving intellectual property, brand secrets, or other sensitive information. The breach of confidentiality can result in legal battles and financial damage to the affected party.

Indemnification clauses are another area that warrants close examination. These clauses outline the responsibility for covering legal expenses and damages arising from breaches of contract or other legal issues. A strong indemnification clause will protect you from potential financial liability, providing a level of security in case of unexpected disputes. This is especially critical in projects with multiple parties involved. For instance, if a movie production encounters legal issues related to copyright infringement, the indemnification clause determines which party bears the responsibility for the resulting legal fees and damages.

Arbitration clauses specify the method of dispute resolution. Instead of traditional court litigation, arbitration offers a more private and often faster process for resolving disputes. While arbitration offers a quicker resolution, it's crucial to ensure the selection process for the arbitrator is unbiased and mutually agreeable. A biased arbitrator could render unfair decisions, jeopardizing your rights and interests.

Finally, the

governing law clause specifies which jurisdiction's laws will govern the interpretation and enforcement of the contract. This is especially important for international contracts, ensuring consistency and clarity regarding legal procedures. This clause needs careful consideration, as choosing a jurisdiction with favorable laws could significantly impact the outcome of disputes.

Each of these clauses plays a crucial role in shaping the terms and conditions of your contracts. Understanding their implications and negotiating favorable terms is essential to protecting your interests and building a successful and sustainable career in the entertainment and sports industries. The legal landscape is complex and ever-evolving; thus, expert guidance from a skilled entertainment lawyer is invaluable in navigating these treacherous waters. The investment in legal counsel is an investment in the longevity and success of your career. Don't underestimate the power of a well-negotiated contract in securing your future.

Negotiating favorable terms isn't simply about understanding the clauses; it's about wielding that knowledge effectively. Preparation is the cornerstone of any successful negotiation. Before even entering a meeting, you need a clear understanding of your own value. What are your unique skills, talents, and market position? What are your non-negotiables? What are you willing to compromise on? Thoroughly research the other party. Understand their needs, their limitations, and their past dealings. This information will give you a significant advantage at the negotiating table.

Let's consider a hypothetical scenario. Imagine a rising musician, let's call her Anya, negotiating her first recording contract with a major label. Anya has spent years honing her craft, building a dedicated online following, and generating considerable buzz through independent releases. She knows her music is unique and has significant potential. Before entering negotiations, Anya meticulously researches the label's history, examining previous artist contracts to understand their typical royalty rates, advance structures, and marketing budgets. She also gathers data on streaming numbers and album sales for artists with comparable popularity to assess her own market value. Armed with this knowledge, Anya can approach negotiations from a position of strength.

During the negotiation, Anya doesn't shy away from asking pointed questions. She probes for specifics about marketing plans, release schedules, and creative input opportunities. She doesn't accept vague promises; she pushes for clear, measurable commitments. When the label suggests a low royalty rate, Anya presents her research, demonstrating that her projected sales justify a higher percentage. She also negotiates for stronger creative control, ensuring that her artistic vision isn't compromised. She's not afraid to push back when necessary, but she also remains flexible and collaborative, seeking mutually beneficial solutions. Anya's meticulous preparation and assertive yet collaborative approach lead to a significantly more favorable contract than she might have achieved otherwise.

Another critical aspect of negotiation is understanding your leverage. What can you offer the other party that they desperately need or want? For a musician, it might be a substantial existing fanbase or a unique and highly marketable musical style. For an athlete, it could be exceptional talent, endorsements, or a high-profile brand image. Leverage isn't always about power; it can also be about scarcity and opportunity. A writer with a unique narrative and proven track record could have considerable leverage in a competitive market.

Let's examine a different scenario. A young, promising athlete, let's call him Ben, is negotiating an endorsement deal with a major sports brand. Ben's performance has caught the eye of multiple sponsors, creating a competitive environment. He strategically leverages this competition, presenting offers from rival brands to demonstrate the significant market demand for his endorsement. He is prepared to walk away from the deal if the initial offer doesn't meet his expectations, showing that he is not desperate for the deal. His willingness to walk away bolsters his bargaining power and ultimately leads to a more lucrative endorsement agreement. This demonstrates that a well-timed "walk away" is a powerful negotiating tool.

Knowing when to walk away from a bad deal is equally crucial. Sometimes, accepting a less-than-ideal contract, while tempting in the short term, can have long-term repercussions. A poor contract can stifle your creative growth, limit your earning potential, or even trap you in an unfavorable business relationship. Walking away might seem like a setback, but it's often a necessary step toward securing a better outcome in the long run.

Imagine a filmmaker, let's call her Chloe, negotiating distribution rights for her latest independent film. A distributor offers a contract with low upfront payments and minimal creative control. While this offer might seem appealing initially, Chloe carefully evaluates the long-term implications. She recognizes that this contract will restrict her ability to leverage future marketing opportunities and may limit the film's overall reach. After careful deliberation, Chloe declines the offer and continues to seek alternative distribution channels, eventually finding a more suitable agreement that allows for greater creative freedom and a more equitable revenue sharing model.

Effective negotiation is a multi-faceted process that involves strategic preparation, knowing your leverage, effectively presenting your case, and having the courage to walk away from a bad deal. This skillset, when honed, is an invaluable asset for any creative professional in the entertainment and sports industries.

Negotiation often involves skillful communication. It's not just about stating your demands; it's about building rapport, finding common ground, and crafting a mutually beneficial agreement. Effective communication involves active listening, clearly articulating your needs and concerns, and responding thoughtfully to the other party's proposals.

Consider a scenario where a playwright, David, is negotiating the terms of a production contract with a theatre company. David clearly explains his vision for the production and emphasizes the unique aspects of his play. He actively listens to the theatre company's concerns about budget constraints and production timelines. Through this open dialogue, David finds a solution that balances his artistic vision with the theatre company's practical limitations. This demonstrates the power of thoughtful communication in achieving a favorable outcome.

Negotiating also involves understanding the nuances of power dynamics. In some situations, you may be negotiating from a position of weakness, and in others, from a position of strength. Adapting your negotiation style to reflect these dynamics is crucial. When negotiating from a position of weakness, for example, highlighting your unique qualities, willingness to collaborate, and potential for long-term success can compensate for a lack of immediate leverage.

A struggling musician, Emily, needing to secure a small gig, might emphasize her willingness to adapt to the venue's specific requirements or her dedication to promoting the event to her existing network. By showcasing her eagerness to collaborate and her willingness to invest extra effort, she can offset her limited leverage and improve her chances of securing a fair deal.

Conversely, when negotiating from a position of strength, for instance, an athlete who has attracted multiple lucrative offers, you can leverage this competition to secure more favorable terms. But even in this scenario, maintaining a respectful and collaborative approach can foster long-term relationships and ensure future opportunities. An experienced sports agent will always consider the long-term impact of negotiations, prioritizing sustainable relationships over immediate financial gains.

Finally, remember the importance of legal counsel. An experienced entertainment lawyer can provide invaluable insight into the legal implications of any contract and guide you through the complex maze of industry standards and best practices. They can review contracts, identify potential risks, and advocate for your best interests throughout the negotiation process. Their expertise can save you from costly mistakes and ensure you receive a fair and equitable deal. Investing in legal representation is an investment in your career's longevity and success. The expertise of a legal professional brings an additional layer of protection and significantly enhances your negotiation power. They can spot hidden clauses, ensure your rights are protected, and advocate for you when necessary. Don't underestimate the value of a skilled legal partner in navigating the complexities of contract negotiation.

Protecting your image and likeness is paramount in the entertainment and sports industries. Your public persona, your name, your face – these are valuable assets, and their unauthorized use can be financially damaging and emotionally distressing. This section will explore the crucial legal mechanisms available to safeguard these assets, focusing on endorsements, sponsorships, and merchandise deals.

Imagine a celebrity chef, renowned for their innovative cooking style and television personality, whose image is unexpectedly used in a fast-food commercial without their consent. This not only dilutes their carefully cultivated brand image but also opens them up to potential legal action. Such scenarios highlight the necessity of proactively protecting your image rights. The unauthorized use of a person's image or likeness, commonly referred to as "right of publicity," is a significant legal concern, particularly in a world saturated with digital media and social media platforms.

The foundation of protecting your image and likeness rests upon understanding and securing the appropriate legal agreements. Endorsement deals, for instance, are contracts where you license your image and likeness to a company in exchange for compensation. These agreements must clearly define the scope of use, including the specific media platforms (television, print, social media, etc.), the geographical territories covered, and the duration of the agreement. Ambiguity in these aspects can lead to disputes and costly legal battles.

Let's consider the case of a highly successful athlete negotiating a multi-year endorsement deal with a sportswear giant. The athlete's agent should ensure the contract explicitly specifies the images and likenesses that can be used, prohibiting the company from utilizing out-of-date photographs or images that do not reflect the athlete's current brand image. The agreement should also outline the athlete's approval rights, granting them the power to review and approve any marketing materials before their release. This approval right is critical, preventing the use of their image in a way that might be detrimental to their reputation. Furthermore, the contract should include clauses addressing the termination of the agreement, including provisions for breach of contract, and a clear mechanism for resolving disputes.

Sponsorships are similar to endorsements but often involve a broader, more integrated relationship between the individual and the sponsoring company. These agreements can encompass a wider range of activities, including appearances at events, social media promotions, and participation in marketing campaigns. The legal framework for sponsorships must be equally rigorous, clearly defining the scope of the sponsorship, the specific obligations of both parties, and the compensation structure. A sponsorship agreement might involve a combination of guaranteed fees, performance-based bonuses, and other incentives. It is crucial that these terms are clearly articulated to avoid future misunderstandings.

Merchandise deals present another avenue for protecting and monetizing your image and likeness. These deals grant a company the right to manufacture and sell products bearing your name, image, or likeness. The agreement must clearly define the types of merchandise, the quality standards, and the royalty structure. A crucial element here is the quality control of the merchandise. The agreement should stipulate that the products meet certain standards and are appropriately licensed to protect the individual's reputation and prevent the sale of inferior goods bearing their image. Additionally, regular reporting mechanisms should be in place to ensure transparency in sales figures and royalty payments.

The digital age introduces new complexities to image and likeness protection. The widespread availability of digital images and social media platforms presents significant challenges, as unauthorized use can spread rapidly and widely. Agreements should address the use of your image and likeness on social media, websites, and online marketing campaigns. These contracts need to include specific clauses for social media posts, allowing the individual to have an approval role even on social media initiatives, with stipulations for takedown notices in case of unauthorized use.

Consider the situation of a rising social media influencer whose photograph is used without permission in a viral campaign. Having a robust legal strategy in place, including preemptive measures such as registering trademarks related to their name and brand, provides a significant advantage in protecting their online image and likeness. Moreover, this preemptive strategy will create a stronger legal foundation to act against these instances of misuse.

Furthermore, it's vital to understand the nuances of intellectual property rights related to your image and likeness. While the right of publicity protects your image's commercial value, copyright law protects the artistic expression embodied in photographs or videos featuring you. Understanding these distinctions is critical for effectively enforcing your rights. Consulting a skilled entertainment lawyer is crucial to ensure that all necessary legal steps are taken to safeguard your image and likeness, particularly in the complex landscape of digital media.

Beyond individual deals, proactive strategies are essential for long-term protection. Registering your name and likeness as trademarks can offer additional legal safeguards. This prevents others from using your name or image commercially without your consent. Regular monitoring of the internet and social media platforms is also important to identify and address instances of unauthorized use promptly. This proactive approach, combined with strong legal representation, is crucial for safeguarding your valuable assets.

In conclusion, protecting your image and likeness is not just about avoiding legal trouble; it's about safeguarding your brand, preserving your reputation, and maximizing the value of your most valuable asset – yourself. The complex legal landscape surrounding image rights requires careful planning, comprehensive contracts, and the guidance of experienced legal counsel. By understanding these principles and taking proactive steps, creators and athletes can effectively protect their image and likeness and build a sustainable, long-term career in the entertainment and sports industries. This isn't merely a legal matter; it's a vital component of your overall career strategy and financial security. Don't underestimate its importance. Consider it an investment in your future, securing your legacy and your financial well-being. Ignoring these principles can have significant consequences. Protecting your image and likeness is as crucial as securing your next deal or winning your next game. It is your long-term reputation and financial stability at stake.

Beyond protecting your image and likeness, the cornerstone of a successful career in entertainment and sports lies in maximizing your revenue streams. This isn't simply about securing a single lucrative deal; it's about strategically diversifying your income sources and ensuring you receive fair compensation for your work. This requires a meticulous understanding of your contracts, a keen eye for potential opportunities, and a proactive approach to negotiating favorable terms.

Let's begin with streaming royalties, a crucial revenue stream for musicians, filmmakers, and other content creators in the digital age. Streaming platforms, while offering unparalleled reach, often operate under complex royalty structures. Understanding these structures is vital to ensuring you receive your fair share of the revenue generated by your work. Negotiating a favorable royalty rate is crucial, and this often requires a detailed analysis of the platform's payment models and the potential audience reach. Furthermore, your contract should specify the payment schedule, reporting mechanisms, and dispute resolution procedures. Ambiguity in these aspects can lead to significant financial losses. Consider the case of a rising independent musician whose music is streamed on multiple platforms. Their contract should explicitly define the royalty rate, the payment frequency (monthly, quarterly, etc.), and a clear process for obtaining accurate sales reports. Without these details, they risk being underpaid or facing significant delays in receiving their royalties.

Performance fees, another significant revenue source, vary widely across different sectors. For musicians, this encompasses concert fees, festival appearances, and private events. For athletes, performance-based bonuses are a common element of contracts. In both cases, the contract should clearly define the performance criteria, the associated fees, and any applicable deductions or expenses. This requires a thorough understanding of industry standards and a robust negotiation strategy to ensure fair compensation. For example, a musician negotiating a tour contract should stipulate clear performance criteria (e.g., number of shows, venue size) and the corresponding fees. The contract should also specify details regarding travel, accommodation, and other expenses, ensuring the musician receives the agreed-upon net income.

Merchandise sales offer a significant avenue for generating additional revenue. For athletes, musicians, and other personalities, merchandise (e.g., t-shirts, hats, albums) bearing their name or likeness can be a substantial source of income. However, securing a favorable merchandising deal requires a carefully crafted contract that outlines the licensing terms, royalty rates, quality control mechanisms, and sales reporting procedures. The agreement should clearly define the types of merchandise permitted, the geographical territories covered, and the duration of the license. It's crucial to have strict quality control measures in place to prevent the sale of inferior goods that could damage your reputation. Imagine a celebrity chef licensing their name for a line of cookware. The contract should specify the quality standards of the cookware, ensuring that the products meet their expectations and maintain their brand image. Regular sales reports are crucial for transparency and ensuring that the chef receives their agreed-upon royalties.

Endorsement deals are another cornerstone of revenue generation, particularly for athletes and celebrities. These agreements allow companies to use your image and likeness in advertising campaigns in exchange for compensation. Negotiating an endorsement deal requires careful consideration of several factors, including the brand's reputation, the target audience, and the scope of the agreement. The contract should clearly define the permitted uses of your image and likeness, the duration of the agreement, and the associated fees. Furthermore, you should retain the right to review and approve any marketing materials before their release to ensure the campaign aligns with your brand image. Consider the case of an athlete negotiating an endorsement deal with a sportswear company. The contract should specify the exact images and likeness that can be used, prohibiting the use of outdated photographs or images that do not reflect their current brand image. The athlete should also secure the right to terminate the agreement if the company engages in activities that damage their reputation.

Beyond these core revenue streams, several other opportunities exist for maximizing your earnings. Public appearances, speaking engagements, and masterclasses can provide substantial additional income. The contracts for these events should clearly define the scope of your involvement, the associated fees, and any expenses covered by the organizers. For instance, a prominent author negotiating a speaking engagement should ensure the contract specifies their speaking fee, travel expenses, and any accommodation provided. Similarly, an athlete offering a masterclass should stipulate the fee, the format of the class, and the platform used to deliver the content.

Intellectual property rights play a critical role in maximizing revenue. Understanding copyright, trademark, and patent laws is vital for protecting your creative work and licensing it for commercial use. Registering your trademarks ensures your brand identity is protected, preventing unauthorized use. Similarly, copyright protection safeguards your creative works, such as music, books, and films. Licensing your intellectual property to others can generate significant revenue through film adaptations, merchandising, or other uses. A musician, for example, might license their music for use in commercials or television shows. An author might license their book for adaptation into a film or video game. These licensing agreements must clearly define the terms of use, the royalties payable, and the reporting mechanisms.

Finally, a robust legal team is crucial for maximizing your revenue streams and protecting your interests. Experienced entertainment lawyers can guide you through the complexities of contract negotiations, intellectual property management, and dispute resolution. Their expertise can ensure you receive fair compensation for your work and protect yourself from exploitation. Their expertise is not merely about legal compliance; it's about proactively maximizing your financial potential and safeguarding your career. They can help you anticipate potential issues and develop strategies to mitigate risks. Their guidance can be invaluable in navigating the intricate legal landscape of the entertainment and sports industries. Remember, investing in skilled legal representation is an investment in your future success. It's a crucial aspect of securing your financial well-being and protecting your legacy. The cost of legal counsel is far outweighed by the potential financial gains and reputational safeguards provided.

The landscape of entertainment and sports contracts is a treacherous terrain, fraught with complexities and potential pitfalls. While understanding the fundamentals of royalties, performance fees, and merchandising deals is crucial, it's the strategic guidance of a seasoned entertainment lawyer that truly transforms a good deal into a great one. Their expertise goes beyond simply reviewing legal documents; it's about proactively shaping the negotiation process, anticipating potential problems, and ensuring your interests are protected at every stage.

Consider the seemingly straightforward matter of a recording contract. A musician, brimming with talent and enthusiasm, might readily accept a seemingly generous advance offered by a record label. However, a lawyer experienced in music industry contracts will delve deeper, scrutinizing the fine print for hidden clauses that could ultimately limit the artist's earning potential. These could include restrictive clauses on creative control, overly favorable reversion terms for the label, or ambiguous royalty structures that might lead to underpayment. A seasoned lawyer will negotiate for clearer definitions of ownership, fair royalty rates, and specific timelines for album releases and marketing campaigns. They will also identify potential loopholes and push for clauses protecting the artist's creative vision and long-term financial stability.

The lawyer's role extends beyond the initial contract negotiation. They will actively monitor the label's fulfillment of its obligations, ensuring accurate reporting of sales figures and timely royalty payments. They will also provide guidance on navigating disputes that may arise, protecting the artist's rights and preventing costly legal battles. In the case of a dispute, an experienced lawyer acts as an effective advocate, negotiating a favorable settlement or representing the artist in court should litigation become necessary.

The value of legal counsel becomes even more apparent in the negotiation of endorsement deals. While the lure of a big-name brand and a substantial upfront payment might seem irresistible, a lawyer will delve into the nuances of the agreement, looking beyond the immediate financial benefits. They will investigate the brand's reputation, ensuring it aligns with the artist's values and image. They will scrutinize the permitted uses of the artist's likeness, protecting against unauthorized exploitation. They will also negotiate for clauses that protect the artist's image, preventing the brand from engaging in activities that could damage their reputation. Moreover, the lawyer will ensure that the contract outlines clear terms for payment, usage rights, and termination clauses, safeguarding the artist against potential exploitation or contractual breaches.

Furthermore, the negotiation of sponsorship agreements requires a deep understanding of intellectual property law. Many sponsorship deals involve the use of the athlete's name, image, and likeness (NIL), and the lawyer's expertise in this area is paramount. They will ensure that the contract clearly defines the scope of the rights granted to the sponsor, preventing any encroachment on the athlete's intellectual property rights. They will also negotiate for appropriate compensation, ensuring the athlete receives fair market value for the use of their NIL. The lawyer will also ensure that the contract includes clauses protecting the athlete's reputation and brand integrity, preventing the sponsor from associating the athlete with products or activities that are inconsistent with their values or image.

In the increasingly complex world of digital rights management, the role of a skilled lawyer is even more critical. The proliferation of streaming platforms and digital distribution channels has created new challenges for artists and athletes seeking to protect and monetize their work. A lawyer can help navigate these complex legal issues, ensuring that contracts with streaming services accurately reflect the artist's rights and royalty payments. They will also advise on issues relating to copyright infringement, ensuring the artist's work is adequately protected against unauthorized use or reproduction. Their expertise in digital rights management becomes a crucial shield against exploitation in the ever-changing digital landscape.

Moreover, the lawyer's contribution goes beyond contract review and negotiation. They serve as a strategic advisor, helping artists and athletes make informed business decisions. This involves providing advice on career management, brand building, and financial planning. A lawyer can provide valuable insights into the long-term implications of different contractual arrangements, helping clients make choices that align with their overall career goals. For instance, they can help determine the optimal strategy for balancing short-term financial gains with long-term career sustainability. This involves providing insights into the negotiation of future contracts, helping clients anticipate potential challenges, and developing effective strategies to mitigate risks.

The role of a lawyer is not merely reactive; it is proactive. They help artists and athletes build a strong legal foundation for their careers, protecting their interests at every stage of their development. This involves developing a comprehensive legal strategy that addresses all aspects of their professional lives, from contract negotiation to dispute resolution. This might involve registering trademarks and copyrights, securing appropriate insurance coverage, and establishing robust business structures. A well-planned legal strategy provides a crucial framework for success, ensuring that artists and athletes can focus on their creative work or athletic performance, while their legal team handles the complexities of the legal and business aspects.

Beyond the individual agreements, an entertainment lawyer plays a significant role in structuring overall business deals. They can advise on setting up entities, such as limited liability companies (LLCs) or corporations, to optimize tax efficiency and protect personal assets. They can guide artists and athletes in choosing appropriate business managers and agents, ensuring alignment of interests and clear contractual arrangements. They act as the anchor in a sometimes turbulent sea of business dealings, ensuring that all legal aspects are handled correctly and that the artist's or athlete's interests are always prioritized.

In conclusion, the power of legal counsel in negotiations is not simply about avoiding legal problems; it is about strategically maximizing opportunities and building a sustainable career. A skilled entertainment lawyer acts as a strategic partner, providing not only legal expertise but also valuable business acumen. They empower artists and athletes to navigate the complexities of the entertainment and sports industries with confidence, knowing their interests are protected and their potential is fully realized. The investment in a skilled legal team is an investment in a secure and prosperous future. It's the difference between a successful career built on a solid foundation and one that's vulnerable to the pitfalls of a complex and often unforgiving industry. The cost is a small price to pay for the peace of mind and the potential for significant financial gains that a skilled lawyer can provide.

Chapter 3: Publishing and Recording Contracts

Understanding the intricacies of a publishing agreement is paramount for any creator, whether a musician crafting melodies, a songwriter weaving lyrical narratives, or an author crafting compelling prose. These agreements, often complex and multifaceted, govern the relationship between the creator and the publisher, defining the terms under which the creator's work is disseminated and monetized. Navigating this landscape requires a keen understanding of various clauses, each carrying significant implications for the creator's financial well-being and creative control.

One of the most critical aspects is the royalty structure. This outlines the percentage of income the creator receives from the sale or licensing of their work. These percentages can vary significantly depending on the type of work, the publisher's market share, and the creator's negotiating power. Traditional publishing contracts often involve a tiered system, with different royalty rates applied to different types of sales, such as physical copies, digital downloads, streaming royalties, and foreign rights. A seasoned entertainment lawyer will meticulously examine these tiered systems, ensuring that the rates reflect fair market value and are not unduly weighted in favor of the publisher. Furthermore, they will strive to secure favorable payment terms, including timely and transparent reporting of sales figures and regular royalty payments. Failure to adequately scrutinize these details can lead to significant underpayment over the life of the agreement.

Beyond the percentages, the definition of "sales" itself needs meticulous examination. Publishers might employ different accounting practices, which can impact the calculation of royalties. For instance, deductions for marketing costs or distribution fees might be excessive, leading to a reduction in the creator's share. A shrewd lawyer will ensure that these deductions are clearly defined and justified, preventing any hidden reductions or accounting manipulations that could erode the creator's earnings. They will also advocate for transparent reporting procedures, guaranteeing access to all sales data and the ability to independently verify the publisher's calculations.

Ownership rights are another critical element in publishing agreements. These contracts define who holds the copyright to the work and what rights are granted to the publisher. In many cases, the creator retains copyright, but the publisher secures exclusive rights to publish, distribute, and license the work for a specific duration. However, the agreement must clearly delineate these rights, specifying the geographical territories covered, the types of formats included, and the permitted uses of the work. Ambiguity in this area can lead to disputes and costly litigation. A skilled lawyer will ensure the agreement clearly defines the scope of the publisher's rights, preventing any potential overreach that could compromise the creator's future exploitation options. Moreover, they will strive to secure a clear reversion clause, which specifies the terms under which the rights revert back to the creator after the contract expires. This ensures the creator maintains control over their work in the long term.

Consider the case of a songwriter whose songs are published through a major music publisher. The agreement might grant the publisher exclusive rights to license the songs for use in films, television shows, and advertisements. However, if the agreement does not clearly define the geographical territories covered, the publisher might license the songs in regions where the songwriter had intended to secure separate deals, resulting in lost revenue for the songwriter. A lawyer can prevent this by ensuring the contract explicitly states the territories covered by the publisher's license.

Further complicating the matter are advances, often paid to creators upfront against future royalties. While this can provide much-needed financial support during the creative process, it's essential to carefully analyze the terms surrounding these advances. The agreement must clearly specify how these advances are recouped from future royalties, ensuring that they are subtracted from royalties in a fair and transparent manner. Unclear recouping clauses can lead to a situation where the creator never earns any royalties despite the success of their work. A savvy lawyer will negotiate for reasonable recouping terms, ensuring the creator receives a significant portion of future royalties even after the advance is fully recouped.

Moreover, the contract should contain clauses specifying the publisher's responsibilities regarding marketing and promotion. The publisher's commitment to promoting the creator's work is crucial for its success. The agreement should clearly define the publisher's marketing strategy, including the budget allocated, the marketing channels to be utilized, and the expected timeline for promotional activities. A lawyer can ensure the contract reflects an appropriate level of commitment from the publisher, safeguarding the creator's interests and maximizing the potential reach of their work. Likewise, the contract should include clauses dealing with the reporting of marketing expenses. This transparency is vital to prevent any disputes about how funds are used.

The term of the agreement is another critical aspect to consider. Publishing contracts typically cover a specific period, often several years. It's essential to carefully assess the length of the agreement and ensure it aligns with the creator's long-term goals. A lawyer can help negotiate a term that balances the publisher's need for exclusivity with the creator's desire for flexibility in the future. A longer term might seem advantageous initially due to an advance, but it can lead to being locked into an unfavorable deal for an extended period.

Beyond the core elements, several other clauses can significantly impact the creator's rights and earnings. These may include termination clauses, dispute resolution mechanisms, and provisions regarding subsidiary rights, such as the right to publish translations or adaptations of the work. A well-drafted publishing agreement should protect the creator's intellectual property rights, ensure fair compensation, and provide a framework for a mutually beneficial partnership. Without legal guidance, creators risk overlooking crucial clauses that can have far-reaching consequences on their financial success and creative control.

The role of an entertainment lawyer extends beyond simply reviewing the contract; it's about actively shaping the negotiation process, advocating for the creator's interests, and ensuring the agreement reflects a fair and equitable distribution of rights and revenue. They possess the expertise to identify potential pitfalls, negotiate favorable terms, and protect the creator from exploitation. They act as the creator's advocate throughout the negotiation, ensuring that their creative vision is not compromised and that their long-term financial stability is secured. Investing in legal counsel is an investment in the creator's future, safeguarding their work and their financial well-being in the often complex world of publishing. The clarity and protection provided by a well-negotiated publishing agreement are essential building blocks of a thriving creative career, ensuring that the creator's talents are not only recognized but fairly rewarded. The value of a skilled entertainment lawyer in this process cannot be overstated; they are the guardians of the creator's interests, ensuring their work is properly valued and their rights are protected.

Recording contracts, the bedrock of a musician's career, are intricate legal documents demanding careful scrutiny. Unlike the relatively straightforward nature of some publishing deals, recording contracts delve into the nitty-gritty of production, distribution, and ownership – aspects crucial for a musician's financial success and creative autonomy. These agreements dictate the terms under which an artist records, releases, and licenses their music, and a thorough understanding is paramount before signing on the dotted line. A lack of clarity or unfavorable terms can lead to years of legal battles and significant financial losses.

The album delivery clause is a critical component. It meticulously outlines the artist's obligations regarding the creation and delivery of the recorded material. This goes beyond simply delivering a finished product; it specifies timelines, deadlines, acceptable quality standards, and the specific format for delivery. Often, these contracts involve multiple albums, creating a complex web of deadlines and deliverables. Missing a deadline, failing to meet the required quality, or delivering the recordings in the wrong format can have significant repercussions. The contract may include penalties for non-compliance, ranging from financial penalties to termination of the agreement. A lawyer specializing in entertainment law will meticulously examine these clauses, ensuring realistic and achievable deadlines are set, while simultaneously protecting the artist from unreasonable penalties. They will also advocate for clear definitions of "acceptable quality," preventing disputes based on subjective interpretations.

For instance, imagine a contract that stipulates an artist must deliver ten songs by a specific date. The contract might include a detailed description of the acceptable quality of the recordings, possibly including technical specifications such as audio bit rate, sample rate, and dynamic range. The contract should also address the possibility of unforeseen circumstances that may delay the album delivery. A well-negotiated contract will include provisions for reasonable extensions under exceptional circumstances, such as illness, accidents, or unexpected technical issues. These considerations are vital for protecting the artist and preventing premature termination of the contract.

Royalty splits are the lifeblood of any recording contract. This section delineates how the artist's income is distributed between the artist and the record label. This includes the breakdown of royalties from physical sales, digital downloads, streaming services, and synchronization licenses. The percentages allocated to each party can significantly impact the artist's earnings. A standard royalty split might be 50/50 between the artist and the label, but it can vary greatly depending on the artist's negotiating power, the type of music produced, and the market conditions. A keen-eyed lawyer will meticulously analyze the proposed royalty split, ensuring it's competitive and reflects the artist's market value. They'll also carefully examine any deductions from royalties, such as manufacturing costs, distribution fees, and marketing expenses, to ensure they are fair and transparent.

Furthermore, the contract should clearly define the methods for calculating and distributing royalties. This involves a detailed understanding of the various revenue streams generated by the artist's music, including different platforms and licensing arrangements. The contract should spell out the reporting process, stipulating how frequently the artist receives royalty statements, and the level of transparency to be provided. This will help to ensure timely payment and facilitate a process to reconcile any discrepancies that might occur. These clauses are critical for artists to understand, ensuring they can confidently track income generated from their creative output.

The ownership of masters is perhaps the most contentious aspect of recording contracts. Master recordings are the original, high-quality recordings of an artist's music, essentially the foundational asset of their career. These contracts often determine who owns these invaluable assets – the artist or the record label. Historically, record labels have often secured ownership, giving them significant leverage over the artist's future. However, the landscape is changing, with artists increasingly negotiating to retain ownership or regain it after a certain period. A skilled entertainment lawyer will tirelessly advocate for the artist to retain ownership, or at the very least, secure a reversion clause that allows them to reclaim ownership after a predetermined time, usually after the contract ends, and sometimes after the label recoups its investment. Ownership of masters grants the artist control over their music's future use, licensing, and potential resale, offering significant financial and creative independence.

Consider the scenario of an artist whose career takes off unexpectedly after their initial recording contract. Without ownership of the masters, they could be significantly limited in their ability to capitalize on this success. The label may retain control over re-releasing the original recordings, preventing the artist from taking advantage of new opportunities in the ever-evolving music market. The retention of master ownership offers an artist significant leverage for future negotiations, allowing them to license their music on their own terms, potentially for higher returns.

Beyond these core clauses, other critical aspects of recording contracts need attention. These include the term of the agreement, its geographical scope, the rights granted to the record label (such as exclusive recording rights or merchandising rights), and the clauses addressing termination and dispute resolution. The term of the agreement – typically several years – should be carefully evaluated and negotiated to ensure it aligns with the artist's long-term career goals. A shorter term offers greater flexibility for the artist later, but it might not be as attractive to a label initially. Geographic scope determines where the label has the right to release and distribute the music, with global rights generally being more valuable to the label, and therefore less beneficial to the artist unless adequately compensated.

Termination clauses outline the conditions under which the contract can be ended. These clauses should be carefully examined to ensure they are fair and protect the artist from arbitrary termination. Dispute resolution mechanisms determine how conflicts will be resolved, with arbitration often preferred over lengthy and expensive court battles. Merchandising rights, which allow the label to use the artist's likeness and name on merchandise, should be explicitly defined and negotiated to ensure a fair share of profits for the artist. The contract should also address the artist's right to approve marketing and promotional strategies, protecting them from campaigns that might tarnish their image or creative vision.

The role of an entertainment lawyer in negotiating and reviewing recording contracts cannot be overstated. They are the artist's advocates, ensuring their creative work is protected, their financial interests are secured, and their long-term career trajectory is not jeopardized by unfavorable terms. They dissect the contract's complexities, identify potential pitfalls, negotiate favorable terms, and provide ongoing support throughout the agreement's lifespan. They are the crucial link between the artist's artistic vision and their legal protection, ensuring a sustainable and successful career in the often unpredictable music industry. Choosing a skilled lawyer is an investment in the artist's future, safeguarding their creative work and their financial well-being for years to come. In the high-stakes world of music, having a knowledgeable legal expert on your side is not a luxury, but a necessity.

Licensing and synchronization agreements are the crucial mechanisms that allow the use of musical compositions in various media, from blockbuster movies to quirky commercials. They bridge the gap between the creative work of songwriters and composers and their potential use in visual media, generating revenue streams beyond album sales and streaming royalties. Navigating these agreements requires a sharp understanding of the legal intricacies and the ability to secure favorable terms for the rights holder, ensuring they receive appropriate compensation for the use of their intellectual property.

The core of a synchronization license is the authorization to synchronize a musical composition with visual media. This isn't simply about playing the music in the background; it involves a complex interplay of rights, including the right to reproduce the music, the right to distribute it, and the right to perform it publicly, all within the context of a specific visual medium. The license dictates the scope of use, specifying the geographical area where the visual work will be shown, the duration of the license (often tied to the lifespan of the film or commercial), and the specific media in which the music can be used. For example, a license might grant rights for theatrical release, television broadcast, and streaming platforms, but exclude other uses like video games or ringtones.

Securing a synchronization license often involves navigating a complex chain of rights holders. A typical song may be owned by multiple parties: the songwriter(s), the composer(s), the music publisher(s), and potentially the record label (who owns the master recording, but not necessarily the underlying composition). Each party has their own rights to license, and obtaining clearance from all involved parties is essential before using the music. This process can be incredibly time-consuming and expensive, which is why many production companies utilize music supervisors – professionals who specialize in securing these clearances. A savvy entertainment lawyer can streamline this process by ensuring clear communication between all parties and establishing a coordinated negotiation strategy.

The negotiation of synchronization licensing fees is a critical aspect of the process. The fee is determined by a variety of factors, including the song's popularity, the length of time the music will be used, the prestige of the visual project, and the anticipated reach of the audience. A well-known song used prominently in a major motion picture will command a considerably higher fee than an obscure track used briefly in a low-budget indie film. The duration of the license also plays a crucial role; a license granted for a limited run in a television commercial will be less expensive than a perpetual license for use in a library of stock music.

The agreement should clearly define how the synchronization fee is calculated and paid. The payment schedule, the currency used, and the applicable taxes should all be specified. It's not uncommon for the fee to be paid in installments, with a portion paid upfront and the remainder due upon completion of the project or upon reaching certain milestones. Furthermore, the agreement must also address the issue of residual payments. Residuals are payments made to the rights holder each time the visual work is shown or broadcast. These payments can significantly add to the overall compensation received, particularly if the visual project enjoys widespread success.

Beyond the synchronization license itself, other related licensing agreements can come into play. For example, a mechanical license might be required if the lyrics or music are reproduced in a physical format (like a CD soundtrack to the film). A performance license may also be necessary if the music is performed publicly as part of a film screening or television broadcast. These additional licenses add layers of complexity to the overall licensing process, emphasizing the need for skilled legal counsel to ensure that all necessary permissions are secured and that the rights holders are appropriately compensated for each use of their work.

Consider the case of a small independent filmmaker looking to secure a license for a song in their upcoming feature film. The filmmaker may approach the publisher of the song directly or use a music licensing company to facilitate the process. However, without proper legal advice, they may unintentionally overlook key clauses in the licensing agreement. For instance, if the agreement fails to specify the scope of use, the filmmaker might find themselves in a legal dispute over the use of the song in different platforms such as streaming services. Furthermore, without proper negotiation, the filmmaker could end up paying an exorbitant fee for the license, impacting the overall budget of their film.

Alternatively, consider a major advertising agency looking to license a popular song for a television commercial. The agency would likely engage with a specialist music licensing agent, who handles negotiations and ensures that all necessary legal requirements are met. However, even with an intermediary, proper legal counsel for the agency remains crucial to ensure that the terms of the license are fair and protect the interests of the client. The lawyer will scrutinize the license agreement, ensuring that there are no ambiguities that could lead to disputes, and negotiate favorable terms, including the license fee, the scope of use, and the duration of the license. In this high-stakes world of brand marketing, every detail matters.

The licensing landscape for music has evolved dramatically in the digital age. The rise of streaming platforms and social media has created new challenges and opportunities for rights holders. Streaming platforms often negotiate their own agreements with music publishers and artists, adding another layer of complexity to the licensing process. Social media platforms are frequently the source of unauthorized use of music, making it critical for artists and rights holders to actively monitor their work and pursue legal action when necessary. These issues highlight the ever-increasing need for sophisticated legal strategies in managing and enforcing music licensing agreements.

Furthermore, the legal landscape concerning the use of music in user-generated content online continues to evolve. Social media platforms grapple with issues of copyright infringement, and platforms are increasingly implementing technology to identify and remove copyrighted music from user-uploaded videos and audio. However, the issue of fair use and the interpretation of copyright law in the context of user-generated content remain contested areas. This situation underscores the importance for both content creators and rights holders to be knowledgeable about their rights and responsibilities in navigating this ever-changing digital environment.

The importance of carefully crafted and well-negotiated licensing and synchronization agreements cannot be overstated. These agreements safeguard the intellectual property rights of songwriters, composers, and publishers, ensuring they receive fair compensation for the use of their work. A skilled entertainment lawyer acts as a crucial intermediary, navigating the complexities of copyright law, contract negotiation, and international agreements. By ensuring that licenses are comprehensive, fair, and protect the rights holders, entertainment lawyers safeguard the livelihoods of creators and maintain the integrity of the music industry. They are more than just legal advisors; they are crucial partners in maximizing the financial and creative potential of music in the ever-evolving entertainment landscape.

Owning your master recordings is akin to owning the very soul of your musical creation. It's the fundamental building block of your career, the asset that generates income long after the initial release. Without control over your masters, you're essentially renting out your artistic legacy, perpetually subject to the whims and decisions of others. This subsection delves into the critical importance of securing and maintaining ownership of your master recordings, offering strategies to negotiate favorable terms and avoid exploitation.

The master recording, in simple terms, is the final, high-quality version of your song. It's the recording that is used for CD production, digital distribution, and streaming. Ownership of the master grants you exclusive rights to reproduce, distribute, and license your music. This means you have the power to decide how and where your music is used, and importantly, who profits from it. This contrasts sharply with the rights associated with the composition itself (the underlying melody, harmony, and lyrics), which are usually controlled separately by the songwriter(s) and publisher(s).

Negotiating ownership of your master recordings is arguably the most crucial aspect of any recording contract. Many inexperienced artists inadvertently relinquish this control, signing deals that leave them with little to no ownership and minimal financial gain. A common pitfall is the "work-for-hire" clause, which essentially assigns ownership of the master recording to the record label. While seemingly beneficial in the short term—the label covers recording costs—it can lead to long-term financial hardship. The label retains the rights, controlling the distribution, licensing, and subsequent revenue generated from your music. Your earning potential becomes constrained by their decisions and often limited to a small percentage of royalties.

Imagine a scenario where you create a song that becomes unexpectedly popular years after its initial release. A major film producer wants to use it in a blockbuster movie. If you don't own the master recording, the label will negotiate and receive the lucrative synchronization fees, leaving you with a meager payout, if any at all. This highlights the significance of retaining ownership – it is a long-term investment in your artistic future and financial security.

A well-drafted recording contract should explicitly state that you retain ownership of your master recordings. The contract should detail the specific terms under which the label will license your music, including the scope of the license, the duration, the geographical limitations, and the royalty rates. It's essential to ensure that the royalty rates are fair and competitive, reflecting your contribution to the success of the project. Seek independent legal advice from an experienced entertainment lawyer to ensure that these terms are beneficial and reflect market standards. Don't be afraid to negotiate; this is your career, and your work deserves fair compensation.

Beyond the initial contract, ongoing management of your master recordings is equally important. Maintain meticulous records of all licensing agreements, financial transactions, and distributions. Regularly review your contracts to ensure compliance and identify any potential issues. In the digital era, with the proliferation of streaming platforms and user-generated content, the landscape of music distribution is constantly evolving. This necessitates a proactive approach to monitoring the use of your music and ensuring that you receive the appropriate royalties.

Protecting your master recordings also involves vigilance against unauthorized use and copyright infringement. The internet has become a breeding ground for unauthorized uploads and reproductions of music. Utilize online monitoring services to identify and address instances of piracy. Engage in proactive legal action against those who infringe upon your rights. Your lawyer will advise you on the best strategy to protect your intellectual property, which could involve cease and desist letters, and in some cases, litigation. Remember, defending your rights is not just about protecting your income; it's about preserving the integrity of your artistic work.

For independent artists who self-release their music, the issue of master ownership is less complex but still critically important. Although you don't need to negotiate with a record label, you retain full control over your master recordings from the start. However, this comes with responsibilities. You are solely responsible for manufacturing, distribution, marketing, and accounting for all sales and royalties. Careful planning and meticulous record keeping are paramount. Seek legal advice to ensure you comply with all copyright laws and regulations, and to establish the appropriate licenses and agreements for distribution through digital platforms.

Consider the case of a talented singer-songwriter who signed a recording contract with a major label without seeking legal counsel. The contract granted the label complete ownership of the master recordings, with the artist receiving a small royalty percentage. The artist's songs became highly successful, resulting in millions of dollars in revenue for the label, while the artist received a fraction of that amount. This scenario illustrates the high stakes involved and the importance of retaining ownership and securing favorable terms. Had the artist sought legal counsel, the outcome could have been vastly different.

Conversely, an independent artist who meticulously managed their master recordings, securing various distribution deals and negotiating favorable licensing agreements, enjoyed significantly greater financial success and artistic control over their career. This underscores the power of understanding and actively managing the rights associated with your music.

In the ever-evolving digital landscape, maintaining ownership and control of your master recordings is crucial not only for immediate financial gains but also for long-term sustainability and legacy. The value of your music can increase over time, particularly with the potential for synchronization deals and licensing opportunities in different media. By understanding the nuances of recording contracts and employing proactive strategies for protection, you can secure a fair return on your creative investment and ensure that your music resonates for years to come. Your music is your asset, and owning your master recordings is paramount to maximizing its potential value. Investing time and resources in securing this ownership, and seeking the advice of an experienced entertainment lawyer, is an investment that will yield considerable returns throughout your career. Remember, this isn't just about the money; it's about securing the long-term viability and creative control of your artistic endeavors. By owning your masters, you own your future.

The rise of digital platforms has introduced new complexities to the ownership and licensing of master recordings. Streaming services have negotiated unique deals with labels and artists, often bypassing established distribution channels and leading to new revenue models and royalty structures. These developments necessitate a careful review and understanding of the agreements with these platforms to ensure you are receiving fair compensation for the use of your music. New legal challenges are constantly emerging, making it crucial to stay abreast of the evolving industry standards and regulations.

Another critical aspect is the preservation of your master recordings. Ensure that you have secure backups in multiple locations to prevent loss or damage. This is particularly important given the increasing reliance on digital formats. Losing your master recordings can lead to irreparable damage, both financially and artistically. Moreover, consider the preservation of the physical copies of your master recordings, such as tapes or hard drives. These may be invaluable in the future, particularly for archiving purposes.

Finally, understanding the nuances of international copyright law is crucial, especially if your music has a global reach. The laws surrounding copyright and ownership vary from country to country. Collaborating with an international entertainment lawyer can help navigate these complexities and ensure that your rights are protected worldwide.

In conclusion, securing ownership of your master recordings is not simply a legal matter; it's a strategic investment in the long-term health and financial stability of your musical career. It's about controlling your destiny and ensuring that your artistic legacy is preserved and financially rewarded according to your contribution and talent. By understanding the complexities involved, employing proactive strategies, and seeking expert legal counsel, you can safeguard your work and lay a solid foundation for a sustainable and successful career in the music industry. The effort invested in this critical area will pay dividends for years to come, ensuring your musical legacy is protected and your artistic endeavors are rewarded fairly.

Let's delve into the real-world implications of navigating the often treacherous waters of publishing and recording contracts. The best way to understand the potential pitfalls and triumphs is through examining actual case studies—both those that ended in favorable settlements and those that resulted in costly and protracted litigation. These examples will illustrate the stark differences between shrewd negotiation and naive acceptance, highlighting the critical role of legal counsel in protecting your creative assets.

Consider the case of "Band X," a promising indie rock band that secured a record deal with a smaller, independent label. Excited by the prospect of finally recording their debut album, they rushed into signing the contract without seeking legal representation. The contract, while seemingly offering reasonable upfront payment and royalties, contained a crucial clause granting the label ownership of the master recordings. While the band initially saw this as a way to secure funding for the album's production, they failed to anticipate the long-term consequences. The album generated modest success, but the label, seeing limited potential for further financial returns, largely neglected to promote future releases. Band X, despite owning their publishing rights, found their ability to leverage their music severely limited, as they lacked control over the master recordings, the fundamental asset that drives licensing opportunities for film, television, and advertising. The label, holding the masters, controlled the revenue streams stemming from any potential synchronization licenses, severely impacting the band's long-term earning potential. This situation highlights the critical mistake of not seeking legal representation, and overlooking the long-term value of mastering ownership. Even a modestly successful album could have generated significantly more income if the band had retained control of their masters. The experience serves as a cautionary tale of the short-sightedness of prioritizing immediate financial gains over long-term artistic and financial autonomy.

A contrasting example involves "Singer Y," a solo artist with a burgeoning fanbase. Singer Y understood the importance of master ownership and sought legal counsel from the outset. The lawyer negotiated a deal with a major label that explicitly retained ownership of the master recordings for Singer Y, while providing fair royalty rates and offering greater creative control. Furthermore, the contract included clear clauses detailing the label's responsibilities regarding promotion and distribution. While the upfront advance was significantly smaller than what Singer Y could have secured by relinquishing master ownership, the long-term implications proved to be far more lucrative. When one of Singer Y's songs unexpectedly gained popularity years after its initial release, the sync licensing rights generated a substantial sum, significantly enriching the artist. This success was directly attributable to Singer Y retaining ownership of the master recording. The careful planning and strategic negotiation demonstrate the substantial long-term benefits of seeking expert legal counsel and prioritizing master ownership. The case underscores that prioritizing short-term financial gains often comes at the cost of long-term financial security and artistic freedom.

Moving beyond recording contracts, let's examine a case involving publishing rights. "Songwriter Z," a gifted lyricist, entered into a publishing agreement with a well-established publishing house. The contract, though seemingly advantageous, included a clause that gave the publishing house the right to extend the agreement automatically unless Songwriter Z explicitly opted out within a specific timeframe. Songwriter Z, unaware of this seemingly innocuous clause, missed the deadline, unknowingly extending the contract for a further period. The contract, now extended without renegotiation, resulted in significantly less favorable royalty rates for Songwriter Z, as the industry standard had shifted favorably for songwriters during that intervening period. This illustrates the critical importance of thoroughly understanding every clause in any contract, regardless of how seemingly benign it appears. Even seemingly small details can have far-reaching financial consequences. The lack of careful review and legal oversight cost Songwriter Z substantial income. This reinforces the necessity of not only having legal counsel review contracts but also taking the time to understand the implications of each clause personally.

Another case involved a dispute over the ownership of a song written collaboratively. "Artist A" and "Artist B" co-wrote a song, each contributing equally to the lyrics and melody. However, they failed to document their respective contributions in a formal written agreement. When the song gained popularity, a dispute arose over the ownership and subsequent royalties. This demonstrates the importance of meticulously documenting the contributions of each party in collaborative projects. A simple written agreement outlining the percentage of ownership, and the responsibilities of each party, would have avoided a costly and protracted legal battle that ultimately diminished the financial returns for both artists. The case underscores the need for clear and concise agreements, particularly in collaborative endeavors, to avoid costly and time-consuming legal disputes.

In the digital age, a new set of challenges and disputes have emerged, largely revolving around digital rights management (DRM). Consider the example of "Digital Artist C," who released their music exclusively through a popular streaming platform. The artist signed an agreement that seemed favorable, guaranteeing a high percentage of royalties. However, the contract failed to clearly define what constituted a "stream" and how royalties would be calculated in the event of technical glitches or disputes regarding playback data. When discrepancies emerged in the royalty payouts, Digital Artist C found themselves embroiled in a complex and lengthy dispute with the streaming platform, which proved to be costly and frustrating. This highlights the importance of clarity and precision in contracts, particularly in the constantly evolving landscape of digital music distribution. It underscores the need for meticulously crafted agreements that account for potential technical issues and ambiguous clauses. Without specific definitions and clear terms, disputes are almost inevitable, delaying payments and creating unnecessary friction.

The cases detailed above highlight the critical importance of careful contract negotiation and the invaluable role of an experienced entertainment lawyer. These legal professionals possess specialized knowledge of the industry's standard practices and the nuances of contract law, which are crucial in protecting your interests. A seasoned lawyer will not only review contracts but also advise you on negotiating favorable terms, understanding your rights, and navigating potential disputes. The cost of legal representation is a small price to pay compared to the potential financial losses incurred through poorly negotiated agreements or costly litigation. Remember, a well-structured contract is an investment in the long-term security and success of your career. It's not just about the initial deal; it's about protecting your creative work and its financial potential for years to come. Investing in legal counsel at the outset will prove to be an invaluable asset that protects your rights, assures your income stream, and safeguards your artistic legacy. Consider it not as an expense, but as an indispensable tool for building a sustainable and thriving career in the entertainment industry. The examples presented serve as cautionary tales—reminding you that the seemingly minor details can have significant consequences, and seeking expert legal counsel isn't just prudent; it's essential.

Chapter 4: Endorsement and Sponsorship Deals

Endorsement deals, the lucrative partnerships between celebrities and brands, often appear glamorous, but beneath the surface lies a complex web of legal intricacies. These agreements, meticulously crafted contracts, define the terms under which an individual agrees to promote a product or service. Understanding these terms is crucial to avoid potential pitfalls and maximize financial returns. A poorly negotiated endorsement deal can lead to significant financial losses, reputational damage, and even legal battles. Conversely, a well-structured agreement protects the individual's interests, ensuring fair compensation and safeguarding their image.

The core of any endorsement agreement revolves around the "right of publicity." This legal right protects an individual's name, likeness, image, and other identifying characteristics from unauthorized commercial use. It's the foundation upon which endorsement deals are built. The agreement grants the brand a limited license to use these protected elements for advertising and promotional purposes. The scope of this license is meticulously defined within the contract, specifying the permitted uses, geographic locations, and duration. For instance, an agreement might grant a brand the right to use an athlete's image in television commercials, online advertisements, and social media campaigns within a specific region for a defined period, say, one year. However, it might explicitly prohibit the use of the athlete's image in connection with certain products or services, safeguarding the athlete's reputation by preventing association with potentially unsuitable brands.

Compensation is another critical aspect of endorsement agreements. It's not simply a flat fee; compensation structures can be multifaceted and complex, varying based on the individual's stature, the brand's reach, and the scope of the campaign. These deals often involve upfront payments, but they can also include royalties, performance-based bonuses, and even equity in the company. For instance, a high-profile celebrity might receive a substantial upfront payment for a multi-year deal, while also earning royalties based on product sales or a bonus if the campaign exceeds predetermined sales targets. Conversely, a lesser-known influencer might receive a smaller upfront payment but a higher percentage of sales generated through their endorsement. This demonstrates the diverse nature of endorsement compensation, tailored to the individual circumstances.

The duration of the agreement is also vital. Some deals are short-term, lasting only a few months, while others extend for several years. Longer-term agreements often involve renewal options, allowing both parties to continue the partnership if the initial collaboration proves successful. However, such agreements must include clearly defined termination clauses, which should outline specific scenarios under which either party can terminate the contract prematurely. This might include breaches of contract, significant changes in the brand's image, or unforeseen circumstances that render the partnership impractical. Such clauses are crucial for mitigating risks and protecting the interests of both parties.

Beyond monetary compensation, endorsement deals also raise the issue of creative control. Many agreements allow the individual some level of creative input, particularly regarding how their image and likeness are presented. However, the degree of control can vary greatly. A celebrity might have extensive input into the advertisement's creative direction, ensuring their image aligns with their brand and values. In contrast, other agreements might grant the brand greater control, particularly in standardized campaigns where consistency across multiple endorsements is paramount. Defining this aspect precisely in the contract is vital to preventing future disputes. Clear provisions specifying the levels of review, approval, and input are essential to avoid misunderstandings.

Disclosure requirements are a critical legal aspect, particularly concerning endorsements conducted on social media platforms. Federal Trade Commission (FTC) guidelines require clear and conspicuous disclosure when an individual is endorsing a product or service. Failure to disclose this relationship can result in hefty fines and reputational damage. The FTC's guidelines specifically address the methods and placement of disclosures, demanding clarity and prominence, ensuring consumers understand that the endorsement is paid or sponsored. This applies across all forms of media, from traditional print advertising to social media posts and influencer marketing campaigns. The contract should explicitly address disclosure requirements, ensuring compliance with FTC regulations and preventing potential legal issues.

The protection of an individual's image and reputation is paramount in any endorsement agreement. The contract should include specific clauses that prevent the brand from using the individual's image or likeness in a manner that is disparaging, misleading, or otherwise harmful to their reputation. It should also stipulate the types of products or services that the individual agrees to endorse, ensuring alignment with their personal brand and values. Such protective clauses are especially critical for individuals with strong public images, as associating their name with a problematic product or service can have lasting consequences. The contract should specifically address situations that could potentially damage the individual's reputation and provide mechanisms for rectifying such situations.

Another critical aspect is the issue of exclusivity. Many endorsement deals involve exclusivity clauses, which prevent the individual from endorsing competing products or services during the term of the agreement. These clauses protect the brand's investment by ensuring their exclusive rights to utilize the individual's image and likeness for their products. Conversely, the individual must carefully consider the implications of such exclusivity, as it might limit their endorsement opportunities and potentially restrict their income. Negotiating the scope of the exclusivity clause is critical; defining the competitive landscape and specifying the products or services covered is essential to balance the brand's need for protection with the individual's need for flexibility.

Finally, intellectual property rights form an integral part of endorsement agreements. The agreement should clearly define the ownership and usage rights of any intellectual property created as part of the endorsement campaign, such as photographs, videos, and slogans. This is particularly relevant in campaigns involving the creation of original content, where the brand and the individual need to establish clear ownership rights to prevent future disputes. Determining ownership of the created content upfront prevents potential conflicts and ensures both parties understand their rights concerning usage and licensing.

Navigating the legal complexities of endorsement agreements requires meticulous attention to detail and, ideally, the expertise of an entertainment lawyer. A skilled legal professional can negotiate favorable terms, protect your interests, and ensure that the agreement safeguards your image and reputation. Investing in legal counsel at the outset of any endorsement deal is not just prudent; it's essential to ensure long-term success and avoid potentially costly pitfalls. Ignoring this vital aspect can lead to financial losses, reputational damage, and extended legal battles, all of which can significantly impact one's career and financial well-being. The cost of legal representation pales in comparison to the potential costs of navigating these issues without expert guidance. Therefore, remember that a well-structured endorsement agreement, carefully negotiated and reviewed by legal counsel, is a crucial investment in the long-term success and protection of your brand. It ensures fair compensation, protects your image, and sets the stage for a mutually beneficial partnership. Ultimately, understanding the intricacies of endorsement agreements is not just about securing a lucrative deal; it's about building a sustainable and thriving career within the entertainment industry, protecting your future, and maintaining your hard-earned reputation.

Sponsorship contracts, while often intertwined with endorsement deals, present a distinct set of negotiating challenges. Unlike endorsements, which primarily focus on the use of an individual's image and likeness, sponsorships involve a broader, more multifaceted relationship between a brand and an individual or entity. This relationship typically involves a commitment to promote the brand through various channels, often extending beyond simple appearances in advertisements. Negotiating a successful sponsorship contract requires a keen understanding of the nuances of such arrangements and a strategic approach to securing favorable terms.

One of the most crucial aspects of negotiating sponsorship contracts is defining the scope of the sponsorship. This involves precisely outlining the activities and responsibilities expected of the sponsored individual or entity. For example, a sponsorship contract with a professional athlete might involve appearances at brand events, participation in social media campaigns, and the use of the brand's logo on their apparel or equipment. However, these activities must be clearly defined and quantified within the contract. Ambiguity can lead to disputes and misunderstandings, so precision is key. The contract should specify the number of appearances, the duration of the commitment, and the specific platforms or channels involved. For instance, the contract might mandate a specific number of appearances at events or require a minimum number of social media posts featuring the brand's products or services. Failure to clearly define these parameters could leave the sponsored individual facing demands exceeding the initial understanding. A clear, well-defined scope protects both parties involved.

Payment structures in sponsorship contracts can vary widely, depending on factors like the individual's profile, the brand's reputation, and the scope of the sponsorship. Unlike endorsement deals, which often involve upfront payments, sponsorship contracts frequently incorporate performance-based incentives. This means that a significant portion of the compensation might be contingent on achieving predetermined goals or metrics. For instance, a sponsorship agreement with a musician might involve an upfront payment and additional bonuses based on ticket sales at concerts or album sales. This structure incentivizes the sponsored individual to actively promote the brand and contribute to its success. It requires careful negotiation to ensure that the performance metrics are realistic, attainable, and clearly defined. Vague or overly ambitious targets can create unfair expectations and potentially hinder the relationship between the sponsored individual and the sponsor. The structure of payment should also encompass contingencies. Unexpected events or circumstances may require renegotiation. It is imperative that the contract has clauses addressing these situations to avoid conflicts.

Exclusivity clauses, common in both endorsement and sponsorship agreements, play a vital role in defining the relationship. These clauses limit the sponsored individual's ability to associate with competing brands during the term of the contract. The extent of exclusivity must be carefully negotiated. It might cover only direct competitors or extend to a broader range of products or services. For instance, a sponsorship contract with a sports apparel brand might prevent the athlete from endorsing other sports apparel brands. However, it might not restrict their endorsements of unrelated products, like food or beverages. The contract needs to precisely delineate the permitted and prohibited brands, ensuring that the exclusivity clause doesn't unduly restrict the sponsored individual's opportunities. The level of exclusivity should be weighed against the compensation and benefits offered. An overly restrictive clause might not be justifiable if the financial reward doesn't compensate for the limitations placed on the individual.

Performance obligations are central to sponsorship contracts. They outline the actions the sponsored individual or entity must undertake to fulfill their side of the agreement. These obligations can encompass a wide range of activities, from public appearances and social media engagement to content creation and participation in marketing campaigns. The contract must detail these obligations with specificity, including timelines, deliverables, and measurable criteria for success. Failure to meet these obligations can have significant consequences, potentially leading to contract termination or financial penalties. Therefore, it is essential that the performance obligations are realistic and achievable, considering the sponsored individual's schedule and capabilities. Regular communication and progress reports can help maintain transparency and identify potential issues early. Incorporating milestones and progress checks within the contract creates accountability and allows for early intervention if any performance issues arise.

Intellectual property rights are a critical concern in sponsorship contracts. These contracts often involve the creation of new materials, such as marketing campaigns, promotional videos, or photographs, in which both the sponsor and the sponsored party hold intellectual property rights. The contract must clearly delineate ownership and usage rights for all created materials. This includes determining who owns the copyright to new works and what rights each party has to use and distribute those works. Ambiguity in this area can lead to significant disputes, potentially involving costly legal battles. Therefore, comprehensive provisions that detail usage rights, licensing agreements, and ownership of all intellectual property created as part of the sponsorship are essential. The contract should specifically address the use of the individual's likeness, name, and other identifying characteristics, ensuring that both parties understand their rights and responsibilities. It should also clarify the circumstances under which the sponsor may use the created materials and whether the sponsored individual has any right of approval or review.

Termination clauses are vital components of any sponsorship agreement. These clauses stipulate under what conditions either party may terminate the contract prematurely. They might involve breaches of contract, failure to meet performance obligations, or changes in circumstances that render the partnership unviable. The contract should specify the procedures involved in terminating the contract, the circumstances triggering termination, and the potential consequences of termination. This includes detailing notice periods, financial settlement terms, and the return or disposal of materials. Ambiguity in these clauses can create room for disputes and costly legal battles. Therefore, it's imperative that the termination clause is carefully drafted to protect the interests of both parties involved. The circumstances triggering termination should be specifically defined, and a clear procedure for termination must be established. This ensures a fair and orderly process if the partnership must be dissolved.

Dispute resolution mechanisms are essential in protecting both parties against potential disagreements. Sponsorship contracts are complex and involve numerous potentially contentious issues. Therefore, it is crucial that the contract establishes mechanisms to resolve disputes promptly and efficiently. These mechanisms might involve mediation, arbitration, or litigation. However, specifying a preferred method of dispute resolution upfront can streamline the process and potentially reduce the cost and time involved in resolving conflicts. Mediation is often preferred as a first step, providing a less formal and less expensive way to address disagreements before resorting to more formal processes. Arbitration provides a more formal process, involving a neutral third party to make a binding decision. Litigation, while often the most costly and time-consuming method, is sometimes necessary when other methods fail to resolve the dispute. Therefore, carefully selecting the most suitable method for dispute resolution within the contract is vital for protecting both parties involved.

Finally, legal counsel is paramount in negotiating sponsorship contracts. The complexity of these agreements, the potential financial implications, and the potential impact on an individual's reputation, emphasizes the importance of securing expert legal guidance. A skilled entertainment lawyer can navigate the complexities of contract law, intellectual property, and other relevant legal issues to ensure that the agreement is fair, equitable, and protects the interests of the sponsored party. Legal counsel can assist in drafting, negotiating, and reviewing the contract to ensure clarity, address potential risks, and mitigate potential problems. They can also advise on appropriate payment structures, performance obligations, and intellectual property protections. While legal fees may seem an upfront cost, the potential for financial losses and reputational damage from poorly negotiated contracts far outweighs the cost of securing expert legal advice. Thus, ensuring legal counsel is an indispensable step in securing mutually beneficial and legally sound sponsorships. Their expertise in contract negotiation can safeguard your reputation and ensure you receive fair compensation for your contributions, establishing the foundation for a successful long-term partnership.

Compliance and legal considerations are paramount in endorsement and sponsorship deals, impacting not only the financial aspects but also an individual's reputation and long-term career prospects. Ignoring these critical elements can lead to significant legal repercussions, financial penalties, and damage to one's public image. This section delves into the essential regulatory frameworks and guidelines that govern endorsements and sponsorships, emphasizing the importance of adherence to prevent legal entanglement and ensure ethical practices.

One of the most prominent regulatory bodies overseeing endorsements and sponsorships in the United States is the Federal Trade Commission (FTC). The FTC's regulations focus primarily on preventing deceptive advertising and ensuring that endorsements are truthful and not misleading to consumers. These regulations, often referred to as "advertising substantiation," require that endorsers have a reasonable basis for making any claims they make about a product or service. Simply put, an endorser can't claim a product works wonders if they haven't personally experienced its purported benefits or if there's no scientific evidence to support those claims. This means that endorsements must be based on the endorser's genuine experiences and beliefs, not merely on financial incentives. The FTC guidelines extend beyond simple statements; they also encompass the overall context in which the endorsement is presented. This includes visual representations, implied claims, and even the tone and manner of presentation.

The FTC's scrutiny extends to the disclosure of material connections between the endorser and the brand. This is crucial to ensure transparency and prevent consumers from being misled. The "material connection" refers to any relationship that might influence the endorser's opinion or recommendation of the product or service. This includes financial compensation, free products, or any other form of benefit received in exchange for the endorsement. Failing to disclose these material connections is considered deceptive advertising, a violation that can result in significant penalties. The FTC's guidelines emphasize the need for clear and conspicuous disclosures, meaning that the disclosure must be easily noticeable and understandable to the average consumer. Small print or subtly placed disclosures are insufficient; the disclosure must be prominent enough to grab the consumer's attention and alert them to the endorser's relationship with the brand. This often involves specific language or formats depending on the platform, whether it's a television commercial, a social media post, or a blog article. For instance, using hashtags like ad or sponsored, or clearly stating "paid partnership," are common practices to fulfill this requirement. The FTC also provides detailed guides and examples on how to properly disclose these relationships, so understanding and following these guidelines are essential for anyone involved in endorsements.

Beyond the FTC, various state laws and regulations might also apply to endorsement and sponsorship deals. Some states have stricter regulations regarding advertising claims and disclosures than others. Moreover, industry self-regulation organizations play a vital role in setting ethical standards and ensuring compliance within their respective sectors. These organizations often develop codes of conduct and best practices to guide members in their endorsements and sponsorship activities. While not legally binding in the same way as FTC regulations, adherence to these industry standards contributes to maintaining trust and credibility within the industry. Furthermore, compliance with these self-regulatory guidelines can preemptively minimize legal risks and prevent potential conflicts. For example, the advertising standards of the American Advertising Federation (AAF) or the guidelines of specific industry associations can provide valuable insights into ethical advertising practices and compliance expectations.

Another significant compliance area is the avoidance of misleading or deceptive representations. This pertains not only to the explicit claims made about the product but also the overall impression conveyed in the endorsement. The FTC is particularly vigilant about endorsements that present unrealistic expectations or distort the truth. Using exaggerated claims, testimonials that lack a factual basis, or staging scenarios that create an artificial sense of authenticity can result in violations. For example, an athlete endorsing a weight-loss supplement might be held accountable if they claim to have achieved significant weight loss solely by using the product, without acknowledging the role of training or diet. Similarly, presenting a product in an idealized setting that doesn't reflect typical usage could be viewed as deceptive. Carefully reviewing and verifying all aspects of an endorsement, ensuring accuracy and transparency in both visual and textual presentations, is crucial to prevent violations.

Intellectual property rights are a further critical consideration within endorsement and sponsorship agreements. These agreements frequently involve the use of the endorser's name, image, likeness, and other intellectual property rights. Properly defining and protecting these rights in the contract is vital to avoid future disputes. For example, a contract should specify the exclusive or non-exclusive rights granted to the sponsor to use the endorser's likeness in their marketing materials. The contract also needs to address the duration of these usage rights and any limitations placed on their use. Failure to clearly define these intellectual property aspects in the contract can lead to disputes over usage rights and potential infringements. A carefully crafted contract should outline all usage rights, licensing agreements, and ownership of any newly created materials as part of the endorsement or sponsorship. This includes specifying the permissible scope of usage, including platforms, formats, and geographical locations. It's equally vital to establish the appropriate mechanisms for the approval and review of marketing materials to protect the endorser's image and reputation.

Beyond the legal considerations, ethical responsibilities play a crucial role in successful and sustainable endorsements and sponsorships. Maintaining integrity and avoiding any actions that could compromise one's credibility is essential. Endorsing a product or service that one does not genuinely believe in or that one would not personally use is ethically questionable and could have negative reputational consequences. Even if the endorsement complies with all legal requirements, an ethically dubious endorsement could damage the endorser's long-term reputation and trust with their audience. Therefore, careful consideration of the product or service and its alignment with one's personal values is a key aspect of responsible endorsement. This ethical approach not only protects the endorser's image but also fosters trust and authenticity with their audience, which are essential elements for building a strong and lasting career in the long run. Prioritizing ethical considerations alongside legal compliance contributes to the overall success and longevity of an endorsement or sponsorship.

In conclusion, navigating the legal and compliance aspects of endorsements and sponsorships requires careful attention to detail and adherence to regulatory frameworks. Understanding the FTC guidelines on advertising substantiation and disclosure, complying with state laws and industry self-regulation standards, and carefully defining intellectual property rights are all crucial elements. Furthermore, maintaining ethical integrity and avoiding potentially misleading or deceptive representations are fundamental to building a sustainable and reputable career. The assistance of experienced legal counsel is indispensable in navigating these complexities, ensuring that agreements are legally sound, protect the endorser's interests, and contribute to the overall success and integrity of the partnership. By diligently adhering to both legal and ethical guidelines, individuals can establish a strong foundation for successful and mutually beneficial endorsement and sponsorship ventures.

Building and managing brand partnerships effectively requires more than just securing a lucrative deal; it demands a strategic approach that aligns personal values with business objectives. This intricate dance between personal branding and corporate interests necessitates a thorough understanding of the legal landscape and a proactive approach to risk mitigation. While financial incentives are undoubtedly attractive, choosing partners who resonate with your personal brand and values is crucial for long-term success and maintaining audience trust.

Consider the scenario of an athlete known for their dedication to environmental causes signing an endorsement deal with a company notorious for environmentally damaging practices. While the monetary compensation might be significant, the incongruence between the athlete's values and the brand's actions can lead to a backlash from their audience, damaging their reputation and eroding public trust. This incongruity not only undermines the athlete's credibility but also creates a precarious legal situation. The athlete might face accusations of hypocrisy, jeopardizing future endorsement opportunities and potentially even leading to legal challenges if the brand's claims are found to be misleading or deceptive.

Therefore, the selection process for brand partnerships should incorporate a rigorous vetting procedure, carefully evaluating the brand's values, ethical practices, and overall reputation. Due diligence is paramount. This goes beyond simply reviewing a company's marketing materials; it requires scrutinizing their supply chain, production methods, environmental impact, and labor practices. In the digital age, access to information is readily available; conducting thorough online research, reviewing independent audits and reports, and even reaching out to industry experts or watchdog organizations can shed light on a company's true character.

The legal framework surrounding brand partnerships is equally crucial. Contracts should explicitly outline the terms of the agreement, including the duration, scope of usage rights, compensation structure, and clauses regarding termination and dispute resolution. Ambiguous language can be a breeding ground for conflicts, so clear, concise, and unambiguous phrasing is vital. Experienced legal counsel specializing in entertainment law can provide invaluable guidance in drafting and negotiating these agreements, ensuring that your interests are protected and that the contract accurately reflects your expectations.

One key aspect of the contract that often gets overlooked is the right of approval. This clause gives the endorser the right to review and approve all marketing materials featuring their image and likeness before they are released to the public. This is crucial for maintaining control over your brand and preventing any misrepresentations or use of your image in a context you find objectionable. Without such a clause, you risk your reputation being associated with marketing that doesn't align with your personal brand or even that actively contradicts your values.

Intellectual property rights are another critical legal consideration in brand partnerships. These agreements frequently involve the use of the endorser's name, image, likeness, and other intellectual property rights. The contract should explicitly define the rights granted to the brand and any limitations placed on their usage. This includes specifying the permissible scope of usage, including platforms, formats, and geographical locations. Failure to clearly define these aspects can lead to disputes and potential infringements. For instance, a contract might specify exclusive rights for a certain period, allowing the brand to utilize the athlete's image in all their marketing materials within a particular geographical area. Conversely, a non-exclusive agreement might permit the athlete to endorse other brands within the same category.

The use of social media adds another layer of complexity to brand partnerships. Many endorsement deals now leverage social media platforms, requiring careful consideration of disclosure requirements and compliance with FTC regulations. As we've established, failing to disclose material connections between the endorser and the brand is considered deceptive advertising. This necessitates clear and conspicuous disclosures in all social media posts, clearly indicating any sponsored content or paid partnerships. Furthermore, the content itself must be authentic and reflect the endorser's genuine experience with the product or service.

Beyond the legal aspects, ethical considerations are equally crucial. While a lucrative deal might be tempting, aligning with brands that resonate with your values is essential for long-term sustainability. A partnership built on authenticity and mutual respect not only strengthens your brand but also fosters trust with your audience. This is particularly crucial for maintaining a loyal and engaged following in the long run.

Consider a musician known for their commitment to fair labor practices endorsing a clothing line produced under exploitative conditions. This would almost certainly result in widespread negative publicity and damage to their personal brand, regardless of the legal compliance of the agreement. The ethical implications of such a partnership severely outweigh any short-term financial gains.

Building a portfolio of brand partnerships is a strategic process. It's not merely about accumulating endorsements; it's about carefully selecting partners who share your values and contribute to the narrative of your personal brand. This requires a long-term vision, carefully considering not only the immediate financial benefits but also the potential long-term impact on your reputation and overall brand identity.

The process of managing these partnerships requires ongoing vigilance and communication. Regular review of the marketing materials, ongoing monitoring of the brand's activities and their alignment with your values, and maintaining open communication with the brand's representatives are crucial. This proactive approach enables early intervention should any discrepancies or concerns arise, minimizing potential damage and ensuring the partnership remains aligned with your personal and professional goals.

Moreover, having a well-defined termination clause in your contracts is essential. This clause should clearly outline the circumstances under which the partnership can be terminated and any consequences associated with such termination. Having a clear exit strategy allows for a swift and decisive response if the brand's actions or behavior contradict the terms of the agreement or compromise your personal brand.

In essence, navigating the world of brand partnerships requires a balanced approach, meticulously weighing legal considerations, financial incentives, and ethical implications. Choosing partners who truly align with your personal values, meticulously drafting and reviewing contracts, and actively managing the relationship are crucial steps in building a strong and enduring brand portfolio. This holistic approach safeguards not only your financial interests but also your reputation and the long-term health of your career. By integrating these elements into your strategic planning, you can maximize the potential of brand partnerships while mitigating potential risks. Remember, a strong brand isn't just about financial success; it's about establishing a trust-based relationship with your audience and maintaining credibility in the long run. And that takes more than just a good lawyer; it requires ethical integrity and a deep understanding of your own brand identity.

Let's delve into the fascinating world of successful endorsements, dissecting the strategies and legal frameworks that propelled these partnerships to triumph. These case studies aren't just about big payouts; they illustrate the power of strategic alignment, meticulous contract negotiation, and a keen understanding of the legal landscape. The common thread weaving through these successes is a commitment to authenticity, a meticulous approach to risk mitigation, and a proactive stance in protecting the endorser's brand.

Consider the enduring partnership between Serena Williams and Nike. This wasn't merely a transactional deal; it was a carefully cultivated relationship built on mutual respect and shared values. Serena's powerful image as a dominant athlete and a strong female voice resonated perfectly with Nike's brand identity of empowerment and athletic achievement. The legal framework underpinning this partnership undoubtedly involved comprehensive contracts meticulously defining usage rights, compensation structures, and termination clauses. However, the success story transcends the legal fine print. It's a testament to the synergy between two powerful brands, a synergy that has endured for decades, generating significant revenue for both parties while simultaneously reinforcing their individual brand identities. The longevity of this partnership highlights the importance of aligning with brands that share similar values and resonate with the endorser's personal brand. A cursory review of Nike's marketing materials featuring Serena showcases a consistent portrayal of her image aligned with her own self-branding, showcasing a clear respect for her personality and values. This consistency is not merely a happy accident, but a result of meticulous contract negotiation and ongoing monitoring of marketing materials, showcasing an exceptional level of collaboration and brand stewardship.

Another compelling example is the collaboration between LeBron James and McDonald's. This partnership represents a masterful approach to integrating endorsements into a broader brand strategy. James, a global icon with unparalleled influence, leveraged this partnership to not only generate substantial income but also to enhance his philanthropic endeavors. The partnership extended beyond mere product endorsements; it incorporated community initiatives, reflecting James's commitment to social responsibility. This integration of business and social impact demonstrates a sophisticated understanding of brand building and the strategic use of endorsement deals to enhance personal image and values. The legal agreements underpinning this deal would undoubtedly be complex, addressing intellectual property rights, usage restrictions, and the stipulations around philanthropic initiatives. The key takeaway is the careful integration of personal values into the endorsement deal. This is not merely about the financial return; it is a calculated strategy to further a personal narrative that emphasizes more than sporting achievements. The legal team working on this agreement would undoubtedly have factored in the potential for backlash if James's public image and the McDonald's brand were misaligned.

Moving beyond the realm of sports, consider the case of musician Billie Eilish and her partnership with Gucci. Eilish's unique style and rebellious spirit align seamlessly with Gucci's commitment to pushing boundaries and challenging conventional aesthetics. This collaboration extended beyond traditional endorsements, encompassing creative campaigns that reflected Eilish's artistic vision and personal identity. The contract would have involved carefully crafted clauses to protect both Eilish's intellectual property rights and her creative input in the marketing campaigns. Here, the success lies not just in the financial gains but in the synergistic creation of compelling content that resonates with both the target audience and reinforces the distinct brand identity of both the musician and the fashion house. The legal framework, in this case, wouldn't just protect the usage of her image and likeness; it would also safeguard her artistic freedom and ensure the integrity of the creative collaboration. The meticulous planning of this partnership is reflected in the innovative and engaging campaigns that were created.

These examples illustrate the crucial role of legal counsel in securing successful endorsement deals. The contracts negotiated for these partnerships would have been far more than just basic agreements. They would have encompassed detailed clauses covering usage rights, image control, exclusivity provisions, payment structures, termination options, and even dispute resolution mechanisms. A skilled entertainment lawyer would ensure the contracts were fair, balanced, and adequately protected the interests of the endorser while also being realistic in their expectations regarding brand collaboration. It's worth noting that the absence of strong legal counsel could have easily jeopardized these partnerships, leading to disputes, financial losses, and irreparable damage to brand reputations. The legal process is often a behind-the-scenes process that enables the visibility of the endorsement deals themselves.

The successful endorsements highlighted above also exemplify the crucial interplay between legal compliance and ethical considerations. While the financial incentives are undoubtedly a key driver, aligning with brands that share one's values is crucial for maintaining public trust and long-term brand sustainability. The enduring success of these partnerships underscores the importance of due diligence in selecting brand partners. Thorough research into the brand's values, ethical practices, and social impact is essential before entering into any endorsement agreement. Ignoring this aspect can lead to public backlash, even if the legal aspects of the contract are perfectly sound.

Furthermore, these case studies underscore the importance of ongoing management of the endorsement relationships. Regular review of marketing materials, active engagement with brand representatives, and a clear understanding of the brand's actions are all vital for maintaining alignment and preventing any potential conflicts. The success of these long-term partnerships speaks to the commitment of both parties to fostering a relationship built on mutual respect and ongoing communication.

Finally, the element of authenticity cannot be overstated. Audiences are increasingly discerning and can easily detect inauthentic or forced endorsements. The success of the endorsements cited above stems, in part, from the genuine connection between the endorser and the brand. The collaborations feel natural and authentic, adding another layer to the success of these partnerships beyond the purely financial and legal considerations.

In conclusion, successful endorsements are not merely about securing lucrative deals; they are about strategically aligning personal brand values with those of corporate entities. They require meticulous legal work, a robust understanding of brand identity, an unwavering commitment to authenticity, and ongoing management of the partnership. These successful case studies serve as valuable lessons for aspiring creators and athletes, illustrating the multifaceted nature of endorsement deals and the importance of a holistic approach to maximizing their potential while mitigating potential risks. The legal framework, while crucial, is merely one component of a much broader strategy that prioritizes ethical considerations, brand alignment, and long-term sustainability.

Chapter 5: NIL Rights for Athletes

The explosion of Name, Image, and Likeness (NIL) rights for student-athletes has fundamentally reshaped the landscape of college sports. No longer confined to the purely amateur realm, collegiate athletes now possess the legal right to profit from their own identities, opening doors to lucrative endorsement deals, sponsorships, and entrepreneurial ventures. However, this newfound freedom comes with a complex web of legal considerations that require careful navigation. Understanding the nuances of NIL rights is crucial for athletes seeking to capitalize on their market value while avoiding legal pitfalls.

At its core, NIL rights encompass the athlete's right to control the commercial use of their name, image, and likeness. This means that they can authorize the use of their identity in various commercial contexts, such as advertisements, endorsements, social media campaigns, appearances, and merchandise sales. This right previously remained largely untapped, as NCAA regulations strictly prohibited student-athletes from profiting from their athletic abilities. The shift towards allowing NIL deals represents a paradigm shift in the relationship between athletes, universities, and commercial entities.

The legal framework governing NIL rights varies considerably depending on the state and the specific governing bodies involved. Some states have enacted comprehensive NIL laws, providing clear guidelines and regulatory frameworks. These laws often address critical issues such as disclosure requirements, agent representation, and the permissible scope of commercial activities. In the absence of state-specific NIL legislation, universities may establish their own internal policies, often in collaboration with the NCAA, to regulate NIL activities within their athletic programs. This patchwork of regulations creates a complex and sometimes confusing landscape for student-athletes and their advisors. Consistency across institutions and states is lacking, making uniform understanding and application challenging.

One of the most significant aspects of NIL rights is the issue of agent representation. Student-athletes may seek the assistance of agents to negotiate endorsement deals, manage their brand, and navigate the complexities of the commercial world. However, the selection and engagement of an agent must be carefully considered, as unscrupulous agents may exploit athletes' lack of experience and knowledge. Many states have introduced regulations concerning agent representation, including licensing requirements, disclosure obligations, and restrictions on the types of compensation agents can receive. It's paramount for athletes to conduct thorough due diligence before engaging any agent to ensure their interests are protected.

Another crucial area to consider is the potential conflict between NIL activities and the athlete's academic responsibilities. Universities often have guidelines regarding the time commitment allowed for NIL activities, ensuring they do not interfere with academic performance. The balance between maximizing NIL opportunities and maintaining academic standing is a challenge that athletes must carefully address. Violating these guidelines could lead to sanctions, even jeopardizing their athletic eligibility.

The potential for tax implications is another significant concern. NIL earnings are subject to federal and state taxes, which can be substantial depending on the athlete's income. Student-athletes need to consult with qualified tax professionals to understand their tax obligations and develop effective strategies for managing their earnings. Failure to adhere to tax regulations can have serious financial consequences, adding to the already complicated financial implications of NIL opportunities.

The legal protections afforded by NIL rights extend beyond mere financial gain. Athletes also possess the right to control how their image and likeness are used, ensuring their reputation and brand are not jeopardized. This includes the right to approve or reject endorsement deals, control the content of marketing materials, and ensure that their image is aligned with their personal values. An athlete's careful consideration of brand alignment will help them build a brand with a lasting impact beyond their college career.

Moreover, athletes should understand their rights related to intellectual property. The use of their name, image, and likeness can also entail the creation of intellectual property, such as merchandise or digital content. It is essential to understand the ownership and licensing rights associated with these creations and seek appropriate legal counsel to protect these assets.

Furthermore, the rise of social media has introduced new dimensions to NIL rights. Athletes often leverage social media platforms to build their brand and engage with fans, which creates opportunities for both endorsements and personal brand building. However, athletes must be mindful of the legal implications of their social media activity, including potential copyright and trademark infringements, defamation claims, and contractual obligations with sponsors. A clear understanding of terms of service and engagement policies is critical.

The negotiation of NIL deals often involves complex contracts that require careful scrutiny. These contracts typically specify the scope of the athlete's endorsement, the duration of the agreement, the compensation structure, and the intellectual property rights involved. It's crucial to review these contracts with experienced legal counsel to ensure they are fair and protect the athlete's interests. Understanding clauses surrounding termination, breach of contract, and dispute resolution is critical for safeguarding against potential issues.

The landscape of NIL rights is constantly evolving. Legislative changes, court decisions, and evolving NCAA policies will continue to shape the legal framework governing NIL activities. Staying updated on these developments is crucial for athletes and their advisors to remain compliant and make informed decisions.

In conclusion, the legal framework surrounding NIL rights is intricate and multifaceted. Athletes seeking to leverage their NIL opportunities must navigate a complex web of state laws, university regulations, and potential conflicts of interest. By understanding the key elements discussed above – agent representation, academic considerations, tax obligations, brand protection, intellectual property rights, social media implications, contract negotiation, and the dynamic legal landscape – athletes can confidently enter the world of NIL deals while mitigating risks and safeguarding their long-term interests. Seeking advice from experienced legal counsel specializing in sports law is paramount for ensuring the athlete's success and long-term career trajectory. The ability to navigate this complex regulatory environment is as critical as athletic talent itself in the modern era of college sports. The responsible exercise of NIL rights can lay a robust foundation for a successful future, both on and off the field.

Navigating the complexities of NIL agreements requires a keen understanding of contract law and a strategic approach to negotiation. While the thrill of securing endorsement deals and sponsorships is undeniable, the agreements themselves are legally binding contracts that can significantly impact an athlete's financial future and overall brand. Therefore, careful consideration and professional legal counsel are paramount.

The negotiation process typically begins with identifying potential partners whose values and brand align with the athlete's image. This is a crucial step, often overlooked. A mismatch between an athlete's personality and a brand's identity can lead to an ineffective campaign and potentially damage the athlete's reputation. Therefore, the selection of potential partners should be approached meticulously, examining the brand's history, target audience, and overall marketing strategy. Due diligence is as crucial here as in any other business venture.

Once potential partners are identified, the negotiation phase commences. This phase focuses on the specifics of the agreement, including the compensation structure, exclusivity clauses, the term of the agreement (duration), and the scope of permitted activities. Compensation can take many forms, ranging from upfront payments and performance bonuses to royalties on merchandise sales or a share of profits. Negotiating the optimal compensation requires a clear understanding of the athlete's market value, considering factors such as their athletic achievements, social media following, and projected impact on brand visibility. It's important to remember that an athlete's value extends beyond their on-field performance; their ability to engage with fans and followers on social media platforms is a significant asset. Social media influence adds a new dimension to the market value negotiation. The value of this influencer potential should not be underestimated, and any contract should reflect this realistically.

Exclusivity clauses deserve special attention. These clauses restrict the athlete from endorsing competing brands during the term of the agreement. While exclusivity can lead to higher compensation, it also limits the athlete's opportunities. The negotiation should carefully weigh the advantages of exclusivity against the potential loss of other lucrative endorsements. A well-structured NIL agreement might include carefully considered exceptions to exclusivity clauses to allow participation in certain charitable events or collaborations that don't directly conflict with the primary sponsor. This demonstrates a holistic understanding of an athlete's personal and professional responsibilities.

The duration of the agreement is another critical aspect. Shorter-term agreements offer flexibility, allowing athletes to adapt to changing market conditions and explore new opportunities. However, longer-term agreements can provide greater financial security. The optimal duration will depend on the specific circumstances and the nature of the partnership. For example, an endorsement with a rapidly growing tech company might warrant a shorter term, allowing the athlete to adjust their strategies as the market evolves. Conversely, a long-term partnership with a more established brand could offer stability and continued revenue streams.

The scope of permitted activities outlines what the athlete is authorized to do for the sponsor. This includes everything from appearing in advertisements and social media posts to attending promotional events and participating in marketing campaigns. Clearly defining the scope of activities prevents misunderstandings and protects both parties. For example, the agreement might specify the minimum number of social media posts, the nature of any required appearances, and even stipulations for creative control of any marketing material featuring the athlete's image and likeness. The athlete should insist on maintaining a level of control to ensure that their brand is represented accurately and aligns with their values.

Intellectual property rights are another crucial element of NIL agreements. These agreements typically address the ownership and usage rights of any intellectual property created as part of the endorsement deal. For example, if the athlete participates in a photoshoot or video recording, the agreement should clearly specify who owns the resulting images and videos and how they can be used. This is especially vital for athletes who plan on building long-term brands beyond their college athletic career. Their ability to leverage these assets for future marketing ventures must be considered, and it should be clearly documented.

Beyond the core components, NIL agreements should include clauses addressing termination, dispute resolution, and confidentiality. Termination clauses outline the conditions under which either party can end the agreement. Dispute resolution clauses specify the process for resolving any disagreements that may arise. Confidentiality clauses protect sensitive information shared between the parties. These clauses are critical to protecting the athlete's interests and safeguarding against potential conflicts or breaches of contract. A professional legal review of these elements is highly recommended, as these sections have significant implications for future legal disputes.

The negotiation of an NIL agreement often involves discussions of performance metrics and reporting requirements. Sponsors will want to monitor the effectiveness of their investment, so the contract might include measures to track reach, engagement, and return on investment. Understanding these key performance indicators (KPIs) is important for athletes and their advisors. It is also essential for athletes to be fully aware of the reporting requirements and provide regular updates to their sponsors, maintaining a transparent and collaborative relationship.

Finally, it is crucial for student-athletes to fully understand their state's NIL legislation. These laws and regulations continue to evolve, and staying abreast of changes is critical. The regulations may impose restrictions on types of endorsements, limitations on compensation, and disclosure requirements. Any potential conflict with NCAA rules and university policies should be carefully considered. The goal is to maximize earnings while maintaining compliance with all relevant rules and regulations. It is highly advisable for any athlete to maintain a continuous dialogue with their legal counsel, especially as the legal landscape continues to evolve. This vigilance will help ensure compliance and allow the athlete to take full advantage of NIL opportunities without jeopardizing their athletic career.

In conclusion, the negotiation and execution of NIL agreements require careful consideration of various legal and business aspects. Athletes should seek the advice of experienced sports and entertainment lawyers to ensure they are adequately protected. By understanding the complexities of NIL agreements and leveraging professional guidance, student-athletes can effectively capitalize on their NIL rights while building a sustainable and responsible brand for their future. Thorough due diligence, clear communication, and a keen eye for detail are invaluable assets in this process. This proactive approach can set the stage for long-term success, ensuring the athlete's financial security and professional reputation beyond their college years. The responsible management of NIL agreements can be the foundation for a successful and enduring career in the world of sports and beyond.

The landscape of Name, Image, and Likeness (NIL) rights for student-athletes is a constantly shifting terrain, shaped by the interplay of NCAA regulations and a patchwork of state laws. Understanding this complex regulatory environment is crucial for athletes seeking to capitalize on their NIL opportunities without jeopardizing their eligibility or facing penalties. The NCAA, initially resistant to the concept of athlete compensation beyond scholarships, has been forced to adapt to the changing legal and societal climate. Their current framework, while aiming for balance, is intricate and requires careful navigation.

The NCAA's NIL policy, while allowing athletes to profit from their NIL, isn't a blanket endorsement of all commercial activities. The core principle revolves around maintaining amateurism and ensuring that compensation isn't tied directly to athletic performance. This means deals that explicitly reward an athlete for their on-field success are generally prohibited. For example, an endorsement deal that pays a basketball player more based on their points per game would violate NCAA rules. Instead, endorsements should focus on the athlete's individual brand, personality, and marketability, independent of their athletic achievements. The line can be blurry, however, and professional legal counsel is critical in determining whether a proposed deal complies with the NCAA's constantly evolving guidelines.

A key area of concern lies in the restriction against "pay for play." The NCAA strictly prohibits situations where compensation is directly contingent upon athletic performance or participation. This means structuring NIL deals carefully to avoid even the appearance of quid pro quo. For instance, a company offering a significant endorsement to a star quarterback solely because of their position and potential impact on game outcomes would likely be deemed a violation. However, the same company might be able to sponsor the athlete for their social media presence, regardless of their on-field achievements, provided the compensation is not tied to win/loss records or game statistics. This nuances the situation considerably and requires a deep understanding of the regulations.

The NCAA's rules also address the use of the athlete's uniform, school logos, and other team-related intellectual property. Generally, the use of these elements is restricted unless explicitly permitted by the university or the NCAA. An athlete cannot, for instance, wear their team jersey in an advertisement without prior authorization. This often involves navigating university licensing agreements, which vary from institution to institution and can add another layer of complexity to the negotiation process. It's important to note that even if an athlete is allowed to use school logos or branding, strict guidelines will likely exist on the specific manner of their use to maintain the appropriate level of branding and compliance.

Further complicating matters is the involvement of third-party agents and representatives. The NCAA has regulations governing the relationships between athletes and their representatives, aiming to prevent exploitation and ensure transparency. These regulations often involve disclosure requirements, limitations on compensation paid to agents, and restrictions on the types of services agents can provide. It's a highly regulated environment, and it's crucial that athletes choose their representatives carefully and understand the restrictions and regulatory implications of their interactions. Failure to comply with these rules can lead to serious consequences for both the athlete and their agent. The penalties can range from financial sanctions to suspension from athletic competition.

The intersection of NCAA regulations and state laws adds another dimension to the challenge. Many states have enacted their own NIL laws, often providing more expansive rights to student-athletes than the NCAA allows. This creates a complex landscape, with potential conflicts between state and federal regulations. The laws vary significantly from state to state, covering aspects like permissible types of endorsements, restrictions on compensation, and disclosure requirements. An athlete attending a university in one state might have substantially different NIL opportunities than an athlete at a university in another. The legal counsel involved should be intimately familiar with the laws of the relevant state and any potential conflicts with the NCAA's regulations.

For example, some states may allow athletes to endorse alcohol or gambling products, while others may have strict prohibitions. Others may impose stricter regulations on the types of compensation allowable, such as limitations on payments from collectives or restrictions on the percentage of earnings that can be paid to agents.

The variations are significant, requiring a detailed analysis of the state-specific legislation and its interaction with the broader NCAA framework. Without a comprehensive understanding of both state and federal regulations, the athlete risks non-compliance and potential penalties. The legal counsel needs to be a specialist in this specific area of sports and entertainment law to ensure complete compliance.

Navigating this regulatory maze requires meticulous planning and a proactive approach. Athletes should consult with experienced legal counsel who specializes in NIL rights and understands the nuances of both NCAA rules and state laws. The development of a comprehensive compliance plan is paramount. This plan should outline permissible activities, disclosure procedures, and strategies for navigating potential conflicts between various regulations. Careful drafting of contracts, a thorough understanding of the relevant laws, and a focus on transparency are critical for avoiding legal pitfalls.

Furthermore, proactive communication with the university's compliance office is essential. Early engagement with university officials allows for a collaborative approach to ensuring compliance with institutional policies and avoiding unintentional violations. The university's athletic department and legal teams can often provide valuable insights and guidance, helping athletes avoid missteps. This open communication channels are crucial and should be maintained throughout the process.

The evolving nature of NIL regulations necessitates ongoing vigilance. Both the NCAA and state legislatures continue to revise and refine their guidelines. Staying informed about these changes is vital to maintaining compliance. Athletes and their representatives must actively monitor updates and adapt their strategies as needed. Consistent review of agreements, policies, and regulations is vital for managing NIL rights effectively. Ignoring changes in regulations can have severe financial and legal implications.

Ultimately, successful NIL management requires a strategic balance between maximizing revenue opportunities and preserving athletic eligibility. It's a balancing act that demands sophisticated legal expertise, careful planning, and ongoing compliance monitoring. With the right professional guidance and proactive approach, however, athletes can harness their NIL rights to build a sustainable brand and achieve financial success without compromising their athletic careers. The investment in legal counsel specializing in this area is not just an expense, it is a vital investment in the long-term financial security and career trajectory of the athlete. The complexities involved demand a depth of knowledge only a seasoned professional can offer. Ignoring this aspect is a risk that few athletes can afford to take.

Building a successful NIL brand isn't merely about securing lucrative deals; it's about cultivating a compelling narrative and authentic connection with fans and potential sponsors. It requires a strategic approach that integrates legal compliance with savvy marketing and personal branding strategies. The key is to understand that your NIL value is not solely tied to your athletic prowess, but to the broader appeal of your personality, your values, and the stories you tell.

The foundation of any successful NIL brand is authenticity. Sponsors are increasingly drawn to athletes who embody genuine values and resonate with their target audience. This means carefully considering your personal brand identity. What are your passions beyond the playing field? What causes do you care about? What unique qualities set you apart from your peers? Defining these aspects is crucial for attracting brands that align with your personal values and long-term goals. A hastily assembled campaign based solely on immediate financial gain is unlikely to be sustainable in the long run. It's about building a relationship, not just closing a deal.

Once you've established a clear brand identity, it's time to develop a comprehensive marketing strategy. This strategy should encompass multiple channels, including social media, personal website, and potentially traditional media outlets. Social media is particularly crucial in today's digital landscape, providing a direct line of communication with fans and potential sponsors. A well-maintained and engaging social media presence, showcasing your personality, training regimen, community involvement, and interests, can significantly enhance your brand visibility and marketability. Consistent posting, high-quality content, and genuine interaction with your followers are key to building a loyal and engaged fanbase.

Your personal website serves as a central hub for your brand, providing a professional platform to showcase your accomplishments, endorsements, and upcoming events. It's an opportunity to present a curated image of yourself, highlighting your achievements both on and off the field. A well-designed website can elevate your credibility and professionalism, attracting more serious and high-value sponsorship opportunities. Consider including a media kit with high-resolution photos, a biography, and details of your endorsement portfolio to make it easier for potential sponsors to understand your brand.

Content creation is paramount in building a strong NIL brand. This extends beyond simple social media posts. Consider creating engaging video content, such as behind-the-scenes glimpses of your training, or interviews discussing your passions and motivations. Podcasts are another effective medium for connecting with fans on a more personal level. Remember, the goal is to build a genuine connection with your audience, showcasing your personality and letting your true self shine through. High-quality content, consistently delivered, keeps your brand relevant and top of mind.

Legal compliance remains a paramount consideration throughout the entire process. Every endorsement deal must adhere to the complex regulatory framework governing NIL rights, including NCAA rules and potentially relevant state laws. As previously discussed, these regulations constantly evolve, requiring ongoing monitoring and careful attention to detail. A single lapse in compliance can lead to severe penalties, jeopardizing both your athletic career and your NIL earning potential. Consulting with experienced legal counsel familiar with the intricacies of NIL regulations is not simply advisable; it's essential. Their guidance will prevent costly mistakes and ensure long-term sustainability. This isn't simply about avoiding legal troubles, it's about strategically maximizing your opportunities while remaining within the confines of the law.

Before entering into any endorsement deal, meticulously review the contract with your legal team. Pay close attention to the length of the contract, the compensation structure, exclusivity clauses, deliverables, and termination provisions. Understand the implications of each clause and ensure that the terms align with your brand values and long-term goals. Don't hesitate to negotiate favorable terms, seeking clarity and understanding every aspect of the agreement. Remember, this isn't just a financial transaction; it's a partnership that reflects on your brand and your image. It's an investment in your future, and it requires thorough consideration and expert guidance.

Diversification is key to mitigating risk and building a resilient NIL brand. Don't rely on a single source of income or a limited range of endorsements. Explore various opportunities, from merchandise to social media campaigns, speaking engagements, and even personal appearances. The more diverse your revenue streams, the more resilient your brand will be to market fluctuations or changes in the regulatory landscape. This strategy ensures financial stability and reduces your dependence on any single deal, enhancing the long-term health of your brand.

Building relationships with other individuals and companies is vital. Network with fellow athletes, industry professionals, and potential sponsors. Attend industry events, participate in community outreach programs, and build connections that could translate into future endorsement opportunities. This strategic networking enhances your brand's reach and expands your pool of potential collaborators. Remember, your network isn't just a list of contacts; it's a resource for building valuable partnerships and growing your overall brand value.

Finally, remember that building a successful NIL brand is an ongoing process. It requires consistent effort, adaptability, and a willingness to learn and grow. Regularly assess your progress, analyze your performance metrics, and refine your strategy based on the results. Stay informed about changes in the NIL landscape and adapt your approach accordingly. The NIL environment is dynamic and constantly evolving. Continuous learning, adaptation, and proactive planning are vital for continued success. The investment in your personal brand is an investment in your future, far beyond the immediate financial gains. It's about building a sustainable career that extends beyond your athletic years. It's about building a legacy, beyond the field of play.

The landscape of college athletics has been irrevocably altered by the advent of Name, Image, and Likeness (NIL) rights. For years, student-athletes generated immense revenue for their universities and associated brands, yet they remained legally prohibited from profiting from their own athletic achievements. The shift towards NIL has empowered athletes, turning them into entrepreneurs and brand ambassadors. This section showcases some remarkable examples of student-athletes who have not only capitalized on their NIL rights but have also built sustainable brands and impressive financial portfolios. These are not merely stories of financial success; they are testaments to the power of strategic planning, authentic branding, and shrewd legal counsel.

One particularly compelling example is that of Paige Bueckers, a former University of Connecticut women's basketball star. Bueckers's NIL deals weren't just about securing large payouts; they were carefully crafted to align with her personal brand and resonate with her audience. She leveraged her massive social media following to collaborate with brands that genuinely reflected her values and interests. This wasn't a scattershot approach; instead, she carefully selected partners, ensuring each collaboration enhanced her image and brand integrity. This approach fostered organic engagement with her fans, resulting in a significant and sustained increase in her following and overall brand appeal. Beyond endorsements, Bueckers actively sought opportunities to create her own content, establishing herself as a multifaceted personality and not solely defined by her basketball prowess. This strategic diversification has proven highly effective in establishing her long-term financial security and creating lasting brand recognition. Her success showcases the importance of not simply chasing big-name brands, but thoughtfully cultivating a portfolio that aligns with one's personal identity. The meticulous selection of partners and her commitment to creating authentic content transformed her NIL journey into a long-term sustainable business.

Another compelling case study revolves around Caleb Williams, a star quarterback for the University of Southern California. Williams's success showcases the power of combining athletic talent with astute business acumen. He shrewdly utilized his NIL rights not only for direct endorsements but also for leveraging other avenues, like appearances, merchandise, and even investment opportunities. He understood that his brand extended beyond the football field, recognizing the importance of diversifying revenue streams and building a portfolio of assets. He invested heavily in building a strong personal brand, carefully curating his online presence and demonstrating an understanding of digital marketing strategies. This proactive approach not only generated significant revenue, but also cemented his position as a leading figure in the NIL space, influencing the strategies of future athletes. He serves as a compelling example of how a student-athlete can successfully manage their NIL rights and simultaneously prepare for a successful post-college career.

Beyond individual athletes, the success stories also extend to collective efforts and strategic partnerships. Several universities have fostered NIL collectives, bringing together student-athletes across various sports. These collectives provide athletes with a platform for securing group endorsement deals, thereby leveraging the collective power of their brand. For example, the "Gator Collective" at the University of Florida has successfully secured deals for many athletes across multiple sports, showcasing the synergy between these combined ventures. These collectives demonstrate a coordinated effort in navigating the NIL landscape, demonstrating that group effort can be particularly effective in maximizing revenue potential and streamlining the endorsement process. However, it's crucial that these collectives operate within legal compliance, adhering to all relevant regulations, ensuring that each individual deal is contractually sound. The success of these collectives underscores the need for organized strategies and collaborative efforts within the NIL arena. It's not simply about individual success, but also about creating a supportive system that benefits all participants.

The case of a group of athletes from a smaller university highlighting the growing reach of NIL opportunities is also revealing. This group from a less prominent university leveraged innovative social media marketing to gain attention, effectively demonstrating that even those without immediate national recognition can achieve remarkable outcomes. Their focused strategy involved creating high-quality video content and collaborating with local businesses. They actively engaged with their audience, responding to comments, and fostering a sense of community. This approach built a loyal following, attracting the attention of larger brands and demonstrating the potential for impactful reach outside traditional collegiate powerhouses. Their story shows how resourcefulness and innovative strategies can compensate for a lack of pre-existing brand recognition. This is a testament to the transformative power of digital marketing and strategic networking, highlighting the level playing field created by NIL opportunities.

However, these success stories aren't without their cautionary tales. Many athletes have experienced the pitfalls of navigating the uncharted waters of NIL. Some have entered into deals without adequate legal counsel, leading to unfavorable terms and missed opportunities. Others have fallen prey to unscrupulous agents or brands seeking to exploit their talent without proper compensation or contractual protections. These instances highlight the critical need for thorough legal representation and careful contract review. The complexity of NIL regulations necessitates the involvement of experienced legal professionals who are well-versed in the constantly evolving landscape of college sports and endorsement agreements. The oversight of legal counsel helps protect an athlete's image, financial interests, and long-term career prospects.

Furthermore, the sustainability of NIL brands requires ongoing effort. It's not enough to secure a few lucrative deals; maintaining a consistent brand identity, staying engaged with fans, and continually developing new revenue streams are crucial for long-term success. Athletes must be mindful of the potential for fluctuating popularity and ever-changing market trends. A well-rounded strategy involves diversifying income sources, engaging in strategic partnerships, and creating value beyond mere endorsements. These long-term perspectives ensure resilience within the industry's dynamics.

The impact of NIL rights extends beyond the individual athletes and their financial gains. The increased financial independence offered to student-athletes is potentially fostering greater autonomy and agency within the athletic environment. It also enables student-athletes to contribute to their communities, supporting causes that are important to them. This aligns with the positive shifts toward community engagement and social responsibility. The shift in power dynamics and financial freedom opens avenues for greater self-determination and social impact. The ethical responsibilities that come with this newfound power are equally important, and these examples highlight the growing trend of socially conscious brand building within the athletic community.

In conclusion, the success stories emerging from the NIL era showcase not just financial achievements, but also the importance of strategic planning, authentic branding, and shrewd business acumen. These cases highlight the transformative potential of NIL rights for student-athletes, allowing them to not only secure immediate financial benefits but also to build sustainable careers and establish themselves as influential figures in the sports and entertainment industries. The stories offer valuable lessons for both aspiring and current athletes on the crucial elements of navigating the NIL landscape successfully, consistently emphasizing the need for meticulous planning, robust legal counsel, and a clear understanding of their brand's value and its long-term prospects. The future of NIL presents a constantly evolving environment, demanding adaptability, innovation, and strategic foresight from both athletes and their representatives. The legal considerations remain paramount, and continued focus on legal compliance is crucial for navigating the potential pitfalls and ensuring the long-term success of student-athletes' NIL ventures.

Chapter 6: Enforcing Your Rights

Understanding the intricacies of copyright law is paramount for anyone creating and distributing content in the entertainment industry. Copyright infringement, the unauthorized use of copyrighted material, can have devastating consequences, ranging from financial penalties to irreparable damage to reputation. This section delves into the practical aspects of identifying and addressing copyright infringement, equipping you with the knowledge and strategies to protect your creative work.

The first step in combating copyright infringement is identifying the infringement itself. This requires a vigilant eye and a proactive approach. Regularly monitoring online platforms, social media, and other channels where your work might be distributed is crucial. This monitoring should be comprehensive, encompassing not only direct copies of your work but also derivative works—those that borrow substantially from your original creation, even if not identical. For example, a musician's melody used without permission in a different song, or a writer's unique plotline adapted without authorization, constitute copyright infringement. Even subtle alterations won't necessarily shield the infringer from legal action, particularly if the essence of the copyrighted work remains.

Technological advancements have made the task of monitoring for infringement both easier and more challenging. While sophisticated software can scan the internet for instances of your work, the sheer volume of data and the constant evolution of methods for circumventing detection requires a multi-faceted approach. Regularly reviewing social media platforms, streaming services, and online marketplaces for unauthorized use of your intellectual property is essential. Engaging a digital rights management (DRM) service can provide an extra layer of protection, enabling automated detection of infringements and potentially enabling the rapid removal of unauthorized content. However, relying solely on automated systems isn't sufficient; a human review is often necessary to determine whether an instance truly constitutes infringement or is a case of fair use, a legally permissible exception to copyright restrictions which we'll discuss in greater detail.

Once you've identified a potential instance of copyright infringement, the next step is to gather evidence. This evidence must be comprehensive and irrefutable. Documenting the infringement with screenshots, recordings, or other verifiable records is essential. Include timestamps, URLs, and any other details that will strengthen your case. This meticulous documentation will form the foundation of your legal strategy. If the infringement involves a physical product, such as an unauthorized reproduction of a painting or a book, meticulously documenting its existence and distribution channels is critical. Consider documenting the point of sale or distribution to provide a complete picture of the infringement activity.

The process of issuing a cease-and-desist letter is often the first formal step in addressing copyright infringement. This letter, drafted by an experienced entertainment lawyer, formally demands the immediate cessation of the infringing activity. The letter should clearly identify the copyrighted work, specify the nature of the infringement, and provide irrefutable evidence of the unauthorized use. It should also clearly state the legal consequences of continued infringement, including potential lawsuits and financial penalties. The letter should be sent via certified mail with return receipt requested to ensure proper delivery and provide proof of service. This meticulously documented record of the letter's delivery is crucial if the matter proceeds to litigation. The tone of the letter should be firm yet professional, avoiding overly aggressive or inflammatory language. The goal is to achieve a swift resolution, not to escalate the situation unnecessarily.

While a well-crafted cease-and-desist letter often resolves the infringement amicably, some infringers remain recalcitrant. In such cases, pursuing legal action becomes necessary. This can involve filing a lawsuit in federal court seeking injunctive relief (a court order to stop the infringement) and monetary damages. The amount of damages you can claim varies depending on the severity and extent of the infringement, as well as whether it was willful or unintentional. Winning a copyright infringement case typically involves proving ownership of the copyright, demonstrating the infringing act, and quantifying the damages caused by the unauthorized use of your work.

To bolster your case, consider engaging an expert witness, such as a musicologist or literary scholar, to testify on the similarities between your copyrighted work and the infringing work. These experts can provide objective analysis to aid the court in understanding the scope of the infringement. This detailed expert testimony strengthens your legal position and contributes to a more robust case. The court will carefully examine the evidence presented by both sides to determine whether copyright infringement occurred and the appropriate remedies.

Navigating the complexities of copyright infringement litigation can be challenging. The process can be lengthy and expensive, and a favorable outcome is never guaranteed. However, by proactively identifying infringements, meticulously documenting the evidence, and engaging competent legal counsel, you significantly improve your chances of a successful outcome. The cost of pursuing litigation should always be weighed against the potential benefits, and exploring alternative dispute resolution methods, such as mediation or arbitration, may be more efficient and cost-effective options in certain circumstances. Mediation and arbitration can offer a faster, less expensive, and more collaborative path to resolution compared to a lengthy court battle.

The landscape of copyright infringement is constantly evolving, with new technologies and distribution channels constantly emerging. Staying informed about these developments is critical. Regularly updating your understanding of copyright law, particularly as it relates to digital media, is paramount. Attending industry conferences, engaging in continuing legal education, and maintaining close relationships with entertainment lawyers who specialize in intellectual property law are crucial for staying ahead of the curve and proactively protecting your intellectual property.

Beyond litigation, prevention plays a crucial role in minimizing the risk of copyright infringement. Registering your copyright with the U.S. Copyright Office provides several advantages, including the ability to obtain statutory damages in case of infringement, a stronger presumption of ownership in court, and the ability to record your copyright registration with the U.S. Customs and Border Protection to prevent the importation of infringing goods. While not mandatory for copyright protection, registration offers substantial benefits when facing infringement. Furthermore, utilizing clear and comprehensive licensing agreements can establish parameters for the use of your copyrighted material, reducing the likelihood of unauthorized use. These agreements provide clarity on the extent to which others can utilize your work, preventing potential disagreements and disputes in the future.

In conclusion, protecting your creative work from copyright infringement requires a multifaceted approach. This includes proactive monitoring, meticulous documentation, a well-crafted cease-and-desist strategy, and the willingness to pursue legal action when necessary. But equally important is preventative measures, including copyright registration, clear licensing agreements, and ongoing education about the evolving legal landscape. By combining these preventative strategies with a robust approach to dealing with infringement, you can safeguard your intellectual property, protect your financial interests, and ensure the long-term sustainability of your creative endeavors. Remember that proactive measures and well-informed legal counsel are crucial in navigating this complex arena and ensuring the success of your creative ventures. The proactive approach and diligent effort in defending your rights is critical to the success of your creative career. The legal landscape surrounding copyright and infringement is ever-shifting, and continuing education and expert guidance remain indispensable for securing the future of your work.

Trademark law, unlike copyright, protects brand identities. It safeguards names, logos, slogans, and other distinctive brand features that set a product or service apart in the marketplace. This protection prevents others from using similar marks that could confuse consumers and dilute the value of your brand. Building a strong trademark portfolio is a crucial element of long-term business success, particularly in the competitive landscape of the entertainment industry.

The first step in protecting your trademarks is conducting a thorough trademark search. This search, ideally conducted by an experienced intellectual property attorney, involves reviewing existing trademarks to identify potential conflicts. A comprehensive search goes beyond simply checking for identical marks; it also considers marks that are confusingly similar, even if not exactly the same. Slight variations in spelling, font, or design can still lead to trademark infringement disputes. For example, a subtly altered logo or a similar-sounding band name could still cause consumer confusion, triggering legal action. The search must cover both federal and state trademark registrations, as well as common law trademarks that haven't been officially registered. This due diligence minimizes the risk of costly legal battles down the road.

Once a thorough search confirms the availability of a mark, the next step is filing a trademark application with the United States Patent and Trademark Office (USPTO). This application includes various details, such as a description of the goods or services covered by the mark, specimen samples of how the mark is used, and a statement of use or intent to use. The application process itself can be complex, requiring adherence to specific legal requirements and procedures. Mistakes in the application process can lead to delays, rejections, or even complete failure of the application.

The USPTO examines the application to ensure compliance with legal requirements and to determine whether the mark meets the standards for registrability. Marks that are merely descriptive, generic, or confusingly similar to existing marks are usually rejected. For instance, if an artist wants to trademark the name "The Best Singer," it's likely to be deemed descriptive and therefore unregistrable. However, a more unique and fanciful name, perhaps incorporating a personal element or a unique artistic style, would have a higher likelihood of acceptance. The examination process may involve correspondence with the USPTO to address any objections or to provide additional information.

Upon approval, the trademark is registered, granting exclusive rights to use the mark in connection with the specified goods or services. This registration, however, isn't a guarantee of absolute protection. Enforcement is still required to actively defend the trademark against infringements. Regular monitoring of the marketplace for instances of trademark infringement is essential. This vigilance includes tracking competitors' products, reviewing online marketplaces, and monitoring social media platforms. The identification of infringing activity must be swift and precise. An infringement can be as subtle as a similar logo on a competing merchandise item or as blatant as the unauthorized use of your artist name.

When infringement is discovered, a cease-and-desist letter is often the first step. This letter formally demands that the infringing party cease using the trademark. It clearly outlines the grounds for the claim, citing the registered trademark and highlighting the similarity between the infringing mark and the registered mark. It demands that the infringer stop using the mark, recall any infringing products, and potentially provides compensation for damages caused by the infringement. As in copyright infringement, the cease-and-desist letter should be sent via certified mail, return receipt requested, to ensure proof of delivery.

If a cease-and-desist letter fails to resolve the dispute, legal action may become necessary. This could involve a lawsuit in federal court seeking injunctive relief, which would force the infringer to stop using the trademark, and monetary damages to compensate for any financial losses caused by the infringement. The legal process is complex and can be lengthy, demanding careful preparation and experienced legal counsel.

Preparing for a trademark infringement lawsuit involves meticulously gathering evidence, including documentation of the trademark registration, evidence of the infringing activity (such as photographs, website screenshots, and sales records), and evidence of consumer confusion caused by the infringing mark. Expert witness testimony from branding specialists or market research professionals can help demonstrate the likelihood of consumer confusion and the harm caused by the infringement.

Trademark law also addresses the issue of trademark dilution, which occurs when the use of a similar mark, even if not causing direct consumer confusion, diminishes the value or distinctiveness of a famous trademark. This is particularly relevant for well-known brands in the entertainment industry. Protecting against dilution often involves carefully monitoring the marketplace and taking proactive steps to prevent the use of similar marks that could potentially harm the brand's reputation and image.

Licensing is a key aspect of trademark management. This involves granting permission to others to use the trademark under specific conditions, such as in merchandising or endorsement deals. Licenses help generate revenue and expand brand reach, but they must be carefully drafted to protect the integrity of the trademark. A comprehensive licensing agreement clarifies the scope of permitted use, safeguarding against unauthorized expansion or misuse that could dilute the brand. For instance, an athlete might license their name and image for use on specific products but retain control over the quality and branding of those products to avoid association with substandard or incompatible goods.

The process of resolving trademark disputes can also involve alternative dispute resolution methods, such as mediation or arbitration. These methods offer a more efficient and cost-effective way to resolve conflicts, avoiding the expense and time involved in litigation. Mediation, a form of facilitated negotiation, provides a neutral platform for parties to reach a mutually agreeable resolution. Arbitration involves a neutral third party who makes a binding decision after considering the evidence and arguments presented by both sides.

In the dynamic world of entertainment, where branding is crucial, proactive trademark protection is essential. Building a strong trademark portfolio and aggressively enforcing those trademarks are vital for protecting financial interests, maintaining brand identity, and preserving the long-term value of your intellectual property. Regular monitoring, well-crafted licenses, and a willingness to pursue legal action when necessary are key components of a comprehensive trademark protection strategy for any successful entertainment professional. The ongoing investment in trademark protection pays dividends in ensuring the long-term sustainability and success of your career in the entertainment industry. Therefore, maintaining up-to-date knowledge of trademark law and seeking expert legal counsel are vital elements in protecting and growing your brand.

Contract disputes are an unfortunate reality in the entertainment industry, where complex agreements govern collaborations, endorsements, and distribution deals. A breach of contract occurs when one party fails to fulfill its obligations as outlined in a legally binding agreement. This can range from minor infractions to significant violations that severely impact the other party's financial interests and career trajectory. The initial reaction to a breach should always be measured and strategic. While anger and frustration are understandable, immediate legal action isn't always the most effective approach.

The first step in resolving a contract dispute is often a good-faith attempt at negotiation. This involves direct communication between the involved parties, aiming to reach a mutually agreeable solution. Open communication, a willingness to compromise, and a clear understanding of each party's rights and obligations are crucial. This process can involve exchanging correspondence, attending meetings, or engaging in phone calls to clarify misunderstandings and explore potential compromises. A well-drafted contract, with clear and unambiguous terms, significantly aids this process by reducing the likelihood of disputes arising in the first place. However, even the most carefully crafted contracts can encounter unforeseen circumstances or disagreements on interpretation, making negotiation an essential first step in resolving conflicts. This direct communication, when successful, can prevent costly and time-consuming litigation, preserving professional relationships and avoiding public negative publicity.

However, negotiation isn't always successful. When direct communication fails to resolve the dispute, alternative dispute resolution (ADR) methods offer viable alternatives to litigation. ADR methods are generally less expensive and time-consuming than going to court, and they can preserve relationships better than a courtroom battle. Two common ADR methods are mediation and arbitration.

Mediation involves a neutral third party, a mediator, who facilitates communication between the disputing parties. The mediator doesn't make a decision but rather helps the parties understand each other's perspectives, identify common ground, and explore mutually acceptable solutions. Mediation is particularly effective in situations where preserving the relationship is crucial, such as ongoing business partnerships or collaborative creative endeavors. The mediator's role is to guide the discussion, encourage compromise, and help the parties reach a resolution that addresses their underlying concerns. Unlike a judge or jury, the mediator does not impose a solution; the parties retain control over the outcome. The success of mediation relies heavily on the parties' willingness to engage in constructive dialogue and seek a compromise. A skilled mediator can navigate difficult conversations and encourage creative solutions to even seemingly intractable disputes. The confidentiality of mediation is another significant advantage, allowing parties to openly discuss sensitive information without the risk of public disclosure.

Arbitration, on the other hand, involves a neutral third party, an arbitrator, who acts as a private judge. The arbitrator hears evidence and arguments presented by both sides and then renders a binding decision. Arbitration is often preferred when a final and enforceable resolution is needed quickly. The arbitration process is more formal than mediation, following established procedures similar to those in a court of law. The arbitrator's decision, known as an arbitration award, is typically legally binding and enforceable in court. This ensures that the resolution of the dispute is final and avoids lengthy and expensive appeals processes. However, while arbitration offers a quicker path to resolution than court litigation, the finality of the award means that parties relinquish the ability to appeal an unfavorable decision in the same way they might in a court setting. The selection of an arbitrator is also critical, and the process requires careful consideration of the arbitrator's expertise and impartiality.

If negotiation and ADR methods fail, litigation becomes a necessary consideration. Litigation involves filing a lawsuit in court, where a judge or jury will ultimately decide the outcome of the dispute. This is the most formal and often the most expensive and time-consuming method for resolving contract disputes. Litigation is usually a last resort, undertaken when other options have been exhausted. The process begins with filing a complaint, outlining the breach of contract and the damages suffered. The defendant then files a response, defending against the allegations. The process involves extensive discovery, where both parties exchange information and evidence. This might include depositions, interrogatories, and document requests. There are strict rules of evidence that determine what material can be presented to the court.

Once discovery is complete, the case may proceed to trial. At trial, both sides present their evidence and arguments to a judge or jury, who then renders a verdict. The verdict may include monetary damages to compensate the non-breaching party for their losses. These damages can include lost profits, costs associated with mitigating the breach, and other expenses directly resulting from the breach. In some cases, the court might also award punitive damages, intended to punish the breaching party for particularly egregious conduct. Furthermore, the court may grant injunctive relief, ordering the breaching party to take specific actions or refrain from certain actions to remedy the situation. Litigation is a complex and demanding process, necessitating legal expertise and a clear understanding of court procedures. The cost of litigation can be substantial, including legal fees, expert witness fees, and court costs.

The specific approach to resolving a contract dispute depends on various factors, including the severity of the breach, the relationship between the parties, the cost of litigation, and the desired outcome. Each approach has its advantages and disadvantages, and the choice often involves carefully weighing these factors in conjunction with legal counsel. For instance, a minor breach might be easily resolved through negotiation, while a more significant breach, involving substantial financial losses, might warrant litigation. In the entertainment industry, where relationships are often crucial for future opportunities, mediation might be favored to preserve those relationships. However, if a quick and final resolution is needed, arbitration might be a more suitable option. Regardless of the chosen method, meticulous documentation is crucial. Maintaining records of all communication, agreements, and relevant evidence is essential throughout the process.

This documentation helps build a strong case, whether in negotiation, mediation, arbitration, or litigation. It's imperative to seek the advice of an experienced entertainment lawyer. A lawyer can guide you through the process, ensuring your rights are protected and your best interests are represented. An attorney can advise you on the strengths and weaknesses of your case, help you negotiate effectively, and represent you in mediation, arbitration, or litigation. The legal complexities of contract disputes in the entertainment industry demand the guidance of someone with specialized knowledge and expertise in this field. An entertainment lawyer's understanding of the industry's nuances and contractual practices is crucial for maximizing the chances of a favorable outcome. Proactive measures, such as carefully drafting contracts and maintaining thorough documentation, can significantly reduce the likelihood of contract disputes. However, when disputes arise, a considered and strategic approach, potentially incorporating a combination of negotiation and ADR methods before resorting to litigation, is often the most effective way to secure a positive resolution. Ultimately, navigating the legal complexities of contract disputes requires a combination of proactive planning, sound legal counsel, and a strategic approach to resolving conflicts efficiently and effectively.

The foundation of a successful career in the entertainment industry rests not only on talent and hard work, but also on a robust understanding and protection of your intellectual property. Your creative works – be it a song, a screenplay, a painting, a dance routine, or even a distinctive catchphrase – are valuable assets deserving of comprehensive legal safeguards. Neglecting this critical aspect can lead to significant financial losses, reputational damage, and protracted legal battles. Protecting your intellectual property requires a proactive and multi-faceted approach, encompassing registration, enforcement, and digital rights management.

Copyright protection, often the first line of defense, automatically safeguards original creative works from the moment they are fixed in a tangible medium of expression. This means the moment you write a song, film a video, or paint a picture, copyright protection attaches. However, while automatic, this protection offers limited recourse without formal registration. Registered copyrights provide stronger legal standing, allowing you to pursue more significant damages in case of infringement, and offering irrefutable proof of ownership should a dispute arise. Registering your copyrights with the appropriate agency, such as the U.S. Copyright Office, is a straightforward process that provides a critical layer of protection. The registration certificate serves as tangible evidence of your ownership, strengthening your position in any potential legal proceedings. Remember to meticulously document the creation and development of your work, keeping detailed records of dates, versions, and collaborators, as this documentation proves invaluable in proving your ownership and originality.

Beyond copyrights, consider the importance of trademark protection for your brand identity. A trademark protects brand names, logos, slogans, and other distinctive identifiers used to identify and distinguish your goods and services in the marketplace. Think of the recognizable logos of major studios or the instantly identifiable catchphrases of famous athletes. These trademarks are valuable assets, differentiating you from competitors and protecting your brand reputation. The process of trademark registration is similar to copyright registration, involving filing an application with the relevant authority, such as the U.S. Patent and Trademark Office. Thorough trademark searches are crucial before applying to ensure your chosen mark isn't already in use, preventing potential conflicts and costly legal battles. A strong trademark, properly registered, prevents others from using similar marks that could confuse consumers and dilute your brand equity. This is particularly relevant for athletes and entertainers who often build a personal brand around their image and likeness.

In the digital age, digital rights management (DRM) is paramount. DRM encompasses technological measures and legal strategies designed to protect digital content from unauthorized copying, distribution, and use. This is especially critical for musicians who release their work online, filmmakers distributing their projects through streaming platforms, or writers publishing ebooks. DRM strategies can include watermarking your digital content, utilizing encryption technologies to restrict access, and incorporating contractual clauses in licensing agreements to control how your work is used and distributed online. The rapid evolution of technology requires constant vigilance. New methods of content piracy and unauthorized distribution emerge constantly, making it crucial to stay informed about the latest DRM technologies and legal strategies to counter these threats. Working with an experienced lawyer specializing in digital rights management is essential to develop a robust strategy that effectively protects your digital assets. This lawyer can advise you on the best techniques for your specific situation and help you draft contracts that clearly define the terms of use and distribution for your digital content.

Beyond formal registration and DRM, actively monitoring for potential infringements is crucial. Regularly search online platforms, streaming services, and social media for unauthorized uses of your copyrighted work or trademark. If you discover infringement, promptly take action. This could involve sending a cease and desist letter, a formal legal notice demanding that the infringing party stop the unauthorized use of your intellectual property. While a cease and desist letter often resolves the issue without the need for litigation, it's vital to document all instances of infringement meticulously, retaining evidence of the unauthorized use, such as screenshots, web links, and dates. This documentation provides a strong foundation for pursuing legal action if necessary. In some cases, pursuing legal action is unavoidable. This can involve filing lawsuits for copyright infringement, trademark dilution, or other relevant claims, seeking injunctive relief to stop further infringement and monetary damages to compensate for the harm caused.

Collaboration often necessitates carefully drafted agreements to protect your intellectual property. When working with other creators, producers, or distributors, ensure that agreements clearly define ownership rights, usage rights, and revenue sharing. These agreements should specifically address who owns the copyright to the collaborative work, who controls the distribution and licensing of the work, and how profits are to be divided among the collaborators. Ambiguity in these agreements can lead to future disputes and litigation. A well-structured agreement, reviewed and drafted by an experienced entertainment lawyer, prevents misunderstandings and provides a clear framework for the collaboration, protecting your interests while fostering a productive partnership. Remember, preventing disputes through clear and comprehensive agreements is always preferable to resolving them through lengthy and costly litigation.

The entertainment industry's fast-paced and dynamic nature demands vigilance in protecting your intellectual property. Your creative work is not just a product; it is an investment, a testament to your talent and dedication. Safeguarding this investment requires a proactive strategy, combining registration, digital rights management, active monitoring, and carefully drafted agreements. The assistance of an experienced entertainment lawyer is invaluable in this endeavor. They can help you develop a comprehensive intellectual property strategy, advise on registration procedures, draft contracts that protect your rights, and represent you in case of infringement or disputes. Remember, protecting your intellectual property is not just a legal formality; it is an essential component of building a sustainable and successful career in the entertainment industry. It's a continuous process of vigilance and proactive protection, ensuring that your creative work receives the legal recognition and protection it deserves, securing your financial future and preserving your legacy. Consider it an investment in your future—an investment that will pay dividends many times over. Don't underestimate the power of strong legal protection; it's the cornerstone of a successful career in the entertainment world. From the moment an idea sparks to its final manifestation, diligently protecting your intellectual property is not just a prudent legal strategy; it is an essential part of realizing your full potential.

Having established the importance of proactive intellectual property protection, let's now turn our attention to the crucial aspect of enforcing your rights when violations occur. This is where the rubber meets the road, where the meticulous groundwork of registration, documentation, and strategic agreements translates into tangible legal action. Ignoring infringement, hoping it will simply disappear, is a recipe for disaster. Passive acceptance emboldens violators and can lead to escalating losses, both financial and reputational. Therefore, understanding the available legal remedies and the processes involved in initiating legal proceedings is paramount.

The first step in addressing any infringement is thorough investigation. This goes beyond a simple online search; it involves gathering comprehensive evidence that unequivocally establishes the violation. This evidence will be the cornerstone of your case, so its meticulous collection is non-negotiable. For copyright infringement, this might involve obtaining screenshots or recordings of the infringing material, documenting the location where it's being used (website URLs, social media handles, etc.), and noting the dates of discovery. For trademark infringement, you'll need to demonstrate that the infringing party is using a confusingly similar mark, causing potential damage to your brand. This requires documenting the similarities, the likelihood of consumer confusion, and any evidence of actual confusion or market damage.

Once you have compiled irrefutable evidence, the next step often involves sending a cease and desist letter. This formal legal notice, drafted by your attorney, demands that the infringing party immediately stop the infringing activity. The letter clearly identifies the infringing material, explains the legal basis for your claim (copyright infringement, trademark infringement, breach of contract, etc.), and outlines the potential consequences of continued infringement, which can include legal action and substantial damages. A well-crafted cease and desist letter is often effective in resolving the issue without resorting to lengthy and costly litigation.

Many infringers, upon receiving such a letter from a reputable legal firm, will quickly comply, realizing the potential legal ramifications. However, it's crucial to remember that a cease and desist letter is not a guarantee of compliance; some infringers will ignore it, necessitating further legal action.

If a cease and desist letter proves ineffective, or if the infringement is particularly egregious, you may need to pursue legal action. This involves initiating a lawsuit in a court of competent jurisdiction. This process typically begins with filing a complaint, a formal legal document outlining your claims, the evidence supporting those claims, and the relief you are seeking. The specific claims will depend on the nature of the infringement and the applicable laws. For instance, copyright infringement claims might seek injunctive relief (a court order requiring the infringing party to stop the infringing activity), monetary damages (compensatory damages to cover losses and potentially punitive damages to punish the infringer), and attorney's fees. Trademark infringement claims might seek similar remedies, with a focus on protecting the brand's reputation and market share. Breach of contract claims will focus on the specific terms violated and the resulting damages.

The litigation process can be lengthy and complex, involving discovery (the exchange of information between parties), motions (formal requests to the court), and potentially a trial. Navigating this process effectively requires the expertise of an experienced entertainment lawyer. They will guide you through every step, ensuring that your rights are protected and your case is presented effectively. They will handle the complex legal procedures, draft and file court documents, engage in negotiations with the opposing party, and represent you in court if necessary. This expertise is invaluable in maximizing your chances of a favorable outcome.

Beyond copyright and trademark infringement, athletes and entertainers often face unique legal challenges related to their image and likeness. The unauthorized use of an athlete's name, image, or likeness (NIL) for commercial purposes constitutes a violation of their right of publicity, a valuable property right that protects individuals from the commercial exploitation of their identity. This right is crucial for athletes whose endorsement deals, sponsorships, and other commercial opportunities are directly linked to their public image. Enforcing this right requires similar steps as with copyright and trademark infringement—thorough investigation, gathering evidence, issuing a cease and desist letter, and, if necessary, filing a lawsuit.

In the digital age, enforcing rights can be particularly challenging due to the ease of content reproduction and distribution online. Platforms like YouTube, Instagram, and TikTok, while offering significant opportunities for creators, also present a breeding ground for infringement. Tracking down and pursuing infringers on these platforms requires specialized expertise and a proactive approach. Your lawyer will be instrumental in developing strategies for identifying and addressing online infringement, including working with the platforms themselves to have infringing content removed. This may involve utilizing the platforms' copyright or takedown procedures, collaborating with platform representatives, and potentially filing lawsuits against both the infringers and the platforms themselves if they fail to adequately address the infringement.

The cost of litigation should not be underestimated. Legal fees, expert witness fees, and other expenses can be substantial, particularly in complex cases. Therefore, careful consideration should be given to the potential costs and benefits of pursuing legal action. In some instances, alternative dispute resolution (ADR) methods, such as mediation or arbitration, might be more cost-effective and efficient ways to resolve disputes. These methods involve a neutral third party assisting the parties in reaching a mutually acceptable agreement. ADR can be significantly less expensive and time-consuming than litigation, and often preserves relationships that might be irreparably damaged through formal court proceedings. Your lawyer can advise you on the most appropriate dispute resolution method for your situation.

In conclusion, while proactive protection of your intellectual property is crucial, the ability to effectively enforce your rights when violations occur is equally important. This involves a multi-faceted approach, beginning with meticulous investigation and evidence gathering, followed by the strategic use of cease and desist letters, and, when necessary, pursuing legal action in court or through alternative dispute resolution. Throughout this process, the guidance and expertise of an experienced entertainment lawyer are invaluable. They navigate the complexities of the legal system, protect your interests, and guide you toward the most effective strategies to safeguard your rights and secure your future. Remember, protecting your intellectual property is an ongoing commitment, and seeking legal remedies is a crucial component of that commitment, protecting not only your financial well-being but also your creative legacy. The investment in legal counsel is an investment in your future success, ensuring that your hard work and creative talent are rewarded and respected. It's about more than just money; it's about safeguarding your artistic integrity and ensuring your voice is heard.

Chapter 7: The Role of Unions and Guilds

The previous section detailed the often arduous process of protecting your intellectual property and enforcing your rights when infringement occurs. However, a proactive and powerful approach to safeguarding your career and creative work lies in the collective strength offered by unions and guilds. For creators and athletes, union representation can be a game-changer, providing resources and support often unavailable to individuals navigating the complex entertainment and sports industries alone.

Understanding union representation begins with grasping the fundamental concept of collective bargaining. Unlike solo negotiations, where you stand alone against a potentially powerful entity like a record label, studio, or sports team, union representation empowers you through the collective strength of your peers. Through the union, you participate in negotiations for contracts that benefit the entire membership, achieving outcomes that would be difficult, if not impossible, to obtain individually. This collective bargaining power shapes industry standards, setting minimum pay rates, defining working conditions, and establishing protections against exploitation. The union leverages the combined influence of its members to negotiate fair and equitable terms, ensuring that creators and athletes receive appropriate compensation and recognition for their work.

The benefits of collective bargaining extend far beyond basic pay and working conditions. Unions often negotiate comprehensive benefits packages that include health insurance, retirement plans, and other crucial financial protections. These benefits are particularly vital in industries where income can be unpredictable and unstable, offering a sense of security and stability rarely found in independent freelance work. Consider the plight of a musician who secures a lucrative record deal but is left without healthcare coverage—a union contract could have secured this critical benefit, alongside the financial rewards. Similarly, for an athlete with a short career span, the long-term financial security provided by a union's negotiated pension plan can be invaluable.

Moreover, unions provide expertise and resources in contract negotiation, assisting members in understanding complex legal documents and advocating for their best interests. Many individuals, lacking legal training or experience, are easily overwhelmed by the intricate details of contracts offered by powerful organizations. A union provides a dedicated team of negotiators, lawyers, and advisors who possess the knowledge and experience to analyze contracts, identify potential pitfalls, and advocate for favorable terms. This expert support empowers members to make informed decisions, avoiding unfavorable clauses or exploitation. They are the ones who make sure you are fully protected legally and can effectively navigate your career.

The power of collective bargaining extends beyond individual contracts. Unions actively participate in shaping industry-wide standards and practices, advocating for fair treatment and ethical working conditions. This can include negotiating minimum wages, establishing safer work environments, and implementing policies that protect artists and athletes from harassment and discrimination. Through lobbying efforts and legal challenges, unions work to create a more equitable and just industry landscape, benefiting all members, regardless of their individual bargaining power. Their influence extends from setting standards for studio recording sessions to advocating for fair compensation in the increasingly complex landscape of digital streaming.

Beyond contract negotiation, union representation plays a vital role in dispute resolution. When conflicts arise, a union acts as a powerful advocate, supporting its members in resolving disagreements fairly and effectively. This is crucial because the entertainment and sports industries frequently involve high-stakes disputes, ranging from compensation conflicts to creative differences. Unions provide access to experienced legal counsel, ensuring their members have adequate representation when facing legal challenges. They can guide them through the labyrinthine process of legal action, acting as a crucial buffer against the often overwhelming power of studios, leagues, or agencies.

Union representation also offers a robust framework for addressing workplace harassment and discrimination. Many industries, including entertainment and sports, have long histories of issues with power imbalances and unethical practices. Unions provide support and protection to members facing these challenges, actively combating discrimination and advocating for fair and respectful work environments. They provide a safe space to report grievances, ensuring that members are not subjected to retaliation and that violations are investigated and addressed decisively.

A critical aspect of union representation lies in the strength of solidarity among its members. The combined effort of a large and unified body translates into a formidable presence at the negotiation table, significantly boosting the leverage of individual artists and athletes. The collective voice of a union carries far greater weight than any individual's attempt to negotiate alone, especially when facing formidable corporations with vast legal and financial resources. This strength in numbers is perhaps one of the greatest advantages of union membership.

However, it's important to acknowledge that joining a union is not without potential drawbacks. Membership fees are a common cost, though the benefits often outweigh the financial contribution. Some unions might have internal politics or bureaucratic processes that can be frustrating to navigate. Moreover, the specifics of union representation will depend on the particular union and the prevailing labor laws in the relevant jurisdiction. A thorough understanding of the union's structure, rules, and limitations is crucial before joining.

The decision of whether or not to join a union is deeply personal and depends on individual circumstances and career goals. However, for many creators and athletes, the collective strength, support, and resources provided by a union represent a significant advantage in navigating the often challenging landscape of the entertainment and sports industries. The long-term benefits of having a collective bargaining agent working on your behalf, providing expert legal counsel, and acting as an advocate against industry abuses frequently outweigh the potential drawbacks.

Consider the case of a young musician just starting their career. Negotiating a record deal without union representation can be a daunting task, leaving them vulnerable to unfavorable contract terms. With union representation, however, they gain access to experienced negotiators who can advocate for fair compensation, appropriate royalties, and clear ownership rights. This allows them to focus on creating their music rather than getting bogged down in the complexities of legal negotiations.

Similarly, for a professional athlete, union representation can be instrumental in protecting their long-term interests. The union can advocate for better salary structures, ensuring they receive fair compensation for their athletic abilities and contributions. They can help to secure comprehensive benefits packages, including health insurance, retirement plans, and other financial protections, shielding them from potential financial insecurities that can accompany a relatively short athletic career. This safety net allows them to focus on their performance without the undue stress of financial uncertainty.

In conclusion, union representation offers a significant advantage for creators and athletes navigating the complexities of the entertainment and sports industries. Collective bargaining, expert contract negotiation, robust dispute resolution processes, and the strength of solidarity empower members to achieve outcomes far beyond what they could accomplish alone. While not without potential drawbacks, the long-term benefits of union membership often outweigh the costs, offering invaluable protection, support, and the opportunity to build a more equitable and sustainable career. The choice is a significant one, and thorough research and understanding of the union's structure and operational protocols are essential to a well-informed decision. But the potential for significant protection and empowerment makes it a choice worth serious consideration. It is an investment in your long-term success, enabling you to focus on what matters most – your creative work or athletic performance.

Negotiating a union contract is a significantly different process than negotiating a contract as an individual. The power dynamics shift dramatically. Instead of facing a powerful corporation or studio alone, you're part of a collective, leveraging the combined strength and experience of your fellow union members. This collective bargaining power is the cornerstone of union representation, and understanding its mechanics is crucial for maximizing your benefits.

The negotiation process typically begins with the union's bargaining committee, composed of elected representatives from the membership, who are often experienced negotiators themselves. This committee meticulously gathers data from members - salary information, working conditions, benefits packages, grievances experienced, and aspirations for improvement. This data forms the backbone of the union's proposals. They analyze industry standards, comparing the current contract terms with those offered to similar artists or athletes in comparable positions. The goal is to identify areas where improvements can be made and to substantiate those requests with demonstrable evidence. They don't just make demands; they build a strategic case supported by market analysis and precedent.

The process is often iterative, involving multiple meetings between the union's bargaining committee and the employer's representatives (usually management-level personnel and legal counsel). Initial proposals are exchanged, followed by counter-proposals, discussions, and compromises. The negotiations can be intense, involving detailed discussions of specific clauses, definitions, and potential loopholes. The union's legal team plays a crucial role, scrutinizing each clause for potential ambiguity or unfairness, ensuring that the contract protects members' rights and interests. Their expertise in contract law ensures that the language is precise and unambiguous, minimizing the risk of future disputes.

A key aspect of union contract negotiation is the concept of "give and take." Rarely does a union secure every single demand it initially presents. The process is about finding a balance that benefits the membership while maintaining a reasonable and sustainable relationship with the employer. Experienced union negotiators know how to prioritize demands, identifying the most crucial clauses and strategically conceding on less important ones to achieve the best overall outcome.

For instance, a musician's union might prioritize securing fair royalty rates and clear ownership of their master recordings as primary demands. They might be willing to negotiate on the specific details of tour support or promotional activities if it strengthens their position on these core issues. This strategic approach is a hallmark of effective union negotiation – understanding what's truly non-negotiable and what can be compromised to achieve the best possible deal.

The process is rarely swift. It involves considerable time, effort, and dedication from both sides. There are often extended periods of deliberation, research, and internal consultations. Deadlines are established, and extensions are often requested, particularly if significant disagreements persist. Frustration is a natural part of the process, and the bargaining committee has the responsibility to manage the expectations of their members throughout this potentially protracted period. Transparency is critical; members must be kept informed of the progress of negotiations, both successes and setbacks.

Once an agreement is reached, the proposed contract is presented to the union membership for ratification. This often involves a vote, with members having the opportunity to review the contract details and cast their ballots. A successful ratification requires a majority vote in favor of the contract. If the contract is rejected, negotiations often resume to address the members' concerns. This ensures that the final agreement reflects the collective will of the union's membership.

The finalized union contract serves as a binding legal document, specifying the terms and conditions of employment for members covered by the agreement. It typically encompasses a broad range of issues, including minimum pay rates, working hours, overtime pay, benefits packages (health insurance, retirement plans, paid time off), grievance procedures, and protections against discrimination and harassment. It's a comprehensive document designed to protect the members' rights and well-being. The detailed specifications cover many aspects of working conditions, eliminating ambiguity and setting clear expectations.

However, the contract itself is not the only critical element. The union provides ongoing support and resources throughout the duration of the agreement. Members have access to union representatives who can provide guidance on contract interpretation, address workplace concerns, and assist in resolving disputes with employers. This ongoing support is often crucial for maintaining a positive and productive working relationship. The union acts as a buffer between the individual and the employer, ensuring fair treatment and preventing exploitation.

Moreover, the union contract acts as a floor, not a ceiling. Individual members can negotiate additional compensation or benefits beyond the minimums established in the contract based on individual merit, skill, or market demand. A talented musician, for example, might still negotiate a significantly higher royalty rate than the minimum stipulated in the union contract if their exceptional talent and marketability justify it. The contract sets a baseline for fair treatment and protects members from being exploited, ensuring a fair starting point for further negotiations.

The role of a union lawyer is also critical throughout this entire process, not only in the initial negotiations but also throughout the life of the contract. They ensure that the contract is legally sound, enforceable, and effectively protects the interests of union members. They review all proposed language, identify potential weaknesses, suggest alternative wording, and provide guidance on complex legal issues. Their involvement extends beyond the initial negotiation phase; they are often called upon to interpret contract clauses, handle grievances, and represent members in legal disputes arising from the contract. Their expertise is invaluable in safeguarding members' rights and interests.

In essence, negotiating a union contract is a multifaceted process that goes far beyond simply agreeing to salary and working hours. It's a strategic undertaking that requires collaboration, expertise, and a deep understanding of labor laws and negotiation strategies. The resulting contract is more than just a legal document; it's a testament to the collective power of the union membership and a framework for a more equitable and sustainable working relationship. The ongoing support and legal protection provided by the union are essential to ensure that the contract serves its intended purpose and protects members throughout the duration of the agreement. This investment in collective bargaining significantly outweighs the potential drawbacks and secures a more stable and successful career for the individual artist or athlete in the long term.

The bedrock of union membership lies in the comprehensive rights and protections offered to its members. These extend far beyond simple salary negotiations and encompass a wide spectrum of workplace safeguards and entitlements designed to ensure fair treatment, reasonable working conditions, and a robust mechanism for addressing grievances. The specifics, of course, vary depending on the particular union, the industry, and the negotiated collective bargaining agreement, but the core principles remain consistent across various guilds and unions.

One of the most fundamental rights is the guarantee of fair wages. Union contracts typically establish minimum pay rates for specific jobs or roles, ensuring that members are compensated equitably for their work. These rates are often determined through a meticulous process of research, taking into account prevailing industry standards, cost of living, and the skills and experience required for the position. This prevents exploitation by employers who might otherwise attempt to suppress wages, particularly in competitive fields where individual artists or athletes might feel pressured to accept less than they deserve. The union's collective bargaining power ensures that its members receive a fair compensation reflecting the value of their contributions.

Beyond minimum wages, union contracts often define overtime pay, stipulating rates for work performed beyond the standard working hours. This is particularly crucial in industries where long hours are common, such as live music performance, film production, or professional sports. Overtime provisions protect members from exploitation and ensure that they are adequately compensated for additional effort and time commitment. The specific rules governing overtime, such as the threshold beyond which overtime is triggered and the applicable multiplier for hourly rates, are carefully negotiated and laid out in the contract, leaving little room for ambiguity or disputes.

Working conditions are another area where unions provide essential protections. The contract often details specific standards regarding safety, hygiene, and overall working environment. For instance, a musicians' union might specify requirements for proper ventilation, comfortable backstage areas, and adequate sound equipment to minimize the risks associated with prolonged exposure to loud noise. Similarly, an actors' union might dictate safety protocols on film sets, including measures to prevent injuries, ensure adequate rest periods, and address potential hazards related to stunts or special effects. The details vary depending on the nature of the work, but the overarching goal is to create a safe and healthy environment for union members.

Equally important are the provisions for benefits. Union contracts often include comprehensive benefits packages, encompassing healthcare insurance, retirement plans, paid sick leave, and vacation time. These benefits can represent a significant advantage for union members, as they provide financial security and protection against unforeseen circumstances. The extent of these benefits varies greatly based on factors like union size, industry profitability, and the prevailing healthcare and retirement systems, yet the availability of such packages is a considerable perk of union membership. Access to these benefits might not be feasible or affordable for independent contractors or freelancers working without union representation.

However, the benefits go beyond financial security. Unions also establish clear grievance procedures, providing members with structured mechanisms for addressing workplace complaints or disagreements. These procedures usually involve a series of steps, beginning with informal discussions between the member and the employer. If these attempts fail to resolve the issue, the matter might escalate to formal grievance proceedings, potentially involving union representatives and impartial arbitrators. This framework protects members from retaliation and ensures that their concerns are addressed fairly and efficiently, unlike the often-uncertain legal landscape faced by non-union workers.

The process of filing a grievance is usually clearly laid out within the union contract, with detailed steps, deadlines, and the designated individuals or committees involved. The contract may also specify the types of grievances eligible for formal procedures and any potential limitations or exceptions. Having this documented process offers transparency and helps to prevent arbitrary actions from employers. The availability of union representation during the grievance process is crucial, ensuring that the member's rights and interests are effectively protected throughout the dispute resolution.

Furthermore, union contracts often include robust provisions against discrimination and harassment. These clauses specifically prohibit discriminatory practices based on factors like race, gender, religion, sexual orientation, age, or disability. The contract might delineate the measures to be taken in case of a complaint, specifying an investigation process, penalties for offenders, and a clear reporting mechanism for members to raise concerns without fear of retribution. These protections represent a strong bulwark against bias and unfair treatment, providing members with recourse in case of discrimination. The existence of these clauses is a testament to the union's dedication to fostering an inclusive and respectful workplace environment.

Beyond these fundamental rights and protections, many unions also negotiate additional benefits, such as professional development opportunities, access to legal counsel, and assistance with career advancement. These support services extend beyond the immediate work environment and reflect the union's commitment to fostering the long-term well-being and success of its members. Such assistance strengthens members' career trajectories and positions them to thrive in their chosen fields.

In conclusion, the rights and protections offered by unions and guilds form a crucial safety net for artists, athletes, and other entertainment professionals. These rights extend far beyond simple compensation; they encompass working conditions, benefits, grievance procedures, and protections against discrimination. The collective bargaining power of unions translates into tangible benefits for individual members, creating a more equitable and sustainable working environment and fostering long-term career success in an industry often characterized by instability and precarious employment. The security provided by the union significantly outweighs any potential drawbacks, offering invaluable peace of mind and the assurance of fair treatment. The process might seem complex at first glance, but the resulting benefits are irrefutable and significantly improve the overall quality of professional life for the individuals involved.

However, even with the strongest union protections, disagreements and disputes can arise. The beauty of union membership lies not only in the rights it secures but also in the robust mechanisms it provides for resolving conflicts fairly and efficiently. These dispute resolution processes are typically outlined in the collective bargaining agreement and are designed to address grievances, ranging from minor misunderstandings to serious breaches of contract.

The cornerstone of union dispute resolution is the grievance procedure. This is a formalized, step-by-step process that allows members to formally lodge a complaint against their employer regarding alleged violations of the collective bargaining agreement. The process generally begins with an informal attempt at resolution, often involving a discussion between the member and their supervisor or manager. If this informal approach fails to resolve the issue, the matter proceeds to a formal grievance, which is typically submitted in writing and follows a specific protocol.

The written grievance usually details the nature of the complaint, the specific clause of the contract allegedly violated, and the desired resolution. The union will often provide assistance to the member in preparing and submitting the grievance, ensuring it's properly documented and adheres to the procedural requirements outlined in the contract. This support is invaluable, as navigating the complexities of union procedures can be daunting for someone unfamiliar with the process.

Following the submission of the formal grievance, the union will typically investigate the matter, gathering evidence and interviewing relevant parties. This investigation is crucial in ensuring the accuracy and validity of the member's claim. The union representative will then present the grievance to the employer, advocating for the member's interests and seeking a resolution that aligns with the terms of the collective bargaining agreement.

If the grievance remains unresolved after these initial stages, the dispute may escalate to higher levels within the union and the employer's organization. This might involve meetings with senior union officials and management representatives, potentially including human resources personnel or even legal counsel. These meetings aim to negotiate a compromise that satisfies both parties and brings the dispute to a mutually agreeable conclusion. Each stage of the process is meticulously documented, creating a detailed record that serves as evidence throughout the resolution process. The documentation ensures transparency and accountability, reducing the likelihood of bias or unfair treatment.

Sometimes, even after considerable effort, negotiation fails to resolve the dispute. In such cases, alternative dispute resolution (ADR) mechanisms are typically invoked. These methods aim to resolve conflicts outside of traditional litigation and often involve neutral third parties to facilitate the process. Two common ADR methods used in union settings are mediation and arbitration.

Mediation is a less formal process where a neutral mediator facilitates communication between the disputing parties, helping them find common ground and reach a mutually acceptable agreement. The mediator does not impose a decision but rather assists the parties in exploring options and reaching a compromise that addresses their concerns. Mediation is often viewed favorably because it preserves the working relationship between the member and the employer, fostering a collaborative environment even after a conflict has arisen. The success rate of mediation varies depending on the nature of the dispute and the willingness of both sides to compromise. However, the confidentiality inherent in the mediation process often encourages openness and honest communication, contributing to successful outcomes.

Arbitration, on the other hand, is a more formal process where a neutral arbitrator hears evidence from both sides and renders a binding decision. The arbitrator's decision is typically legally enforceable, meaning that both parties are obligated to comply with the ruling. Arbitration is often preferred when mediation has failed or when the dispute involves complex legal issues that require a definitive resolution. The formality of arbitration ensures a fair and impartial hearing, providing a sense of due process for both the member and the employer. While it is more structured and potentially more expensive than mediation, the binding nature of the arbitrator's decision offers certainty and finality. The selection of the arbitrator is often a crucial step in the process, with both the union and the employer having a say in choosing a neutral and impartial individual with relevant expertise.

The collective bargaining agreement typically outlines the specific procedures for mediation and arbitration, including the selection process for the mediator or arbitrator, the rules of evidence, and the timelines for each stage of the process. This clear framework ensures fairness and transparency, reducing the likelihood of procedural irregularities or disputes regarding the process itself. The procedural clarity eliminates ambiguity and ensures both parties are treated equitably.

Beyond the formal grievance procedure, many unions offer additional resources to members facing disputes. This may include access to legal counsel, who can advise members on their rights and provide guidance throughout the process. Some unions also have dedicated staff who specialize in dispute resolution, providing support and advocacy to members facing conflicts. These resources are especially valuable to members who may lack the experience or resources to navigate complex legal procedures independently.

The availability of these comprehensive dispute resolution mechanisms underscores the value of union membership. While disputes are inevitable in any workplace, the structured and fair processes offered by unions provide a critical safety net for members, ensuring that grievances are addressed promptly, fairly, and efficiently. The existence of these formal structures contrasts sharply with the often precarious position of non-union workers who may lack effective recourse against employer misconduct.

The processes discussed above are not merely theoretical; they represent tangible pathways to justice and redress. Consider, for example, a musician in a symphony orchestra who believes their performance evaluations are unfairly biased due to a personal conflict with the conductor. Through the union's grievance procedure, they can formally lodge a complaint, initiating an investigation and potentially leading to mediation or arbitration to resolve the dispute. Similarly, an athlete who feels their contract has been violated by the team owner can utilize the union's dispute resolution mechanisms to seek a remedy. The union's intervention offers a path to resolution far beyond what an individual might achieve alone.

These processes are not just about resolving individual disputes; they serve a broader purpose. By providing a structured means of addressing grievances, unions help to maintain a stable and productive working environment. The existence of a fair and efficient dispute resolution process discourages arbitrary actions by employers and fosters trust and respect between management and employees. This contributes to a more positive and collaborative work atmosphere, ultimately benefiting both the union members and the organization as a whole.

Ultimately, the robust dispute resolution mechanisms embedded within union structures are a critical element of the overall protection and support they provide their members. They are an integral part of the broader benefits package, extending far beyond basic wages and working conditions. They represent a commitment to fairness, equity, and due process, providing a valuable safety net for artists, athletes, and entertainment professionals navigating the often challenging landscape of their respective industries. The availability of these resources signifies a meaningful difference between unionized and non-unionized work environments, highlighting the significant advantages of collective bargaining and union representation. The intricacies of the process may seem daunting initially, but the ultimate outcome – a fair and equitable resolution – makes the effort worthwhile. The peace of mind and security provided are invaluable assets in any career, particularly in those characterized by volatility and high stakes.

The power of a union lies not just in its ability to negotiate strong contracts but also in its capacity to successfully enforce them. While the grievance procedure and alternative dispute resolution mechanisms provide a framework for resolving conflicts, the true measure of a union's effectiveness lies in its track record of securing victories for its members. The following case studies illustrate the tangible benefits of union representation and the powerful impact collective bargaining can have on individual careers.

Our first case involves Anya Petrova, a renowned concert pianist. Anya, a member of the Musicians' Union, had a long-standing contract with a major record label. The contract, while seemingly lucrative on the surface, contained a clause that allowed the label to significantly reduce her royalty payments if digital sales fell below a certain threshold. This clause, cleverly worded, essentially shifted the risk of declining digital sales entirely onto Anya, despite the label having significant control over marketing and distribution. When digital sales dipped unexpectedly due to a poorly planned marketing campaign by the label, the record company invoked the clause, drastically cutting Anya's royalties. Anya, armed with her union representation, felt this was a breach of the spirit, if not the letter, of her contract. The union immediately stepped in, arguing that the label failed to meet its contractual obligations regarding marketing and promotion. After several months of negotiations, which involved detailed analysis of the label's marketing strategies and the industry standards for similar releases, the union successfully negotiated a renegotiated royalty structure. Anya secured a significantly fairer deal, protecting her income and highlighting the crucial role of proactive union involvement in contract interpretation. This case underscores how unions can leverage industry expertise and collective bargaining power to protect artists from exploitative contract terms. Anya's victory wasn't merely financial; it also sent a clear message to other musicians, reinforcing the value of union membership and its potential to address contractual imbalances.

Another striking example involves the case of the "Hollywood Actors Guild" (a fictionalized example that draws on real-world union struggles). This fictional guild faced a protracted battle with a major streaming platform over residuals for its members. The platform, aiming to maximize profits, argued that its business model differed from traditional television and therefore traditional residual payment structures were inapplicable. This argument threatened to drastically reduce the income of many actors, particularly those appearing in episodic series, severely impacting their livelihoods and future earning potential. The guild, however, refused to back down. They argued that the streaming platform's success was directly tied to the actors' performances and that the platform was unjustly benefiting from their work without providing fair compensation. This dispute escalated into a lengthy legal battle, featuring expert testimony from economists and entertainment industry specialists. Ultimately, after years of negotiation and litigation, including a high-profile media campaign that galvanized public support for the actors, the guild secured a landmark victory. The streaming platform agreed to a new compensation model that included substantial residual payments, ensuring actors receive fairer compensation for their work in a rapidly evolving digital landscape. This case highlights the perseverance and strategic prowess required to win landmark victories against powerful corporations, showcasing the importance of unified action and sustained pressure. It served as a significant precedent for future negotiations involving streaming services and actors' rights.

The sports industry also presents numerous examples of union victories. Consider the case of the "National Basketball Players' Association" (again, a fictionalized representation built upon real-world scenarios). During the negotiation of a new collective bargaining agreement, the players' union successfully fought for significant improvements to healthcare benefits, including enhanced coverage for mental health services. While financial compensation is often the most prominent aspect of collective bargaining, this negotiation demonstrated that unions can successfully advocate for benefits that extend beyond financial matters, securing crucial provisions that directly impact members' well-being. The players' union faced staunch resistance from the league owners who argued that the increased cost of healthcare would be unsustainable. However, the union presented compelling data showcasing the importance of mental health support for athletes, who often face significant pressure and unique challenges. They demonstrated that investing in mental health support could actually reduce long-term costs and improve player performance. The union's success underscores the significant role of data-driven advocacy in negotiating favorable agreements. The enhanced healthcare provisions are a testament to the union's commitment to the holistic well-being of its members, extending their advocacy beyond salaries and other financial concerns. This victory became a benchmark for other sports unions, emphasizing the importance of prioritizing the physical and mental health needs of athletes within collective bargaining agreements.

In another example, the "Screenwriters Guild" (a fictionalized case based on actual industry events) secured a significant victory regarding the use of AI in scriptwriting. As AI tools became increasingly sophisticated, there were concerns that studios might use these tools to replace human screenwriters, leading to job displacement and financial instability. The union anticipated this issue and actively engaged in negotiations with studio executives to develop protective measures. They argued for provisions that ensured human writers maintained control over their creative work and received fair compensation for their contributions, even when AI tools were utilized in the creative process. This resulted in a groundbreaking clause in the collective bargaining agreement that stipulated strict guidelines regarding the use of AI in script development, ensuring writers received appropriate credit and compensation for their work, regardless of AI involvement. This proactive approach of anticipating technological disruptions and negotiating protective measures is a testament to the union's forward-thinking strategy. The clause became a model for other creative unions dealing with similar technological advancements, offering a strong precedent for safeguarding creative professionals' rights in the face of emerging technologies. This case serves as a compelling example of how unions can proactively address emerging technological challenges and successfully integrate those concerns into collective bargaining agreements.

These case studies highlight the diverse range of victories unions have secured for their members, demonstrating the broad spectrum of their impact. They emphasize that the benefits of union membership extend far beyond just wages and working conditions; they encompass a comprehensive approach to protecting members' rights, well-being, and career longevity. The success of these campaigns stems from a combination of factors: thorough preparation, strategic negotiation, effective advocacy, and, importantly, the unified strength of members working collectively to achieve common goals. These examples showcase how unions act as powerful advocates, not just securing immediate improvements in working conditions but also setting precedents that benefit future generations of artists, athletes, and entertainment professionals. The sustained commitment to fairness, equity, and due process, as illustrated in these real-world examples, underlines the enduring value of union representation in a constantly evolving industry.

Chapter 8: Building Your Legal Team

Building a formidable legal team is paramount for anyone navigating the intricate landscape of the entertainment industry. While understanding union representation is crucial, the cornerstone of your legal strategy often rests upon the shoulders of a skilled entertainment lawyer. Choosing the right one isn't a decision to be taken lightly; it's an investment in your future success and the protection of your hard-earned creative work. This choice requires careful consideration and a thorough understanding of what you need from legal counsel.

The first and most crucial aspect to consider is the lawyer's experience. Don't be swayed by flashy marketing or promises of quick riches. Look for demonstrable experience within the specific niche of the entertainment industry that aligns with your field. A lawyer with extensive experience in film contracts won't necessarily be the best fit for a musician navigating publishing deals, and vice versa. Look for a track record of success within your specific area of expertise – be it music publishing, film production, sports agency representation, or digital content creation. This specificity ensures that your lawyer possesses the intimate knowledge of the industry's norms, trends, and legal precedents relevant to your work.

Requesting a list of past clients and case studies is a valuable step in the vetting process. While confidentiality often restricts the release of specific details, the lawyer should be able to provide a broad overview of their involvement in significant cases. This will give you an idea of the scale and complexity of the projects they have handled and the types of challenges they have successfully overcome. Look for cases that mirror your own aspirations and challenges. Did they secure favorable deals for clients in similar situations? Did they successfully defend clients against infringement claims or contract disputes? A lawyer's past successes are a strong indicator of their future potential to achieve similar results for you.

Specialization is another crucial aspect to consider. The entertainment industry is diverse, encompassing film, television, music, sports, and digital content, each with its own unique legal challenges. Look for an attorney who demonstrates expertise in your particular segment. For instance, a lawyer specializing in intellectual property law might be ideal for protecting your musical compositions, while one focused on contract negotiation would be essential for securing favorable endorsement deals. Broad experience is useful, but deep expertise in your niche provides the invaluable edge of nuanced understanding and strategic insight that makes all the difference.

Beyond experience and specialization, consider the lawyer's communication style and overall compatibility. This is a crucial, often overlooked aspect of the attorney-client relationship. Effective communication is essential for a smooth and productive working relationship. You need a lawyer who is responsive, accessible, and explains complex legal matters clearly and concisely. Remember, you'll be entrusting this individual with your career, your creative work, and potentially your finances. Schedule consultations with several lawyers to gauge their personalities and communication styles. Choose someone you feel comfortable with, someone you can trust to represent your best interests with clarity and conviction. A good rapport fosters open communication, mutual respect, and ultimately, a more effective working relationship.

Don't hesitate to inquire about the lawyer's fee structure. While this is a sensitive topic, it's vital to have a clear understanding of the cost involved. Some lawyers charge hourly rates, while others may prefer retainer agreements. Discuss your budget openly and honestly. A lawyer worth their salt will understand your financial constraints and work with you to find a payment plan that fits your needs. Transparency around fees is a sign of professionalism and respect for the client's business. Furthermore, understand what services are included in the fee. Does it cover all aspects of your representation, or are there additional charges for specific tasks or legal actions? Clarifying these points will prevent unexpected costs and maintain a clear financial perspective throughout your collaboration.

Thoroughly researching the lawyer's reputation is essential. Check online reviews and testimonials, contact industry colleagues who might have worked with the lawyer in the past, and seek referrals from trusted sources within your network. A solid reputation speaks volumes about a lawyer's competence, ethics, and reliability. Look for patterns in reviews – consistent positive feedback points to a reliable track record. Conversely, recurring negative comments should raise red flags and prompt further investigation. Don't hesitate to dig deeper into any concerns that surface.

Finally, consider the lawyer's network and industry connections. A lawyer with strong connections within the entertainment industry can be an invaluable asset, providing insights into industry trends, potential opportunities, and strategic partnerships. These connections can extend beyond legal matters, offering valuable guidance and support throughout your career. Inquire about the lawyer's involvement in industry organizations and any relationships with key players in your specific segment of the entertainment industry. These connections can significantly benefit your career trajectory.

Remember, choosing an entertainment lawyer is a critical decision that will have a significant impact on your career. It requires careful consideration of multiple factors, including the lawyer's experience, specialization, communication style, fee structure, reputation, and industry connections. Don't rush into the decision. Invest time in researching potential candidates, interviewing several lawyers, and selecting someone who shares your vision and understands the complexities of the entertainment industry. The right lawyer will be more than just a legal advisor; they will be a crucial partner in your journey to success, ensuring that your creative endeavors are protected and your rights are safeguarded. Your career is a significant investment – choose your legal representation accordingly.

The selection of an entertainment lawyer is an ongoing process, not a one-time event. As your career evolves, your legal needs might change. You might need additional specialized counsel, for instance, in intellectual property litigation or international distribution agreements. Your initial lawyer might not have the expertise for such issues. Staying proactive and evaluating your legal needs regularly is crucial. Never hesitate to seek second opinions or explore alternative legal counsel when circumstances demand it. Your long-term career success depends on the quality of your legal representation; it's an investment that requires both diligent selection and ongoing evaluation. Your legal team is your protective shield in the fiercely competitive world of entertainment.

Selecting the wrong lawyer could lead to costly mistakes, missed opportunities, and even legal battles that could derail your career. You might unwittingly sign unfavorable contracts, neglect to protect your intellectual property, or fail to secure the compensation you deserve. These scenarios can significantly impact your earnings and your professional reputation. The time and effort invested in finding the right legal representation are a small price to pay compared to the potential consequences of a poor choice. Remember, you're not just seeking a lawyer; you're building a long-term partnership that will navigate the challenges and celebrate the successes of your career journey. Make it a partnership based on trust, mutual understanding, and a shared commitment to your professional success.

Having carefully selected your legal team, the next crucial step is cultivating a productive and collaborative working relationship. This is not simply about hiring the best lawyers; it's about building a partnership built on trust, mutual understanding, and open communication. A strong attorney-client relationship is the bedrock of effective legal representation, ensuring your interests are consistently prioritized and your legal strategy is implemented seamlessly.

One of the most important elements of this relationship is clear and consistent communication. Regular updates on the progress of your cases, contract negotiations, or any legal matters are essential. Don't hesitate to schedule regular meetings with your legal team – whether it's weekly, bi-weekly, or monthly – to discuss ongoing projects and address any questions or concerns. These meetings shouldn't be viewed as mere updates but rather as opportunities for collaborative brainstorming and strategic planning. Consider them a forum to not only receive information but actively participate in shaping the direction of your legal strategy.

Effective communication also involves utilizing the appropriate channels. Emails are ideal for conveying routine updates or documents, while phone calls might be necessary for more immediate issues or discussions requiring nuanced understanding.

For particularly complex matters or those involving extensive documentation, consider video conferencing or in-person meetings. The medium should always be tailored to the complexity and urgency of the matter at hand. Choose the method that best facilitates effective and efficient communication. A prompt response from your legal team is crucial; a lack of timely communication can lead to missed deadlines, lost opportunities, or even detrimental legal setbacks.

Furthermore, fostering open and honest communication necessitates asking clarifying questions. Legal jargon can be dense and confusing. Don't be afraid to ask your lawyers to explain complex legal concepts in plain language. Understanding the nuances of your contracts, legal options, and potential risks is vital for informed decision-making. Remember, your legal team is there to serve you, and a robust understanding of your legal position empowers you to participate actively in the decision-making process. Don't shy away from asking detailed questions; thorough understanding is crucial for making sound strategic decisions.

Beyond the specifics of your legal matters, building a strong relationship with your legal team involves establishing a personal rapport. Regular interaction fosters mutual understanding and trust, building a foundation for more effective collaboration. Sharing your creative vision, your career aspirations, and the challenges you face helps your legal team understand your overall goals, enabling them to provide more tailored and insightful advice.

This holistic perspective allows them to consider the legal implications of your decisions not only in isolation but within the larger context of your career path.

Regularly review your legal contracts and agreements. Contracts can be complex and multifaceted, requiring careful review and understanding. Don't simply sign documents without thoroughly reviewing each clause. Your legal team should assist you with this process, explaining any unclear terms and highlighting potential risks or benefits. This process is not just about complying with legal formalities; it's about proactively safeguarding your rights and interests. Treat contract reviews as opportunities to understand the implications of your legal commitments and ensure they align with your career aspirations.

Remember that your legal team is an extension of your professional network. They are not merely legal advisors; they are partners in your professional success. Therefore, maintaining regular communication and actively engaging in the decision-making process is crucial. The more involved you are, the stronger your partnership will be, and the more effective the legal representation you receive. This collaboration significantly impacts your legal outcomes and overall career trajectory.

Building a positive working relationship involves handling disagreements professionally and constructively. Disagreements can arise; it's inevitable. However, approaching disagreements with mutual respect and a commitment to finding common ground is vital for maintaining a healthy and productive partnership. Remember that your legal team is there to advise you, not dictate your actions. Openly expressing your concerns and listening to their perspectives are key components of resolving conflicts and ensuring that the best possible outcome is achieved.

Furthermore, your legal team should be transparent regarding their fees and billing practices. Regularly review the invoices to ensure that the charges are accurate and reflect the services rendered. Transparency and clear communication regarding billing practices are integral to maintaining a strong attorney-client relationship. This also helps prevent unexpected financial burdens and keeps you informed about the financial aspects of your legal representation.

Understanding the limits of your legal team's expertise is also important. While your core legal team might excel in specific areas, recognizing when specialist advice is required is crucial. Don't hesitate to engage other legal professionals—intellectual property specialists, tax advisors, or international law experts—as needed. Building a network of specialized legal advisors helps ensure that your legal representation covers all facets of your professional life. This holistic approach safeguards your interests and maximizes the effectiveness of your legal strategy.

Finally, always remember that your legal team is a resource. They are not only there to react to crises but also to proactively help you navigate the complexities of your career. Utilize their expertise for preventative measures, such as ensuring your contracts are robust, protecting your intellectual property, and strategically managing your financial affairs. This proactive approach can minimize legal risks and maximize your long-term success in the entertainment industry. Regular consultations, proactive planning, and clear communication will build a solid foundation for achieving your career ambitions.

In conclusion, establishing and maintaining a strong working relationship with your legal team is a crucial ingredient for success in the entertainment industry. It's an ongoing process that demands consistent communication, mutual respect, and a proactive approach to legal matters. Your legal team isn't merely a group of professionals; they are your partners, working alongside you to achieve your creative and professional goals. Building a strong partnership with them ensures that your legal strategies are effectively implemented, your rights are protected, and your journey to success is navigated with clarity and confidence.

Understanding the financial landscape of legal representation is paramount to effectively managing your career. Entertainment law, in particular, can involve a complex array of fees and costs, making transparency and clear communication with your legal team absolutely crucial. This isn't just about paying bills; it's about understanding the value you receive for your investment and ensuring you're making informed financial decisions that support your long-term success.

One of the most common fee structures is the hourly rate. This is a straightforward method where you are charged a predetermined amount for each hour of a lawyer's time, as well as the time of paralegals and other support staff. Hourly rates vary widely based on the lawyer's experience, specialization, and geographic location. A seasoned entertainment lawyer in a major city like Los Angeles or New York will naturally command a higher hourly rate than a newer lawyer in a smaller market. It's important to inquire about the hourly rates for all members of the legal team who will be working on your case, as these costs can quickly accumulate. Understanding the nuances of hourly billing is vital, as even seemingly small tasks can accumulate significant charges over time.

To manage costs associated with hourly billing, it's helpful to be very clear with your legal team about the scope of work involved from the outset. Clearly define your objectives, the specific tasks you expect them to perform, and the desired outcome. Regularly checking in with your lawyers to ensure you're staying within budget and that work is progressing as planned is crucial. Ask for regular updates on time spent, providing an opportunity for proactive adjustments to the work plan if necessary.

Another common fee structure is the flat fee. This involves an upfront payment for a specific legal service, such as reviewing a contract or drafting a simple agreement. Flat fees offer a degree of predictability, allowing you to budget more effectively. However, it's essential to ensure the scope of work is clearly defined within the agreement. Any tasks falling outside the original scope could result in additional charges, possibly converting the flat fee arrangement into a hybrid approach with added hourly billing for the extra work. Negotiating the terms of a flat fee arrangement carefully is essential to avoid unexpected expenses later. Always obtain a detailed breakdown of what is included in the flat fee to prevent misunderstandings and potential disputes.

Contingency fees are another option, primarily used in litigation cases. In a contingency fee arrangement, your lawyer's fees are contingent on a successful outcome. If the case is won, the lawyer receives a percentage of the recovery, typically ranging from 25% to 40%. If the case is lost, the lawyer receives nothing beyond any costs already advanced. Contingency fees can be beneficial for clients who can't afford upfront legal costs but risk is transferred to the attorney. However, it's essential to weigh the potential risks and rewards carefully. The success of a case is never guaranteed, and even a partially successful outcome might not yield enough to compensate for the percentage your lawyer will take.

Hybrid fee arrangements often combine elements of hourly rates and flat fees. For instance, a lawyer might charge a flat fee for reviewing a contract and then an hourly rate for negotiating it. This structure provides a balance between predictability and flexibility, allowing you to budget for certain aspects while remaining adaptable to evolving needs. Clearly understanding the breakdown of fees within a hybrid arrangement is vital to prevent unexpected costs. Ask your attorney for a detailed fee schedule outlining all aspects of the arrangement to ensure clarity and avoid any potential surprises.

Beyond the core legal fees, other costs can significantly impact your overall expenses. These include court filing fees, expert witness fees, travel expenses, copying and printing costs, and service charges. Some of these costs are non-negotiable and determined by external factors, such as court fees set by the judicial system. However, your lawyer can advise you on ways to potentially mitigate some of these expenses, such as employing strategies to reduce the need for extensive expert witness testimony or utilizing cost-effective methods for document management. Transparency in these additional costs is crucial; don't hesitate to ask your lawyer for a detailed breakdown of all anticipated expenses.

Negotiating legal fees is perfectly acceptable, especially when considering different fee structures. Don't be afraid to discuss your budget and explore options that fit your financial circumstances. Many lawyers are willing to work with clients to reach a mutually agreeable arrangement. However, remember that undercutting fees excessively might compromise the quality of legal representation. Focus on finding a lawyer who offers a balance between affordability and competence, ensuring their experience and expertise align with your needs. Remember, investing in a skilled legal team is an investment in your career, and the potential cost savings of a less experienced or less suitable lawyer can quickly outweigh any initial savings.

Furthermore, the value of legal counsel goes beyond simply handling legal disputes. Proactive legal planning, like securing strong contracts and protecting intellectual property rights, can prevent costly problems down the line. The long-term cost of neglecting preventative legal measures can often far exceed the cost of proactive legal guidance. Consider this as an investment in protecting your future earnings.

Regularly review your invoices and raise any questions or concerns you may have immediately. Open communication with your legal team about billing is crucial for maintaining trust and transparency. Don't hesitate to ask for clarification on any item you don't understand. Early identification of discrepancies can prevent significant misunderstandings and financial burdens down the road. Building a relationship with your lawyer based on open financial communication ensures that you're both on the same page regarding costs and expectations.

In conclusion, navigating the financial aspects of legal representation requires careful planning, open communication, and a thorough understanding of different fee structures. By understanding your options, negotiating effectively, and maintaining regular communication with your legal team, you can manage your legal expenses effectively while ensuring you receive the high-quality representation necessary to protect your interests and build a thriving career in the entertainment industry. The initial investment in strong legal counsel is a crucial element of your overall career strategy, protecting your creative work, financial security, and future success. Don't view legal fees as mere expenses, but as investments in your long-term professional growth and stability. Choosing the right lawyer and structuring your financial relationship correctly can make all the difference in navigating the complex legal world of the entertainment industry.

Beyond the crucial role of your legal team, another indispensable member of your professional support system is the business manager. While lawyers handle the legal intricacies of your career, your business manager acts as your financial strategist and overall business advisor, guiding you through the complex world of financial management, investments, and long-term career planning. Think of them as your financial quarterback, calling the plays to ensure your financial success.

Their responsibilities extend far beyond simply balancing your checkbook. A skilled business manager is a multifaceted professional, offering expertise in areas such as financial planning, investment management, tax strategy, and contract negotiation support. They are your trusted advisor, providing an objective perspective on financial decisions and ensuring your resources are allocated strategically to maximize your long-term financial well-being.

One of their core functions involves comprehensive financial planning. This goes beyond simply tracking income and expenses. A good business manager will create a detailed financial plan tailored to your specific circumstances, considering your current income, expenses, short-term and long-term financial goals, and risk tolerance. This plan often includes budgeting, forecasting, and investment strategies designed to secure your financial future, even beyond your active career. They'll help you understand your net worth, cash flow projections, and potential tax liabilities, enabling you to make informed financial decisions.

Furthermore, they'll guide you through the intricacies of investment management. This isn't just about investing in stocks and bonds; it involves understanding your risk tolerance, diversification strategies, and long-term investment goals. They will likely work with financial advisors to structure your investments, carefully considering your overall financial health and future plans. Their understanding of your career trajectory allows them to make informed investment decisions, balancing short-term needs with long-term growth. They might advise on diversified portfolios including real estate, private equity, and other alternative investments, depending on your specific circumstances and risk profile. They'll also handle the administrative tasks associated with managing your investments, freeing you to focus on your creative endeavors.

Tax planning is another critical area where a business manager provides invaluable assistance. The entertainment industry often presents unique tax challenges due to fluctuating income, deductions, and complex tax laws. A savvy business manager will work with tax professionals to develop a comprehensive tax strategy that minimizes your tax liability while remaining fully compliant with all relevant regulations. They understand the nuances of tax deductions specific to the entertainment industry, helping you leverage opportunities to reduce your tax burden legally and ethically. They can advise on strategies like qualified retirement plans, tax-advantaged investments, and other methods to optimize your tax position. This proactive approach can save you substantial sums over time, ensuring more of your hard-earned income remains available for your personal and professional use.

Contract negotiation support is another important role of your business manager. While your lawyer focuses on the legal aspects of contracts, your business manager helps analyze the financial implications of deals, ensuring they align with your long-term financial strategy. They'll assist in negotiations, ensuring you receive fair compensation and favorable terms, scrutinizing revenue streams, payment schedules, and other financial aspects of any contracts you're considering. They'll act as your advocate, ensuring you're protected from potentially disadvantageous financial clauses, thereby ensuring that the contracts work in your best financial interest. They are your voice in ensuring fair and equitable financial arrangements in all business dealings.

Beyond these core functions, business managers often handle a wide range of administrative tasks related to your finances. This can include managing your bank accounts, paying bills, tracking expenses, and preparing financial reports. This frees you from the burden of administrative tasks, allowing you to concentrate on your creative work and career development. They act as a crucial buffer between you and the complexities of managing your finances, streamlining administrative processes and ensuring your financial affairs are handled with efficiency and transparency.

Finding the right business manager is crucial for your success. Look for someone with a strong understanding of the entertainment industry, experience in managing finances for artists or athletes, and a proven track record of success. Thoroughly research potential candidates, reviewing their credentials, experience, and references before making a decision. Check their professional affiliations, seek recommendations from trusted sources, and schedule interviews to determine their personality and approach to financial management. A strong relationship based on trust and mutual respect is essential for a successful collaboration.

The fees for business managers vary depending on the level of service, experience, and complexity of your financial needs. Some might charge an hourly rate, while others work on a percentage of your income or a retainer fee. Clearly understand their fee structure and payment terms before entering into an agreement. Negotiating fees is perfectly acceptable, just as with your legal team. Make sure the fee is appropriate given their expertise and the scope of their responsibilities. Ensure that all financial arrangements are clearly detailed in writing, so that there's no ambiguity about their services and your obligations.

The value of a business manager far outweighs their fees. They help protect your financial well-being, ensuring that you maximize your earnings, make informed financial decisions, and build a secure financial future. They are an integral part of your professional support system, providing valuable expertise and advice, allowing you to focus on your craft and excel in your chosen field. They are a strategic partner, helping you achieve your professional and financial goals, and they are a vital component in building a sustainable and thriving career in the entertainment industry.

In conclusion, while your legal team safeguards your legal interests, your business manager acts as your financial guardian, helping navigate the complex financial landscape of the entertainment industry. They play a critical role in protecting your financial well-being, providing guidance on financial planning, investment management, tax strategies, and contract negotiation.

Their expertise frees you to focus on your creative work, providing peace of mind that your financial affairs are being expertly managed. The collaborative effort between your legal team and your business manager forms the core of a robust and supportive professional network, paving the way for a long and successful career. Investing in both is an investment in your future success, not just today, but for years to come. The long-term benefits of having a skilled legal and financial team far exceed the initial costs, acting as a bulwark against future unforeseen challenges and securing your financial well-being throughout your career and beyond. This proactive approach to both legal and financial planning lays the foundation for a sustainable and prosperous career in the demanding yet rewarding world of entertainment.

Building a truly robust and effective support system goes far beyond simply securing a top-tier legal team and a shrewd business manager. While these professionals are undeniably crucial, they represent only a portion of the comprehensive network you need to thrive in the fiercely competitive landscape of entertainment. Think of it as an orchestra – your legal team and business manager are the principal soloists, but you need a full ensemble to create a truly harmonious and successful performance. This ensemble consists of other vital players: accountants, agents, and publicists, each bringing their unique expertise to the table.

Accountants, unlike business managers who focus on overall financial strategy, delve into the granular details of your finances. They are the meticulous record-keepers, ensuring your tax returns are meticulously prepared and filed, navigating the intricacies of tax laws, and identifying potential avenues for tax optimization. They are not merely number crunchers; they are strategic advisors, proactively seeking ways to minimize your tax liability while staying fully compliant with all regulations. They will understand the nuances of deductions specific to the entertainment industry, from travel expenses and entertainment costs to equipment write-offs and home office deductions. They are your trusted partners in financial transparency, providing the necessary documentation and insight for accurate financial reporting. A dedicated accountant will work hand-in-hand with your business manager, providing the granular financial data the manager needs for long-term financial planning and strategic investment decisions.

Their role extends beyond yearly tax preparation. They offer ongoing financial guidance, providing real-time feedback on your financial health and identifying potential areas of concern. They can help you establish sound financial habits, providing practical advice on budgeting, expense tracking, and saving for the future. They'll analyze your financial statements, identify trends, and offer insights that can inform your long-term financial strategies. For instance, an accountant can help you understand the implications of various contract offers, analyzing the after-tax income from different deals and helping you make informed decisions that align with your overall financial goals. They will also help you understand and navigate complex financial instruments and investments, ensuring your assets are managed effectively and prudently.

Consider this scenario: you're offered a lucrative endorsement deal, but the contract is filled with complex financial clauses and payment structures. Your accountant can dissect the fine print, breaking down the complexities and helping you understand the true financial implications of the deal. They'll ensure all the numbers add up and that you're getting a fair return on your investment of time and effort. They'll be able to highlight any potential pitfalls or hidden costs, making sure you enter the agreement with your eyes wide open and with a clear understanding of your financial commitments and obligations. This preventative approach is invaluable and can save you from potentially costly mistakes in the future. In essence, they are the unsung heroes of your financial wellbeing, ensuring accuracy, compliance, and strategic financial planning.

Next, let's discuss the indispensable role of an agent. While your lawyer protects your legal interests and your business manager guards your financial well-being, your agent is your champion in the marketplace, tirelessly seeking out opportunities that align with your career goals. They are your advocate, negotiator, and tireless promoter, always working to secure the best possible deals for you. They are the gatekeepers to opportunities, screening offers, and identifying those that best fit your unique skill set and career aspirations. They often have extensive industry connections, providing access to a wider range of projects and opportunities than you might find on your own. They understand the nuances of the industry, having spent years building relationships with producers, directors, casting agents, and other industry professionals.

Your agent's expertise extends beyond simply finding work. They are your primary point of contact with potential clients, negotiating contracts on your behalf, ensuring you receive fair compensation, and protecting your professional interests. They are skilled negotiators, leveraging their industry knowledge and relationships to achieve the best possible terms for you. They'll scrutinize contracts, ensuring they're favorable and protective of your rights and reputation. They'll also manage your schedule, coordinating auditions, meetings, and other industry events. Their deep understanding of the industry enables them to navigate the complexities of contract negotiations, advocating for your interests every step of the way. They'll often have experience working with lawyers and business managers, ensuring a coordinated approach to managing your professional affairs.

A common misconception is that agents work only for actors or musicians. Agents are equally crucial for athletes, securing lucrative endorsement deals, negotiating contracts with teams or sponsors, and managing their public image. In essence, your agent is the bridge between your talent and the marketplace, working tirelessly to build your career, expand your opportunities, and maximize your earning potential. Choosing the right agent is paramount. Look for someone with a proven track record of success, a strong network of contacts, and a reputation for integrity. A good agent will be honest and transparent, providing regular updates on their progress and always putting your interests first.

Finally, in this symphony of support, the publicist plays the crucial role of shaping and managing your public image. They are the architects of your reputation, crafting your narrative and ensuring it resonates with your target audience. In today's hyper-connected world, public perception is paramount. A skilled publicist can leverage media outlets, social media platforms, and other channels to build your brand and connect you with your fans. They are experts in crisis management, swiftly and effectively addressing any negative publicity that may arise. They will create and maintain your online presence, manage interviews, and oversee your media appearances. They will strategize ways to build anticipation for upcoming projects or events, ensuring maximum media coverage and public interest. They understand the power of storytelling and can create compelling narratives that resonate with your audience, captivating them and building a loyal following. They act as your spokesperson and media advisor, meticulously crafting your messages and ensuring they are consistent with your personal brand.

The publicist's role is especially crucial in the modern entertainment landscape, where social media and online reputation can significantly impact an artist's career trajectory. They know how to leverage social media to your advantage, building an engaged following and fostering a strong connection with your fans. They'll monitor your online presence, engaging in positive conversations and addressing any negative comments or criticisms. They might handle press releases, create compelling social media content, and arrange interviews with key media outlets. A good publicist will act as a proactive shield, anticipating potential issues and addressing them before they escalate into significant problems. This proactive approach to reputation management is essential for maintaining a positive image and fostering a strong connection with your fanbase.

Building this holistic support network requires careful consideration and diligent research. Each professional you choose needs to be not only highly skilled in their field but also a good fit for your personality and working style. You'll need to establish trust and open communication with each member of your team, ensuring a collaborative approach to managing your career. The investment in these professionals is an investment in your long-term success, providing you with the tools and support to navigate the complexities of the entertainment industry, protect your interests, and achieve your career goals. Remember, it is not just about individual talent; it's about building a strong, cohesive team that works together to achieve a shared vision of success.

Chapter 9: Dispute Resolution and Litigation

Negotiation and mediation represent powerful tools in your arsenal for resolving disputes without resorting to the often costly and time-consuming process of litigation. These methods offer a more collaborative and less adversarial approach, allowing parties to find mutually acceptable solutions while preserving relationships. While litigation offers a definitive legal outcome, it can be a protracted and emotionally draining experience, potentially damaging personal and professional ties. Negotiation and mediation provide a path to resolution that prioritizes compromise and collaboration, fostering a more positive and productive outcome.

Effective negotiation begins with thorough preparation. Before entering any discussion, you must have a comprehensive understanding of your own position, including your goals, your "walk-away" point, and the evidence supporting your claims. This requires meticulous review of contracts, communications, and any other relevant documentation. Know your leverage – what assets or information do you possess that might influence the other party? Perhaps you have compelling evidence, a strong reputation, or the ability to take alternative actions. Understanding your leverage empowers you to negotiate from a position of strength.

The art of negotiation lies not just in presenting your case, but also in actively listening to the other party's perspective. Empathy and understanding are crucial. Try to see the issue from their point of view. What are their motivations? What are their concerns? By demonstrating a willingness to understand their position, you create an atmosphere of mutual respect and trust, making it more likely that you'll reach a compromise. Remember, negotiation is not a win-lose proposition; it's about finding a solution that satisfies both parties' needs, even if it means making concessions.

The process often involves a series of offers and counter-offers. Begin with a reasonable opening offer, leaving room for negotiation. Be prepared to justify your position with evidence and logical arguments. Avoid making emotional outbursts or personal attacks. Maintain a calm, professional demeanor, focusing on the issues at hand. As the negotiations progress, be willing to compromise, but only to a point where your fundamental interests are protected.

Consider the use of creative solutions. Sometimes, thinking outside the box can lead to unexpected and beneficial outcomes. Perhaps there's a mutually beneficial alternative that neither party had initially considered. Flexibility and adaptability are key to successful negotiation. Be prepared to explore different options and make adjustments as needed.

Document every stage of the negotiation process. Maintain a record of all offers, counter-offers, agreements, and any other relevant communications. This documentation is vital not only for ensuring a clear understanding of the final agreement but also to provide evidence should the negotiation fail and litigation becomes necessary.

Mediation offers a more structured approach to dispute resolution, involving a neutral third party, the mediator, who facilitates communication and helps parties find common ground. Mediators do not make decisions or impose solutions; they act as facilitators, guiding the parties through the process and helping them to identify mutually acceptable compromises. The mediator's expertise lies in their ability to manage the process, defuse tensions, and help parties communicate effectively. They assist in identifying underlying interests and concerns, assisting parties in navigating complex emotional issues. They encourage collaboration and creative problem-solving.

Choosing the right mediator is critical. The mediator's experience and expertise in the relevant area of law or industry are significant. Look for someone with a strong reputation for impartiality, effectiveness, and communication skills. The mediator should be skilled in managing conflict and facilitating constructive dialogue. They should be able to create a safe and respectful environment where all parties feel comfortable expressing their views and concerns.

The mediation process typically begins with a joint session where the mediator introduces the process, sets the ground rules, and encourages parties to explain their perspectives. This is followed by separate caucuses, allowing each party to privately discuss their concerns and interests with the mediator. The mediator then facilitates communication between the parties, helping them to identify common ground and explore potential solutions. The mediator guides the parties through identifying mutually acceptable outcomes.

The mediation process is confidential. Anything said during the mediation cannot be used in subsequent litigation. This confidentiality encourages open communication and encourages parties to explore potential solutions without fear of compromising their position in court. It fosters trust and enables collaborative problem-solving.

The success of mediation hinges on the willingness of all parties to participate in good faith. It requires a commitment to finding a resolution that is acceptable to all. It's a collaborative effort, demanding open communication, compromise, and a willingness to consider alternative solutions. While not all disputes are suitable for mediation, it's often a preferable option to lengthy and costly litigation.

Consider a scenario where a musician is embroiled in a dispute with their record label over royalty payments. Negotiation could begin with the musician reviewing the contract in detail, identifying discrepancies or clauses that support their claim. They may also analyze sales data, streaming statistics, and other relevant financial information. Armed with this evidence, the musician can approach the record label with a reasonable proposal for recalculation, outlining their calculations and emphasizing the contractual basis for their claim. If this negotiation fails, mediation may be the next step, bringing in a neutral party experienced in music industry contracts to facilitate communication and guide the parties toward a mutually agreeable solution. The mediator helps both parties understand each other's perspectives, identify common ground, and explore different ways to resolve the dispute fairly, potentially leading to a revised agreement that satisfies both sides and avoids costly litigation.

Another example: an athlete is involved in a contract dispute with their sports agency. Through negotiation, they might seek a clarification on certain clauses, requesting specific documentation or details. If this fails, mediation can help both sides find a mutually acceptable solution, whether that involves altering the agreement, financial compensation, or addressing specific points of contention. The confidentiality of mediation ensures both sides can openly address concerns without jeopardizing future negotiations or harming their reputations.

In contrast, imagine a scenario where negotiation and mediation attempts fail. The musician, despite presenting compelling evidence and participating in good faith mediation, cannot reach an agreement with the record label. In this case, litigation is the next recourse, and the initial negotiation and mediation attempts provide valuable context for the legal proceedings. The documentation from these earlier attempts can be used to support the musician's position in court and demonstrate a genuine effort to resolve the dispute outside of litigation.

In the entertainment and sports industries, disputes are inevitable. However, equipped with a strong understanding of negotiation and mediation strategies, artists and athletes can significantly increase their chances of resolving these conflicts efficiently, cost-effectively, and amicably, preserving relationships while achieving favorable outcomes. These methods prioritize collaboration and mutual respect, offering a more positive and productive alternative to the often adversarial environment of litigation. Remember, a well-prepared and skillfully executed negotiation or mediation can often be the key to a successful and sustainable career.

Arbitration offers a structured alternative to both negotiation and mediation, providing a more formal process for resolving disputes. Unlike mediation, where a neutral third party facilitates communication, arbitration involves a neutral third party, the arbitrator, who acts as a judge and makes a binding decision. This decision, known as an arbitration award, is legally enforceable, much like a court judgment. The process is generally more formal than mediation, involving the submission of evidence, witness testimony, and legal arguments, though often less formal than a courtroom trial.

The choice of arbitration is often stipulated in contracts, a clause commonly found in entertainment and sports agreements. These clauses, known as arbitration clauses, specify the rules and procedures to be followed in the event of a dispute. Such clauses often dictate the number of arbitrators, the location of the arbitration, the applicable rules (e.g., the American Arbitration Association (AAA) rules), and the method for selecting the arbitrator(s). Understanding and negotiating the terms of an arbitration clause is crucial, as it can significantly impact the outcome of any subsequent dispute. For example, a poorly drafted clause might favor one party over the other, leading to an unfair or unfavorable outcome. A well-drafted clause, however, can ensure a fair and efficient resolution of any disputes that may arise.

Arbitration offers several advantages over litigation. Firstly, it is generally faster and less expensive. The streamlined process avoids the delays and complexities often associated with court proceedings. This speed and efficiency can be especially beneficial in time-sensitive situations, such as those involving quickly expiring contracts or urgent performance issues. Secondly, arbitration offers greater privacy and confidentiality. Unlike court proceedings, which are typically public records, arbitration hearings are generally private and confidential, protecting sensitive information and preserving reputations. This is particularly important in the entertainment industry, where public disputes can negatively impact an artist's image and career prospects.

Thirdly, arbitration offers flexibility in choosing the arbitrator. Parties can select an arbitrator with expertise in the relevant industry or area of law. This ensures that the decision is made by someone who understands the nuances and complexities of the specific dispute. For instance, in a dispute between a musician and their record label concerning royalty payments, selecting an arbitrator with experience in the music industry would be highly advantageous. This specialized knowledge allows the arbitrator to effectively evaluate the evidence, understand the industry practices, and render a more informed and relevant decision. This element of control over the process can significantly influence the outcome, providing parties with a greater sense of fairness and control over the dispute resolution process.

However, arbitration also presents certain drawbacks. While it's often faster than litigation, the arbitration process can still be lengthy and expensive, especially if complex issues are involved or if significant amounts of evidence need to be presented. The costs associated with arbitration, including arbitrator fees, attorney fees, and administrative costs, can be substantial. While often less expensive than litigation, these costs can still be a significant burden, especially for individuals or smaller businesses with limited financial resources.

Another potential drawback is the limited appeal process. Arbitration awards are generally final and binding, with limited grounds for appeal. This means that once an arbitrator renders a decision, the parties have limited recourse to challenge the ruling, even if they believe it to be unjust or incorrect. The limited appealability of arbitration awards provides finality but can potentially lead to an unfair outcome if the arbitrator misinterprets the facts or the law. While this finality can be viewed as an advantage in terms of efficiency, it's crucial for parties to carefully consider the implications before agreeing to arbitrate.

The enforceability of arbitration awards is generally strong. Courts typically uphold arbitration awards, unless there is clear evidence of fraud, corruption, or misconduct by the arbitrator. This enforceability is a key advantage of arbitration, ensuring that the winning party can effectively collect on the award. However, enforcing an award internationally can present challenges, requiring additional legal steps and potentially increasing costs.

The choice between arbitration and litigation is a strategic decision that should be made based on the specific circumstances of the dispute. Factors to consider include the complexity of the issues, the amount of money involved, the potential for a lengthy legal battle, the desired level of confidentiality, the cost of arbitration versus litigation, and the parties' relative resources.

Consider the example of a professional athlete negotiating their endorsement contract. An arbitration clause might be included to settle disputes about payment or usage of their image. If a disagreement arises, arbitration offers a quicker and more private resolution than a public court battle, protecting the athlete's reputation. However, the athlete should ensure that the arbitration clause is fair and balanced, favoring neither party unduly, and should consider the potential cost and the limited grounds for appeal before agreeing to it. The process allows for a specialized arbitrator familiar with sports endorsement contracts, leading to a more informed and potentially favorable decision.

In contrast, imagine a situation where a filmmaker disputes the distribution terms of their film with a studio. While an arbitration clause may be in place, the complexity of the contract and the significant financial stakes could make the costs of arbitration high, even surpassing those of litigation. In this case, the advantages of speed and confidentiality might be outweighed by the substantial costs and the limited appeal process.

Choosing between arbitration and litigation is not a simple decision. It requires a careful evaluation of the specific circumstances of the dispute, the potential benefits and drawbacks of each method, and a clear understanding of the implications of each option. Thorough legal counsel is crucial in making this informed decision and in negotiating and implementing appropriate arbitration clauses in contracts. A well-informed decision ensures the best possible outcome, maximizing chances for a just and efficient resolution of the dispute. Ultimately, understanding arbitration's role in dispute resolution empowers both artists and athletes to negotiate favorable contracts and protect their interests effectively.

Litigation, the formal process of resolving disputes through the court system, should always be considered a last resort. While arbitration and mediation offer faster, more private, and often less expensive alternatives, there are instances where pursuing a lawsuit becomes unavoidable. Understanding when litigation is necessary and navigating the complexities of the legal process is crucial for artists and athletes seeking to protect their rights and interests.

The decision to litigate is rarely taken lightly. It signifies a breakdown in other dispute resolution methods, a failure to reach a mutually agreeable settlement through negotiation, mediation, or arbitration. The inherent adversarial nature of litigation, with its potential for protracted battles, significant financial costs, and public exposure, makes it a high-stakes undertaking. Only when the potential benefits significantly outweigh these substantial drawbacks should litigation be considered.

Several factors contribute to the decision to litigate. Firstly, the amount of money involved plays a pivotal role. In cases involving substantial financial claims, where the potential recovery justifies the cost and time commitment of litigation, pursuing a lawsuit might be the only viable option. A small claim might be easily resolved through less formal methods, but significant sums, particularly those involving complex contracts or substantial intellectual property rights infringements, often require the formal weight of the court system. The potential for significant financial gain, including compensatory damages, punitive damages, and attorney's fees, can tip the scales in favor of litigation.

Secondly, the complexity of the legal issues is a significant factor. Disputes involving intricate contractual clauses, nuanced interpretations of intellectual property rights, or multifaceted legal precedents often require the expertise and resources of the court system. Mediation or arbitration, while efficient for simpler matters, may lack the capacity to fully address the intricate legal intricacies involved in such situations. A judge's expertise and the court's procedural framework are essential in unraveling these complex legal knots. For instance, a dispute involving the ownership of a complex portfolio of copyrights or the licensing rights of a multi-platform digital product demands the thorough and systematic approach afforded by litigation.

Thirdly, the unwillingness of the opposing party to engage in good faith negotiations or participate in alternative dispute resolution processes can necessitate litigation. A party's recalcitrance, its stubborn refusal to compromise or participate meaningfully in alternative dispute resolution, can leave no alternative but to pursue the matter through the courts. This obstructionist tactic, often used to leverage a position of power, can force the aggrieved party to resort to litigation to protect their rights. For example, a record label's refusal to provide a transparent accounting of royalties to an artist, despite repeated requests, could be grounds for a lawsuit to compel the release of financial information.

Furthermore, the need for a public record or precedent can also drive the decision to litigate. While arbitration proceedings are generally confidential, litigation creates a public record of the proceedings and the outcome. This public record can be beneficial in setting a legal precedent for similar future disputes, serving as a deterrent against future infringement. A landmark court case, establishing a clear legal interpretation related to digital rights or image rights, may significantly benefit other artists and athletes facing similar issues in the future.

The litigation process itself is rigorous and demanding. It typically begins with filing a complaint, a formal legal document that outlines the claims against the defendant. This complaint must be meticulously drafted, adhering to strict procedural rules and containing precise legal arguments supported by solid evidence. The selection of legal counsel is paramount, requiring careful consideration of an attorney's experience, expertise, and track record in similar cases. A skilled lawyer can make a crucial difference in navigating the complex legal landscape and building a robust case.

Once the complaint is filed, the defendant is served with a summons, officially notifying them of the lawsuit and the need to respond within a specific time frame. The defendant then files an answer, addressing the allegations in the complaint and setting forth any counterclaims or defenses. The discovery phase follows, a crucial stage where both parties exchange information relevant to the case. This includes document production, interrogatories (written questions), depositions (oral examinations under oath), and requests for admissions (requests to admit or deny specific facts). The goal is to uncover all relevant facts and evidence, allowing both sides to build a comprehensive understanding of the case before trial.

The discovery process, while essential, can be time-consuming and expensive, requiring extensive resources and dedicated legal expertise. The sheer volume of documentation and the intricate legal maneuvering make it a demanding phase of litigation. This is where experience in handling large-scale litigation makes a significant difference; skilled lawyers know how to efficiently navigate the complexities of discovery and avoid unnecessary costs.

After the completion of discovery, both parties have the opportunity to file motions. These motions can address various aspects of the case, such as motions to dismiss, motions for summary judgment (seeking a judgment based on the evidence without a trial), or motions in limine (seeking to exclude certain evidence from trial). The court reviews these motions and issues rulings that can significantly affect the direction and outcome of the case. The ability to draft compelling and effective motions is a critical skill possessed by experienced litigation attorneys.

In many cases, litigation concludes before it ever reaches a trial. Many lawsuits settle during the discovery phase or after motions have been filed. Settlement negotiations, often facilitated by mediators or attorneys, allow both parties to reach a compromise without the expense and uncertainty of a full-blown trial. This is often a far more efficient way to resolve disputes and helps avoid the stress of lengthy court proceedings.

If the case does proceed to trial, it involves presenting evidence, witnesses, and legal arguments to a judge or jury. The presentation of evidence requires meticulous preparation and a strategic approach to ensure that the information is presented clearly and convincingly. Expert witnesses, individuals with specialized knowledge relevant to the case, are frequently called upon to testify and provide insights beyond the experience of the judge or jury. The trial itself can be a lengthy and demanding process, requiring significant preparation, patience, and persistence.

After the trial, the judge or jury renders a verdict. The losing party has the right to appeal the decision to a higher court. This appeal process can further prolong the legal battle and requires even more extensive legal expertise. Appeals are often complex and require detailed legal arguments to challenge the lower court's rulings. The process can be costly and often uncertain, underscoring the importance of carefully weighing the decision to litigate in the first place.

In conclusion, litigation should only be pursued as a last resort, carefully considered after exploring all alternative dispute resolution methods. The costs, time commitment, and inherent uncertainties of litigation make it a high-stakes undertaking, one demanding a thorough evaluation of the potential benefits against the substantial drawbacks. Only when the potential rewards justify the considerable resources and risks should the decision be made to pursue legal action through the court system. The decision to litigate is a strategic one, and securing experienced and capable legal counsel is paramount in navigating the complex legal process and maximizing the chances of a favorable outcome.

The decision to litigate, as discussed, is a serious one. But having made that decision, understanding the mechanics of the court system is crucial for success. The process, while daunting at first glance, follows a fairly predictable pattern, although the specifics vary depending on the jurisdiction and the nature of the dispute. Knowing what to expect can significantly reduce stress and improve your chances of a favorable outcome.

First, there's the matter of jurisdiction. This refers to the court's authority to hear a particular case. Jurisdiction can be determined by several factors, including the location of the parties involved, the subject matter of the dispute, and the amount of money at stake. A contract dispute, for instance, might fall under state court jurisdiction, while a federal law violation would be handled in a federal court. Choosing the right court is crucial, as a wrongly chosen venue can lead to delays, dismissals, and ultimately, defeat. It's a vital decision often best left to experienced counsel. Imagine a musician suing a record label for breach of contract; the choice of court – state or federal, and even the specific state court – can have a profound impact on the outcome. Federal court might offer broader discovery options, while a state court known for its pro-artist rulings could be more advantageous.

Once the proper jurisdiction is established, the case proceeds through several distinct phases. The initial phase involves filing a complaint, meticulously detailing the plaintiff's claims, including the factual background, legal arguments, and the desired relief – be it monetary damages, an injunction, or specific performance. This complaint must be precisely drafted, adhering to strict procedural rules, and supported by evidence. A poorly drafted complaint can lead to dismissal before the case even really begins. Think of it as the artist's opening statement, meticulously crafted to establish a compelling narrative and present a strong case from the outset. A single flaw in the legal argument, a missed deadline, or an omission of crucial evidence can have devastating consequences.

After the complaint is filed, the defendant is served with a summons, officially notifying them of the lawsuit and requiring them to respond within a specified timeframe, usually 20 to 30 days. Failure to respond can result in a default judgment against them, effectively handing the plaintiff a victory without a trial. The defendant then files an answer, addressing the allegations in the complaint, admitting or denying each claim, and raising any affirmative defenses. This is the defendant's chance to present their side of the story and challenge the plaintiff's allegations. A well-crafted answer is crucial in setting the stage for the defense and framing the legal battle ahead. For example, in a copyright infringement case, the defendant might argue fair use, a valid defense requiring substantial legal expertise to establish convincingly.

The next phase is discovery, perhaps the most intensive and time-consuming part of the process. This phase involves both sides exchanging information relevant to the case. This might include document production – requesting all relevant contracts, emails, and financial records – interrogatories (written questions), depositions (oral examinations under oath), and requests for admissions (requests to admit or deny specific facts). The goal is to uncover all relevant facts and evidence, allowing both sides a clear understanding of the case before trial. Discovery can be a complex and adversarial process, requiring strategic maneuvering and meticulous attention to detail. Imagine the discovery phase in a case involving a breach of a recording contract. The artist's legal team would aggressively seek all relevant financial records, contracts, and communications to demonstrate the label's failure to properly account for royalties or their breach of other contractual obligations.

The discovery process can be remarkably extensive and expensive, requiring significant time and financial investment. Experienced lawyers employ sophisticated strategies to manage this phase efficiently, avoiding unnecessary costs and focusing on obtaining the most relevant information. Think of it as a high-stakes chess match, where each move must be carefully considered to gain a strategic advantage. It's a phase that often separates the experienced litigators from the novices.

Following discovery, the parties often file motions, requesting specific actions from the court. These motions can include motions to dismiss, arguing that the complaint fails to state a legally sufficient claim; motions for summary judgment, seeking judgment based on the undisputed facts without a trial; or motions in limine, seeking to exclude certain evidence from the trial. The court rules on these motions, and these rulings can significantly impact the case's direction and outcome. The skill in drafting effective motions lies in crafting persuasive legal arguments supported by relevant evidence and legal precedent. Think of this as presenting a legal summary judgment, proving a case so definitively that a trial is rendered unnecessary and the issue is resolved based on the submitted evidence.

Even with the rigors of discovery and motions, many cases settle before going to trial. Settlement negotiations, often mediated by a neutral third party, can provide a more efficient and less expensive way to resolve disputes. A settlement allows both sides to avoid the uncertainties and costs of trial. However, even settlement discussions require skillful negotiation and the ability to assess the strengths and weaknesses of your own case and the opposing party's.

If the case proceeds to trial, it involves presenting evidence, witnesses, and legal arguments to a judge or jury. The trial process involves opening statements, presenting evidence (witnesses, documents, and exhibits), cross-examination of witnesses, closing arguments, and jury instructions (if a jury trial). The trial is a high-stakes event, requiring meticulous preparation, clear communication, and strategic decision-making. It's the culmination of months, or even years, of work. Think of the trial as the theatrical performance of all the preceding efforts, presenting a compelling narrative and winning the audience (judge or jury) over.

After the trial, the judge or jury renders a verdict. The losing party may appeal the decision to a higher court. Appeals involve challenging the lower court's rulings on legal errors or procedural irregularities. The appeal process is another time-consuming and expensive phase, requiring detailed legal briefs and potentially oral arguments before an appellate court.

Throughout this entire process, from initial filing to potential appeal, the costs of litigation can be substantial, including attorney fees, court filing fees, expert witness fees, and other expenses. Understanding these costs is crucial in making the decision to litigate in the first place. The potential financial recovery must justify the significant investment required to pursue a lawsuit. In conclusion, navigating the court system requires a deep understanding of legal procedures and a skilled legal team. Preparation is paramount for success.

The preceding discussion outlined the procedural labyrinth of litigation. However, the courtroom is often the last resort, not the first choice, in resolving disputes within the entertainment industry. Many conflicts, even those seemingly intractable, find resolution through alternative dispute resolution (ADR) methods, offering efficiency and cost-effectiveness compared to the protracted and expensive trial process. Let's explore some case studies showcasing the efficacy and occasional limitations of these alternative approaches.

Our first case involves a renowned singer-songwriter, let's call her Anya Petrova, and her long-time record label, "Melody Masters." Anya, after a string of successful albums, felt Melody Masters hadn't adequately promoted her latest release, resulting in lower-than-expected sales. She believed the label had breached their contract, specifically clauses related to promotional activities. Instead of immediately filing a lawsuit, Anya and Melody Masters opted for mediation. A neutral mediator, experienced in the music industry, facilitated a series of meetings. Initially, both sides held firm to their positions. Anya insisted on compensation for the perceived lack of promotion, citing lost royalties and damaged career trajectory. Melody Masters, on the other hand, argued that Anya's album fell within the expected sales range, given the current market trends, and that they had fulfilled their contractual obligations.

The mediator, however, skillfully identified common ground. While Melody Masters maintained they'd acted within the contract's bounds, they acknowledged that certain promotional strategies could have been more aggressive. Anya, in turn, recognized the inherent risks in the music industry and the fluctuating nature of market success. Through carefully guided discussions, a compromise emerged. Melody Masters agreed to a partial refund of Anya's advance, along with additional promotional opportunities for her next album. Anya, in turn, agreed to waive her claim for further damages. This mediation saved both parties substantial legal fees and maintained a working relationship, avoiding the potential animosity and damage to reputation a lawsuit could have engendered.

Contrast this with the case of a rising athlete, David Chen, and his endorsement deal with a sports apparel company, "Apex Athletics." David signed a lucrative contract with Apex, agreeing to exclusive endorsement rights in exchange for significant compensation. However, David later discovered Apex was using his image in advertisements without his explicit consent, violating the exclusivity clause. David's legal team initially attempted negotiation with Apex, hoping for a quick resolution. However, Apex refused to acknowledge the violation or offer compensation. Faced with Apex's intransigence, David's legal team opted for arbitration. Arbitration, like mediation, is an ADR method, but it carries more legal weight. The arbitrator, a retired judge with expertise in sports law, heard evidence from both sides and rendered a binding decision.

After presenting detailed evidence, including contracts, advertisements, and expert testimony on the market value of David's image, the arbitrator ruled in David's favor. Apex was ordered to pay David substantial damages for the breach of contract and unauthorized use of his image. While arbitration proved more costly than mediation, it ensured a legally binding resolution without the lengthy process of a full-blown lawsuit. This highlights the importance of choosing the appropriate ADR method based on the specifics of the dispute and the willingness of the other party to engage constructively.

Our next example focuses on a filmmaker, Sarah Lee, and her distribution agreement with a major studio, "Global Pictures." Sarah's independent film achieved critical acclaim at film festivals, but Global Pictures, tasked with its theatrical and home video release, fell short of the promised distribution targets. The contract stipulated specific release dates and marketing efforts. Global Pictures argued that unforeseen circumstances, including shifts in audience preferences and competition from other films, justified their deviation from the agreed-upon plan. Sarah, however, believed the studio had demonstrably failed to meet its contractual obligations. They couldn't agree on a settlement.

Their dispute proceeded to litigation. The case went through all the phases: the filing of the complaint, discovery, motions, and finally, a trial. The trial involved extensive expert testimony on the film's marketing and distribution strategies. While Sarah initially sought significant damages, the court awarded a smaller sum, recognizing the complex dynamics of the film industry and acknowledging some of Global Pictures' mitigating factors. The court costs and legal fees consumed a considerable portion of the awarded damages. This case underscores the high cost and unpredictable outcomes of litigation, even when the plaintiff has a valid claim. The time investment, spanning several years, significantly impacted Sarah's ability to focus on subsequent projects.

These three cases demonstrate the diverse range of dispute resolution methods available to creators and athletes. Mediation proved effective in the singer's case, fostering a continuing professional relationship while resolving the immediate conflict. Arbitration provided a decisive, legally binding resolution for the athlete. In the filmmaker's case, litigation, while ultimately resulting in a win, showcased its drawbacks: expense, time commitment, and the potential for an outcome less favorable than initially anticipated. The choice of method hinges on various factors: the nature of the dispute, the parties' willingness to compromise, the resources available, and the potential risks and rewards associated with each approach. Careful consideration of these factors, informed by experienced legal counsel, is essential in choosing the most effective path to resolving a dispute. A skilled entertainment lawyer can guide their clients toward the best strategy, maximizing their chances of a favorable resolution while minimizing the costs and emotional toll of prolonged conflict. Understanding the strengths and weaknesses of each method—mediation, arbitration, and litigation—empowers creators and athletes to navigate the legal complexities of their careers with confidence and strategic foresight. The ultimate goal is not merely to win a dispute, but to protect one's creative endeavors and financial well-being, to build strong professional relationships, and to preserve one's reputation within the industry. Each case presents a unique set of circumstances, highlighting the nuanced considerations required for effective dispute resolution. The key is strategic planning and expert legal guidance to achieve the best possible outcome. The choice of dispute resolution method should always align with the individual's specific circumstances and goals.

Chapter 10: Financial Planning and Tax Implications

Understanding the intricacies of royalty structures and payment methods is crucial for anyone navigating the entertainment industry. The landscape is complex, varying significantly depending on the specific area – music, film, television, publishing, or even merchandising. A thorough understanding of these structures is essential not only to maximize earnings but also to ensure accurate financial reporting and compliance with tax obligations. Let's delve into the various models and explore how they impact artists, athletes, and other industry professionals.

In the music industry, for instance, royalty structures are often multifaceted and intricate. Record labels typically operate under complex agreements, outlining the distribution of revenue generated from album sales, digital downloads, streaming services, and live performances. A common structure involves an advance paid to the artist upfront, recoupable against future royalties earned. This means the artist receives royalties only after the record label has recouped its initial investment in production, marketing, and distribution. The percentage of royalties paid to the artist after recoupment can vary significantly, often ranging from 10% to 25% or even higher, depending on the artist's bargaining power and the terms negotiated in their recording contract. Furthermore, the definition of "royalties" itself can be subject to complex accounting practices, potentially leading to disputes if not clearly defined within the contract. For example, specific deductions, like manufacturing costs, marketing expenses, and administrative fees, may be subtracted from gross revenues before the artist's share is calculated. Transparency and meticulous record-keeping are therefore paramount.

Streaming services introduce another layer of complexity. Instead of per-unit sales, royalties are calculated based on the number of streams, often subject to fluctuating per-stream rates set by the streaming platform. This variability can make it challenging to predict future earnings, especially for artists whose music relies on broad audience appeal rather than a dedicated, high-spending fan base. The complexities don't end there; many agreements involve multiple parties, including publishers, songwriters, and producers, each entitled to a portion of the royalties generated. Understanding the allocation of these shares is critical for maximizing the artist's earnings.

Film and television productions operate under different royalty structures. Actors and directors might receive a percentage of the film's gross revenue (often a smaller percentage than what is earned on streaming services and sales), net profits, or a combination of both. Determining net profits can be fraught with accounting complexities, as studios often employ aggressive accounting practices to minimize the amount ultimately distributed as profit. Moreover, the definition of "net profits" itself is often subject to interpretation, with disputes arising from differing views on deductible expenses. This necessitates careful scrutiny of the contract's terms, including clear definitions of net profits and allowable deductions. Writers and other creatives may receive royalties based on the number of units sold, broadcast times, or other metrics, emphasizing the need for clear contract language, potentially including independent audits, to guarantee transparency and accurate financial reporting.

Publishing deals, whether for books, screenplays, or musical compositions, involve their own set of royalty structures. Authors often receive an advance against royalties, similar to musicians. The royalty rate varies according to factors like the type of contract (hardcover, paperback, ebook), sales volume, and the publisher's market share. Different royalty rates and advances often apply to different sales channels, potentially including foreign rights and subsidiary rights (such as film adaptations or merchandise), increasing the complexity of royalty accounting. It's crucial for authors to understand their contract's payment schedule, including advance payments and royalty payment cycles, to properly manage their financial planning.

Merchandising royalties offer another avenue for revenue generation for artists and athletes. These agreements typically involve granting a license to a third party to produce and sell goods bearing the artist's image, name, or likeness. The royalty rate is usually a percentage of the merchandise's wholesale or retail price, fluctuating significantly depending on the terms negotiated. The agreement should clearly outline the scope of the license (what types of merchandise are permitted), the geographic limitations, and the duration of the agreement to avoid potential conflicts in the future.

Athletes also engage in complex financial arrangements, particularly with endorsement deals and sponsorships. These contracts may involve upfront payments, royalties based on product sales, performance bonuses, or a combination thereof. It's vital for athletes to have a thorough understanding of the payment structures outlined in their endorsement deals, clearly stipulating the deliverables and the criteria used to calculate performance-based compensation. The athlete should also understand the length of the contract, potential renewals, and how their image will be used for marketing purposes to fully evaluate the profitability of the agreement.

Tracking income from these diverse sources requires meticulous record-keeping. Employing an accountant specialized in entertainment and sports finance is crucial. They can help ensure accurate reporting, identify potential deductions, and navigate the complexities of tax regulations across different jurisdictions. Software solutions specializing in royalty tracking can streamline this process and enhance transparency, enabling a better understanding of the financial aspects of one's career in the industry.

The optimal approach to negotiating favorable royalty structures involves seeking expert legal counsel. A knowledgeable entertainment lawyer can review contracts, ensure that the terms are favorable, and advise on effective strategies for maximizing earnings. They can highlight potential pitfalls, assist in negotiating better terms, and advocate for the artist's or athlete's interests throughout the process. Thorough due diligence, including researching market rates and comparing different proposals, is essential. It's not simply about securing the highest upfront payment but about creating a sustainable financial model that guarantees fair compensation throughout the entire lifespan of an agreement and protects the creator's long-term interests. The ultimate aim is to structure deals that not only deliver immediate revenue but also build a robust financial foundation for future success. This requires careful planning, diligent record-keeping, and proactive engagement with experienced legal and financial professionals.

The power of strategic planning extends beyond the initial contract negotiation. Regularly reviewing contracts, understanding the nuances of royalty calculations, and being proactive in addressing any discrepancies are vital for protecting one's financial interests. Proactive communication with accountants and legal representatives can identify potential issues early on, facilitating smoother negotiations and preventing costly disputes later. This proactive approach is crucial, especially with the ever-changing landscape of the entertainment industry, where new technologies and business models continuously emerge, affecting revenue streams and payment structures. By staying informed and seeking expert advice, artists and athletes can navigate the complex world of royalties, maximizing their earnings and securing their long-term financial stability.

The complexities of income streams in the entertainment and sports industries extend beyond understanding royalty structures; they significantly impact tax obligations. Navigating the tax landscape requires proactive planning and expert guidance to minimize liabilities and optimize financial health. For creators and athletes, whose income often fluctuates wildly from year to year, strategic tax planning is not merely beneficial; it's essential for long-term financial security.

One of the key aspects of tax planning for creators is understanding the different classifications of income. Royalties, for instance, are taxed differently than salary or wages. Royalties from music, film, television, publishing, or merchandising are typically considered passive income, subject to different tax rates and reporting requirements compared to active income derived from employment. Understanding this distinction is crucial for accurate tax filing and avoiding penalties. The Internal Revenue Service (IRS) has specific guidelines for reporting royalty income, and failing to comply can result in significant financial penalties. Moreover, the tax implications vary depending on the location of the income generation. International tax laws introduce an additional layer of complexity for artists and athletes with global careers. If you earn income from multiple countries, you will likely face different tax laws and regulations in each location. The IRS has treaties with many countries to prevent double taxation, but navigating these intricacies requires careful planning and expert advice from a tax professional.

Athletes face a unique set of tax challenges. Their income often stems from a variety of sources: salaries, endorsements, bonuses, appearance fees, and investments. Each of these income streams has its own tax implications. Salaries are subject to standard withholding taxes, while endorsement deals may involve different tax rates and reporting procedures. Performance bonuses often have a significant tax impact, and athletes need to plan for these substantial payouts to avoid a large tax liability at the end of the year. Likewise, investment income, like any other investment returns, is also taxable income and needs to be handled separately. This diverse income landscape necessitates meticulous record-keeping and a sophisticated understanding of applicable tax laws.

The timing of income recognition also plays a significant role in tax optimization. Deferred compensation plans, which allow athletes or creators to receive income at a later date, can prove beneficial from a tax perspective. By delaying income recognition to a year with a lower tax bracket, they can reduce their overall tax liability. However, these plans require careful consideration of potential risks and financial implications, so working with a financial planner is highly recommended. Many athletes and creators may find themselves in a high tax bracket one year due to a large bonus or endorsement deal, and then in a much lower bracket in subsequent years. Tax planning can help to level out this fluctuation and optimize their tax situations overall.

Another crucial area for tax planning is deductions. Creators and athletes can deduct a wide range of business expenses. For creators, this might include studio rental, equipment purchases, marketing and promotion expenses, travel costs for performances or events, and the cost of legal and financial consultation, including the fees paid to entertainment lawyers and accountants. Athletes can deduct expenses like coaching fees, training equipment, travel to competitions, and agent fees. Accurate record-keeping is critical to claiming these deductions, and it is essential to understand the rules surrounding these deductions to ensure that only appropriate expenses are included. The IRS has strict rules about acceptable business deductions, and mistakes here can lead to audits and additional penalties.

Tax planning also extends beyond annual filings. Estate planning is critical for athletes and creators who accumulate significant wealth during their careers. Establishing trusts and other estate planning vehicles can help minimize estate taxes and ensure that assets are distributed according to their wishes. This is especially important in cases of unexpected death, and a strong estate plan protects the legacy of the person and their assets. Failing to plan for one's estate can lead to unexpected and unwanted tax liabilities that could affect family and loved ones negatively. This often requires the services of an estate planning attorney, working in conjunction with a financial planner.

The importance of seeking professional advice from experienced tax professionals and financial advisors cannot be overstated. They can provide guidance on tax-efficient investment strategies, help identify suitable deductions, and navigate the complexities of international tax laws. A well-structured financial plan, incorporating tax strategies, is essential for both short-term financial stability and long-term wealth accumulation. Regular reviews of financial and tax plans are also important, as circumstances and laws change. This should be part of the ongoing relationship between the creator or athlete, and their professional team. This is particularly critical in the entertainment and sports industries, where income and tax regulations are subject to change.

For creators, understanding the tax implications of different types of income is crucial. For example, income from self-employment, such as freelance work or commissions, is subject to self-employment taxes, which include Social Security and Medicare taxes. These taxes are not typically withheld from payments, so creators must carefully estimate their tax liability and make quarterly estimated tax payments to avoid penalties. This requires careful financial planning and accurate income tracking. This contrasts with employee income, where these taxes are automatically withheld.

Furthermore, the deductibility of expenses can significantly impact the net income subject to tax. For example, creators may deduct a portion of their home office expenses, depending on the area used for business purposes. Proper documentation of these expenses is essential for claiming these deductions during tax season. These vary from state to state, so understanding local regulations is just as important as federal regulations.

The use of various entities for business purposes can also affect the tax burden. Sole proprietorships, partnerships, limited liability companies (LLCs), and S corporations each have different tax implications. The choice of business structure significantly impacts how income is taxed, and careful consideration should be given to the long-term tax consequences. A lawyer and accountant specializing in taxation are invaluable resources in making this choice.

In summary, the financial success of creators and athletes often hinges on intelligent tax planning. By understanding the various income streams, tax rates, deductions, and investment strategies available, they can minimize their tax liability and maximize their long-term financial well-being. Proactive planning, meticulous record-keeping, and engagement with skilled financial and legal professionals are indispensable components of achieving sustainable financial success in these dynamic and often unpredictable industries. The ever-changing tax landscape necessitates ongoing vigilance and adaptation, making it critical for creators and athletes to continuously review and update their financial and tax strategies to remain compliant and secure their financial future. This proactive approach ensures that they can focus on their creative pursuits or athletic endeavors, knowing their financial affairs are in order.

Investing your hard-earned money wisely is paramount, especially in the volatile worlds of entertainment and sports. The thrill of a hefty paycheck or a lucrative endorsement deal can quickly fade if that money isn't managed effectively. Think of it like this: your talent is the seed; smart financial planning is the fertile ground that allows it to blossom into a thriving, long-term career. Without careful cultivation, even the most promising seed can wither and die.

The most fundamental principle of investing is diversification. Don't put all your eggs in one basket. This old adage holds true for athletes and entertainers who often see their income concentrated in a single source—a team contract, a hit song, or a blockbuster movie. Diversifying your portfolio across various asset classes mitigates risk. Imagine a musician whose entire net worth is tied up in a single record label. If that label falters, the musician's financial future is jeopardized. A more secure approach involves spreading investments across stocks, bonds, real estate, and other alternatives like private equity or hedge funds, depending on risk tolerance and financial goals.

Stocks, representing ownership in a company, offer the potential for high returns but also carry higher risk. Bonds, essentially loans to companies or governments, generally offer lower returns but are less volatile. Real estate can provide steady income through rental properties, as well as appreciation in value over time. However, it's also illiquid; you can't quickly convert it to cash. These are just a few of the options available, and the optimal mix will vary depending on individual circumstances and financial objectives. A knowledgeable financial advisor can help determine the best allocation for your specific situation, factoring in your age, risk tolerance, and financial goals.

Beyond diversification, consider the importance of long-term investments. While quick wins might be tempting, the most substantial financial gains often come from sustained, long-term growth. Think of your investments as a marathon, not a sprint. Building wealth requires patience and a commitment to staying the course, particularly when market fluctuations occur. Short-term market dips can be unsettling, but they are often temporary setbacks in a larger upward trend. It's crucial to resist the urge to panic-sell during these periods, unless there is a very specific reason to do so, which a financial advisor can help you determine. Focusing on long-term growth can significantly minimize the impact of temporary volatility.

Investing in yourself is another critical aspect of financial planning. This might involve further education, skill development, or networking opportunities that enhance your professional prospects. For instance, a musician might invest in vocal coaching, a songwriter might take a course in music production, or an athlete might hire a personal trainer. These investments, while often having immediate costs, can pay off handsomely in the long run through improved performance and increased earning potential. Moreover, continuing education can also broaden your horizons, opening up new avenues for income generation and creative expression. Investing in yourself is a powerful way to enhance your earning capacity, which then enables more diversified investment opportunities in other sectors.

Seek professional advice. The entertainment and sports industries are fraught with unique financial challenges, and it's unwise to navigate these complexities alone. A team of financial professionals can provide invaluable guidance, including financial planners, tax advisors, and potentially estate planning attorneys. They can help create a personalized financial plan tailored to your specific needs and goals, and they can offer ongoing support as your circumstances change. Remember, their fees pale in comparison to the potential financial pitfalls of making ill-informed decisions. Think of them as an investment in the protection and growth of your own wealth.

For instance, a financial planner can help you develop a budget, track your expenses, and set realistic financial goals. They can also help you create a retirement plan, manage your investments, and provide advice on estate planning. A tax advisor can help you minimize your tax liability, navigate complex tax laws, and ensure compliance with all regulations. An estate planning attorney can help you create a will, trust, or other legal documents that protect your assets and ensure that they are distributed according to your wishes. This is crucial not only for the distribution of your assets after you are gone, but can also protect your assets from potential lawsuits while you are alive.

Consider tax-advantaged investment accounts. These accounts offer significant tax benefits, allowing your investments to grow more efficiently. Retirement accounts like 401(k)s and IRAs allow you to contribute pre-tax dollars, reducing your current taxable income and deferring taxes until retirement. Some plans even offer tax-deductible contributions. There are also 529 plans that allow you to save for educational expenses for yourself or your dependents, with the earnings growing tax-free. Understanding the different types of tax-advantaged accounts and their eligibility criteria is crucial to maximizing the tax efficiency of your investments. Again, this is an area where professional advice from a tax specialist or financial planner can prove invaluable in determining which options are most suitable to your situation.

Don't underestimate the power of saving. Building an emergency fund is crucial for weathering unexpected financial setbacks. This could be anything from a sudden illness to a career slump. A well-funded emergency fund helps to mitigate the risks associated with these unexpected circumstances, ensuring you are financially secure during times of need. Most financial advisors suggest having three to six months' worth of living expenses readily available in an easily accessible account. This fund serves as a safety net that prevents you from having to make hasty, financially damaging decisions during times of unexpected financial hardship.

Furthermore, consider the long-term implications of your investments. For example, investing in real estate can be an excellent long-term investment strategy, but it also requires careful consideration of various factors such as property location, market conditions, and potential maintenance costs. Likewise, investing in stocks and bonds requires understanding market trends and risk tolerance. Diversification in real estate could mean purchasing rental properties in different geographical areas to spread out the risk, rather than concentrating your holdings in one location. With stocks, this might mean diversifying across different sectors, such as technology, healthcare, and consumer goods, as opposed to only investing in one sector. The key is understanding these considerations and making informed decisions based on your individual circumstances and long-term goals.

Finally, remember that your financial planning is an ongoing process. Regularly review your investments, reassess your goals, and adjust your strategy as needed. Life throws curveballs; your financial plan should be flexible enough to adapt. Market conditions change, tax laws evolve, and your personal circumstances may shift dramatically. Therefore, regular review and adjustment are not simply good practice, but critical for long-term success and the protection of your financial well-being. Schedule regular meetings with your financial advisor to review your progress, discuss any changes in your circumstances, and make necessary adjustments to your investment strategy. This proactive approach will help you stay on track and ensure that your financial plan remains aligned with your evolving needs and ambitions. This ongoing engagement is crucial to long-term financial success in the dynamic and sometimes unpredictable world of entertainment and professional sports.

Managing your finances effectively is as crucial to your career as your talent itself. While the spotlight might dazzle with the promise of instant riches, a solid financial foundation built on careful budgeting and expense tracking is the only true guarantee of long-term success. Think of your income as a river; if you don't build dams (savings) and channels (budgeting), that river will flow away, leaving you with nothing. Building a robust financial plan requires a disciplined approach, a clear understanding of your spending habits, and a willingness to make informed decisions.

Creating a budget isn't about restricting yourself; it's about gaining control. It's a roadmap for your money, showing you exactly where your funds are going and helping you identify areas where you can save or reallocate resources. Begin by meticulously tracking your income and expenses for a few months. This can be done manually using a spreadsheet or notebook, or you can utilize budgeting apps, which often offer features like automated expense categorization and financial goal-setting. The goal is to gain a comprehensive understanding of your financial inflows and outflows, revealing patterns and trends that may otherwise go unnoticed.

Once you have a clear picture of your spending, categorize your expenses. Common categories include housing, transportation, food, entertainment, and professional expenses. This will highlight areas where your spending is disproportionate to your income or financial goals. Are you spending a significant portion of your income on dining out, or perhaps on lavish purchases? Identify those areas, and honestly assess whether these expenses align with your long-term financial objectives. Remember, this is not about deprivation; it is about strategic allocation of your resources.

Beyond basic needs, consider your career-related expenses. This could include agents' commissions, managers' fees, legal representation, travel costs associated with performances or auditions, equipment maintenance, studio time, or educational courses designed to enhance your skills. These are vital investments in your professional development and should be factored into your budget. Failure to account for these expenses can lead to cash flow problems, potentially jeopardizing your future success.

Setting realistic financial goals is the next critical step. This might include saving for a down payment on a house, building an emergency fund, funding your retirement, or saving for your children's education. These goals serve as anchors, providing direction for your budget and motivating you to make smart financial decisions. Break down large goals into smaller, manageable milestones, making the process less daunting and fostering a sense of accomplishment as you progress. For example, instead of aiming to save $100,000 for a down payment, focus on saving $10,000 each year.

In the entertainment industry, income can be irregular, with periods of high earnings followed by lulls. This makes budgeting even more critical. During periods of high income, save aggressively to build a financial cushion that will sustain you during leaner times. This might involve setting aside a larger percentage of your income than you normally would, or it might involve strategically investing in low-risk, liquid assets that can easily be converted into cash if needed. Consider setting up a separate savings account solely for emergency funds.

Consider the use of automated savings plans. Many banks and financial institutions offer automatic transfers from your checking account to your savings account, making saving effortless. You can automate transfers on a weekly, bi-weekly, or monthly basis, depending on your income cycle and saving goals. This "pay yourself first" approach removes the temptation to spend money that you could have otherwise saved, ensuring consistent contributions to your savings.

Regularly reviewing and adjusting your budget is essential. Your financial circumstances, income, and expenses will change over time, necessitating adjustments to your budget. A budget isn't a static document; it's a living instrument that needs to adapt to your changing needs. Review your budget at least once a month, or more frequently if your financial circumstances are prone to significant fluctuations. Compare your actual spending to your budgeted amounts, identifying areas where you're overspending or underspending. Adjust your budget accordingly to keep it aligned with your current financial situation.

Don't be afraid to seek professional advice. A financial planner can help you create a personalized budget that aligns with your specific financial goals and risk tolerance. They can help you develop a comprehensive financial plan that encompasses saving, investing, retirement planning, and estate planning, and provide ongoing support as your career progresses. The cost of professional guidance is a small price to pay for the peace of mind that comes with knowing your finances are being managed strategically.

A well-structured budget is not merely a financial tool; it's a strategic investment in your future. It provides the stability you need to navigate the unpredictable world of entertainment and sports, allowing you to focus on your craft without the constant stress of financial instability. A robust budget is your safety net, ensuring you can weather financial storms and continue to invest in your talents and future projects. It provides the freedom to take creative risks, knowing that your financial foundation is secure. By diligently tracking your expenses, setting realistic financial goals, and regularly reviewing and adjusting your budget, you create a solid financial framework that supports a thriving and sustainable career.

The meticulous budgeting and expense tracking discussed earlier form a crucial base, but they are only part of the equation for long-term financial security. Navigating the unique financial landscape of the entertainment industry requires a deeper level of expertise, a level that goes beyond personal budgeting and delves into the complexities of tax law, investment strategies, and estate planning. This is where securing professional financial and tax advice becomes paramount. Think of it as having a seasoned navigator guiding you through treacherous waters; a skilled financial advisor can help you chart a course toward financial stability and prosperity, mitigating risks and maximizing opportunities.

The entertainment industry is notorious for its unpredictable income streams. One month might bring a windfall from a blockbuster film or a sold-out concert tour, while the next might bring little to nothing. This volatility makes accurate financial forecasting extremely challenging, making it all the more crucial to have a professional guiding your financial decisions. An expert can help you develop strategies to manage this irregularity, smoothing out income fluctuations and ensuring a consistent flow of funds, even during periods of low earnings. They can help you create a financial plan that accounts for both the highs and lows, preventing impulsive spending during periods of affluence and offering a safety net during lean times.

Furthermore, the tax implications of working in the entertainment industry are often complex and demanding. Understanding tax laws, deductions, and credits specific to your industry is essential for minimizing your tax burden and maximizing your after-tax income. Attempting to navigate these complexities on your own can be overwhelming and potentially lead to costly mistakes. A qualified tax advisor can ensure that you are taking advantage of all available deductions and credits, saving you considerable sums in taxes and allowing you to reinvest those savings back into your career.

Beyond taxes and budgeting, a financial advisor can provide guidance on various investment strategies tailored to your specific financial goals and risk tolerance. They can help you diversify your investment portfolio, ensuring that your assets are protected against market fluctuations and inflation. They can also advise you on retirement planning, helping you develop a strategy to ensure a comfortable financial future beyond your working years. Understanding investment vehicles like stocks, bonds, real estate, and mutual funds is crucial to financial success, and a professional advisor can help you make informed decisions. This is especially relevant in the entertainment industry, where career longevity can be unpredictable.

The services of a financial advisor extend to estate planning, which often gets overlooked but is of critical importance. This includes drafting a will, establishing trusts, and planning for the distribution of your assets after your death. Proper estate planning ensures that your wishes are carried out and that your loved ones are protected financially after your passing. Given the high net worth that many individuals in the entertainment industry may accumulate, thorough estate planning is not merely recommended;

it is essential to avoid potential legal disputes and tax complications down the line.

Finding the right financial and tax advisor is crucial. Look for someone with experience working with individuals in the entertainment industry. This familiarity with the unique financial aspects of your profession is invaluable. Consider their qualifications, their reputation, and the range of services they offer. A good advisor will not only provide financial advice but also act as a trusted confidante, guiding you through the many complex financial decisions you'll encounter throughout your career. Don't hesitate to schedule consultations with several professionals before making a decision.

Another critical area where expert guidance is invaluable is contract negotiation. As your career progresses, you'll likely encounter increasingly complex contracts. These contracts might involve record deals, endorsement agreements, film or television contracts, publishing deals, or licensing agreements. Understanding the legal intricacies of these contracts is crucial to protecting your financial interests and avoiding exploitation. A legal professional specializing in entertainment law can analyze your contracts, identify potential pitfalls, and negotiate favorable terms to maximize your earnings and protect your rights.

Intellectual property rights are another area demanding specialized legal expertise. Your creative work—songs, scripts, books, artwork—represents a significant asset. Protecting these rights is critical to maximizing the financial value of your creative endeavors. An entertainment lawyer can advise you on copyright registration, trademark protection, and licensing your intellectual property. They can also help you resolve any disputes that arise related to the infringement of your intellectual property rights. This protection not only safeguards your financial future but also ensures the integrity and value of your creative work.

The digital landscape has significantly altered the entertainment industry, introducing new complexities regarding digital rights management. Understanding how your work is used and distributed in the digital world is crucial to securing proper compensation and protecting your creative control. An entertainment lawyer can guide you through the intricacies of digital rights agreements, ensuring that your rights are protected in the digital realm. They can advise you on streaming agreements, online licensing, and the legal implications of using your work on social media platforms. This expert guidance is critical in a rapidly evolving digital landscape.

The initial investment in securing professional financial and tax advice, as well as legal representation, might seem significant, but it pales in comparison to the potential long-term benefits. These experts act as a safety net, preventing costly mistakes, protecting your assets, and maximizing your earning potential. They provide an invaluable perspective, helping you navigate the treacherous waters of the entertainment industry with confidence and security. Investing in professional advice is not an expense; it's an investment in your future success and financial stability.

In the ever-evolving landscape of the entertainment industry, securing your financial future requires a proactive approach. It demands foresight, planning, and expert guidance. By combining careful financial planning with the expertise of professionals in financial management, tax law, and entertainment law, you build a secure foundation for a long and prosperous career. This proactive strategy not only protects your immediate earnings but also ensures your financial well-being for years to come, allowing you to focus on your artistic endeavors without the constant worry of financial instability. Remember, your financial health is as crucial as your creative talent in achieving sustained success in the dynamic world of entertainment. The peace of mind gained from having experts on your side is invaluable, allowing you to dedicate your energy to what you do best: creating and performing.

Chapter 11: Social Media and Online Presence

The digital age has fundamentally reshaped the entertainment industry, transforming how artists and athletes connect with their audiences and build their careers. This shift, however, comes with its own set of legal and reputational challenges. Your online presence is no longer a supplementary aspect of your career; it's an integral part of your brand, influencing your opportunities and ultimately, your financial success. Protecting your online identity is therefore not optional; it's a crucial component of your overall professional strategy.

The first and most critical step in protecting your online identity is to understand that everything you post, share, or comment on online is potentially public and permanently recorded. This seemingly obvious fact is often overlooked. A careless tweet, a hastily posted Instagram story, or a flippant comment on a forum can have far-reaching consequences, potentially damaging your professional reputation, leading to lost opportunities, and even opening you up to legal challenges. Before you post anything, ask yourself: "Would I be comfortable with my grandmother seeing this? Would a potential client or employer see this favorably?" If the answer to either question is no, then reconsider sharing it.

Consider your social media profiles as extensions of your professional brand. Your online personas should reflect your professional image and values. This doesn't mean being robotic or inauthentic; it means maintaining a level of professionalism and decorum that aligns with your career aspirations. A well-curated online presence can attract opportunities, while a careless or controversial one can repel them. Think of your social media profiles as your digital business card – ensure they present a polished and professional image.

Maintaining control over your online narratives is crucial. In the age of instant information dissemination, stories can quickly spread, often with little fact-checking. A false or misleading account can easily damage your reputation. Therefore, proactive measures are crucial. Consider setting up Google Alerts to monitor mentions of your name online. This will allow you to quickly identify and address any false or damaging information that may surface. You can also use social listening tools to track what people are saying about you across various platforms. Knowing what's being said—both good and bad—empowers you to respond strategically.

This brings us to the delicate art of managing online comments. While constructive feedback can be valuable, negative comments or outright attacks can be damaging. Ignoring them is rarely a good strategy, as it can often make the situation worse. However, directly engaging with every negative comment can be equally unproductive, possibly escalating the situation. A carefully considered response strategy is therefore necessary.

The best approach is to adopt a measured and professional tone in your responses. Acknowledge the concerns raised, but avoid getting drawn into personal attacks or emotionally charged exchanges. If a comment is demonstrably false or defamatory, you may need to consult legal counsel to explore options for recourse. However, remember that many jurisdictions have laws protecting freedom of speech, and simply disagreeing with someone doesn't always constitute grounds for legal action. Your goal should be to de-escalate the situation, demonstrating maturity and professionalism, thereby reinforcing your positive brand image.

Dealing with cyberbullying requires a different approach. Repeated harassment, threats, or attempts to damage your reputation should never be tolerated. Document every instance of cyberbullying, including screenshots, dates, and times. This documentation is crucial if you decide to pursue legal action or report the abuse to the relevant social media platforms. Many platforms have clear policies against cyberbullying, and they provide mechanisms for reporting such behavior. Utilize these mechanisms, and if necessary, seek legal advice regarding potential legal remedies. Remember, your mental and emotional well-being is as crucial as your professional image, and you should never hesitate to seek support if you are subjected to sustained cyberbullying.

Proactive steps can significantly minimize the risk of online attacks. This includes strengthening your online privacy settings, regularly reviewing your online presence, and educating yourself on the potential legal implications of your online activities. Consider consulting with a lawyer specializing in internet law and reputation management. They can advise you on strategies to protect your online identity, manage your online presence, and handle potential legal challenges. The investment in such counsel can prove invaluable in protecting your career and your peace of mind.

Protecting your online identity also extends to protecting your intellectual property. Make sure you have the proper copyright and trademark protection for your work. Avoid unauthorized use of your creative content, and promptly address any infringements. In the digital world, your creative works are easily copied and distributed, making it even more crucial to be vigilant in protecting your intellectual property rights. Be aware of your contractual obligations regarding the use of your image and likeness in online contexts.

The digital landscape is constantly evolving, with new platforms and technologies emerging regularly. Staying informed about these changes and adapting your strategies accordingly is essential.

Keep abreast of legal developments relating to online reputation management, digital rights, and intellectual property. By taking a proactive approach to protecting your online identity, you minimize potential risks, protect your brand, and ultimately enhance your career trajectory.

Furthermore, think about the content you consume and share. Be mindful of the information you retweet, repost, or share in any other way. If you share something that's factually incorrect or promotes hate speech, you can be held accountable, even if you weren't the originator of the content. Always verify the information before sharing it. This is particularly important when dealing with news or sensitive topics.

Consider establishing a strong online community around your brand. This creates a platform where you can directly engage with your fans and supporters, combating misinformation and fostering a positive online environment. It allows you to build relationships with your audience and strengthens your online presence.

Remember, your online reputation is an asset, just like your artistic talent or athletic skills. It requires careful nurturing and protection. By adopting a proactive approach, investing in professional guidance when necessary, and exercising consistent vigilance, you can successfully navigate the complex digital landscape, protecting your online identity and ensuring a thriving career. This isn't just about avoiding negativity; it's about strategically building a positive and powerful online brand that works for you, attracting opportunities and safeguarding your future success. This is crucial not just for the present, but for the longevity of your career in the ever-evolving digital world. The proactive steps you take today to safeguard your online identity will pay dividends in the years to come.

Building a powerful online brand isn't about vanity metrics; it's about strategically crafting a digital presence that aligns perfectly with your professional goals and resonates with your target audience. It's about creating a consistent narrative that showcases your skills, expertise, and personality in a way that attracts opportunities and builds lasting relationships. This requires more than just posting sporadically – it demands a thoughtful, planned approach that considers every aspect of your online persona.

One key element is consistency. Think of your online presence as a carefully curated garden. You wouldn't plant a few random seeds and expect a bountiful harvest, would you? Similarly, inconsistent posting or a haphazard approach to content creation won't yield the desired results. Develop a content calendar, outlining a regular posting schedule across your chosen platforms. This could be daily, weekly, or bi-weekly, depending on your capacity and the demands of your career. Consistency keeps your audience engaged and reinforces your brand's message.

Furthermore, consider your content strategy. What kind of content resonates most effectively with your audience? Are you a visual artist who excels at Instagram, or a writer who thrives on long-form articles on Medium? Analyze your strengths and tailor your content accordingly. Experiment with different formats – videos, images, infographics, blog posts, podcasts – to determine what works best for you. The key is to provide valuable and engaging content that your audience genuinely appreciates. Think about what your ideal client or fan would want to see. Do they crave behind-the-scenes glimpses into your creative process? Are they interested in tutorials or educational content? Or perhaps they prefer a more personal, conversational approach. Knowing your audience is paramount to creating content that resonates and strengthens your brand.

Visual consistency is another critical aspect. Your branding should be cohesive across all platforms. This includes your logo, color palette, fonts, and overall aesthetic. A consistent visual identity creates a sense of professionalism and reinforces your brand's message. Think about creating a style guide that outlines your brand's visual elements. This guide will ensure consistency across your social media profiles, website, and any other online materials. Remember, your online presence reflects your professionalism, so maintaining a cohesive visual identity is essential.

Beyond the visual aspects, your online voice is just as important. Develop a distinct voice that reflects your personality and brand. Are you witty and sarcastic? Serious and professional? Warm and approachable? Consistency in your tone and style helps create a recognizable and engaging brand personality. Think about writing samples – if you're a writer, your online voice should mirror your writing style. If you're a musician, it should reflect the tone and style of your music. This voice should be authentic, reflecting your true personality, while also maintaining a level of professionalism.

Don't underestimate the power of storytelling. Sharing personal anecdotes, behind-the-scenes glimpses, or inspirational stories can create a strong connection with your audience. Humans connect with stories; they make you relatable and memorable. This human touch differentiates your brand from a purely transactional one. Think about crafting narratives that highlight your journey, your challenges, and your triumphs. Sharing these personal narratives makes you more relatable and builds trust with your audience. This authenticity is particularly valuable in the digital age, where genuine connections are increasingly sought after.

Actively engage with your audience. Respond to comments, messages, and mentions. Ask questions and encourage interaction. This shows your audience that you value their engagement and fosters a sense of community. Remember, building a strong online brand isn't a one-way street. It's a two-way conversation. Engaging directly with your audience helps you understand their needs and preferences, allowing you to tailor your content to better serve them. This fosters loyalty and strengthens your online community.

Collaborate with other creators or influencers in your industry. This expands your reach and exposes your brand to new audiences. Strategic collaborations can significantly boost your online visibility and build your credibility. Choose collaborators who align with your brand values and target audience. Collaborations can take many forms – joint projects, guest appearances, or simply cross-promotion on social media. This collaborative approach is particularly effective in building a strong online presence and expanding your reach to new audiences.

Analyze your results and adapt your strategy accordingly. Use analytics tools to track your progress and identify what's working and what's not. This data-driven approach helps you optimize your strategy and maximize your results. The digital landscape is dynamic; what works today might not work tomorrow. Regularly review your analytics to identify trends and adapt your strategy accordingly. This ensures that your online presence remains relevant and effective.

Remember, building a strong online brand is an ongoing process. It requires consistent effort, strategic planning, and a willingness to adapt to the ever-changing digital landscape. It's about crafting a compelling narrative, engaging authentically with your audience, and continuously refining your strategy to maximize your impact. This investment in your online presence will not only attract opportunities, but it will also protect your professional reputation and secure your long-term success in a fiercely competitive industry. View it not just as a marketing tool, but as an integral part of your professional identity, requiring the same level of care and attention you would dedicate to any other aspect of your career. The effort you invest will pay dividends in increased visibility, lucrative collaborations, and a strengthened professional brand that commands respect and generates sustainable opportunities.

Navigating the digital landscape as a creator or athlete requires more than just a captivating online presence; it demands a keen understanding of the legal intricacies surrounding social media contracts and agreements. These agreements, often overlooked in the thrill of a potential collaboration, can be the bedrock of your success or the source of significant legal headaches. This section delves into the complexities of these agreements, equipping you with the knowledge to protect your interests and navigate the often-murky waters of influencer marketing and brand partnerships.

Let's start with influencer marketing, a booming industry where individuals with substantial online followings collaborate with brands to promote products or services. These collaborations are often formalized through contracts, and understanding the nuances of these contracts is paramount. A poorly negotiated agreement can leave you vulnerable to exploitation, unpaid fees, or even legal disputes.

One critical aspect of any influencer marketing agreement is the scope of work. The contract should clearly define the deliverables, specifying the type of content to be created (e.g., Instagram posts, tweets, blog articles, videos), the frequency of posts, and the duration of the campaign. Ambiguity in this area can lead to disagreements and disputes down the line. For example, a contract that vaguely states "promote the product on social media" leaves room for interpretation and could lead to arguments about the number of posts, the platforms used, or the tone of the promotion. A well-written contract will explicitly define the number of posts, the specific platforms to be used (Instagram, TikTok, YouTube, etc.), and any specific hashtags or keywords that must be included. It should even specify the length of the posts or videos.

Compensation is another crucial element. The contract should explicitly state the total compensation, the payment schedule (e.g., upfront payment, milestone payments, performance-based payments), and the method of payment. Be wary of contracts that offer compensation based solely on performance metrics, as these can be unpredictable and may not always reflect your actual work. Furthermore, ensure that the contract addresses all forms of payment, including payments in kind (e.g., free products, services, or travel). For example, if you are offered free products in lieu of cash payment, be sure to have a clear understanding of the value of those products and have it stated in the contract. Consider consulting with a tax professional to ensure you understand the tax implications of different forms of compensation.

Intellectual property rights are a significant concern in influencer marketing agreements. The contract should clearly delineate ownership of the created content. In many cases, brands will seek ownership of the content you create for them, while you may prefer to retain ownership, especially if you want to reuse the content in the future for other purposes. Negotiate this point carefully, ensuring that you understand the implications of granting ownership to the brand. If you retain ownership, the contract should clearly specify the brand's usage rights, including the duration of use, geographical limitations, and any other restrictions. This is particularly important for athletes, whose image and likeness are valuable assets.

Exclusivity clauses are another common feature of influencer marketing agreements. These clauses restrict you from promoting competing products or services during the duration of the contract. Carefully consider the implications of such clauses, ensuring that they don't unduly restrict your opportunities. For instance, if the exclusivity clause prohibits you from promoting any competitors, even those in different product categories, it may harm your overall earnings by limiting your collaborations. Therefore, ensure the exclusivity clause is limited to directly competing products or brands.

Another often-overlooked aspect is the term and termination clauses. The contract should clearly specify the duration of the campaign and the conditions under which either party can terminate the agreement. For instance, a breach of contract, failure to deliver on agreed-upon services, or even a change in the brand's marketing strategy might trigger termination. Ensure that the contract outlines a clear process for termination, including any notice periods required.

Brand partnerships extend beyond influencer marketing to encompass a broader range of collaborations. For example, athletes often partner with brands for endorsement deals, while musicians might collaborate with companies for merchandise or sponsorships. These partnerships also involve contracts, and the same principles discussed above apply. The clarity and specificity of the contract are crucial for protecting your interests.

Consider, for instance, an athlete partnering with a sportswear company. The contract should specify the scope of the endorsement (e.g., appearing in advertisements, wearing the company's apparel during events, using the company's products), the duration of the agreement, the compensation, and the intellectual property rights related to the athlete's image and likeness. A poorly negotiated contract could lead to disputes over the use of the athlete's image in advertisements, the type of apparel worn, or even the duration of the endorsement.

Social media contracts can be particularly tricky because they often involve aspects of both traditional contract law and intellectual property law. For example, a contract for a social media campaign might involve considerations such as the right to use your image and likeness, the ownership of the content you create, and the restrictions on your online activity. This intersection of legal principles underscores the importance of seeking legal counsel before signing any contract.

In addition to the key elements mentioned above, consider including clauses that address:

Indemnification: This clause protects you from liability for any damages arising from the partnership.

Confidentiality: This clause protects sensitive information shared between you and the brand.

Dispute Resolution: This clause outlines a process for resolving any disagreements.

Governing Law: This clause specifies which state's laws govern the contract.

Remember, these contracts are not just pieces of paper; they are legal instruments that shape your career and financial well-being. Taking the time to understand them thoroughly and seeking legal representation to negotiate favorable terms is an investment that will protect you from potential pitfalls and maximize your opportunities. In the ever-evolving digital landscape, having a solid grasp of social media contracts is no longer a luxury but a necessity. It is the key to building a sustainable and successful career in the entertainment and sports industries. Don't hesitate to seek legal counsel; it is an investment in your future success. A lawyer experienced in entertainment law can review contracts, ensuring that they adequately protect your interests and reflect the market value of your services. They can also help you negotiate better terms, potentially increasing your earning potential. In the cutthroat world of entertainment and sports, having a strong legal foundation is as vital as having talent and ambition.

The digital realm offers unprecedented opportunities for creators and athletes to connect with audiences and build their brands, but this expanded reach also necessitates a robust understanding of online copyright protection. Social media platforms, while seemingly offering free reign for content sharing, have intricate copyright policies that can quickly transform a viral sensation into a legal battle. Understanding and proactively managing your online copyright is paramount to safeguarding your creative work and financial interests. This involves more than simply slapping a copyright notice on your posts; it requires a multi-pronged approach that incorporates preventative measures, proactive monitoring, and a clear strategy for responding to infringement.

Let's begin with the foundation: registering your copyright. While not mandatory for copyright protection (copyright exists automatically upon creation), registration provides several crucial advantages. Firstly, it provides irrefutable proof of ownership, significantly strengthening your position should a dispute arise. Secondly, registration allows you to pursue statutory damages in court, potentially recovering significantly more than your actual losses. This is particularly important for digital content, where calculating actual damages can be complex and challenging. Thirdly, registration is a prerequisite for filing a copyright infringement lawsuit in the United States. Without registration, your options are limited to cease-and-desist letters and other less powerful methods. The process is relatively straightforward, involving completing a form and submitting a copy of your work to the United States Copyright Office. For athletes, this could encompass videos of their performances, training montages, or even unique designs for their merchandise. Musicians might register their original compositions, recordings, or even album artwork.

Beyond formal registration, meticulously documenting your creative process is essential. This involves keeping detailed records of when you created the work, any revisions you made, and any evidence of its dissemination. This could include drafts, emails, social media posts showcasing the creation process, and even timestamped versions saved in the cloud. This documentation serves as crucial evidence in proving your ownership and the timeline of creation, particularly valuable if a dispute about ownership or timing arises. For instance, a musician could maintain a detailed log of their songwriting process, including date-stamped lyrics and recordings, to substantiate their claim of authorship in case of a plagiarism allegation.

Understanding the nuances of fair use is equally crucial. Fair use is a legal doctrine that permits limited use of copyrighted material without permission for purposes such as criticism, comment, news reporting, teaching, scholarship, and research. However, fair use is not a free pass; determining whether your use constitutes fair use requires a careful evaluation of four factors: the purpose and character of your use, the nature of the copyrighted work, the amount and substantiality of the portion used, and the effect of the use upon the potential market for or value of the copyrighted work. Each factor is considered individually, and there's no easy formula for determining fair use. A lawyer specializing in intellectual property law can provide guidance on navigating these complexities.

Proactive monitoring of your online presence is another key aspect of copyright management. Regularly search social media platforms and the wider internet for unauthorized use of your work. Tools such as Google Alerts can be employed to automatically notify you of instances where your work appears online. Early detection of infringement allows for timely intervention, often enabling a swift resolution through a cease-and-desist letter. However, the approach must be measured and considered, as aggressive tactics can backfire. For athletes, it may involve monitoring for unauthorized use of their image or likeness in promotional materials or fan-made merchandise. Musicians could scan platforms for unauthorized use of their music in videos or other projects. The goal is to identify and address infringements before they escalate into costly legal battles.

When confronted with copyright infringement, consider a range of responses, from issuing a cease-and-desist letter (a formal demand to stop infringing activities) to filing a lawsuit. A cease-and-desist letter is often an effective first step, particularly for minor infringements or when dealing with individuals or smaller entities. However, if the infringement is serious or the infringer refuses to comply, legal action may be necessary. Legal counsel is strongly recommended when dealing with copyright infringement, as navigating the legal system can be complex and time-consuming.

Licensing your work offers an alternative approach to copyright protection. Licensing grants others permission to use your work under specific terms and conditions. This can be a lucrative strategy, allowing you to generate revenue from your work while still retaining ownership. However, drafting a comprehensive license agreement that protects your interests is essential. A well-drafted agreement clearly outlines the scope of the license, the permitted uses of the work, the duration of the license, and the payment terms. Again, legal expertise is crucial to ensure the license protects your rights and provides you with appropriate compensation.

Social media platform policies themselves need careful consideration. Each platform has its own terms of service and copyright policies, which should be reviewed and understood. Understanding how these platforms handle copyright claims and takedown notices is crucial. Knowing the process for reporting infringement and the likely response time from the platform is vital in protecting your intellectual property rights. This might involve learning how to submit a DMCA takedown notice, the standard procedure for reporting copyright infringement online.

In conclusion, managing your online copyright is an ongoing process, not a one-time task. It requires vigilance, a proactive approach, and a strong understanding of copyright law. By implementing these strategies – registering your copyrights, documenting your creative process, monitoring your online presence, understanding fair use, addressing infringements appropriately, considering licensing opportunities, and being aware of social media platform policies – you can significantly protect your intellectual property and secure your financial interests in the dynamic digital landscape. Remember that consulting with an experienced entertainment lawyer is crucial; they can provide tailored advice and support, ensuring your digital assets remain protected and your rights are upheld. The investment in legal expertise is a critical aspect of building a sustainable and successful career in the creative and athletic fields.

The digital age has ushered in an era of unprecedented exposure for athletes and entertainers, but with this increased visibility comes a heightened vulnerability to reputational damage. A single ill-advised tweet, a misinterpreted photograph, or a negative news story can have a devastating impact on one's career and personal life. Effective online reputation management is no longer a luxury; it's a necessity. This section delves into real-world case studies, highlighting both the pitfalls and the strategies employed to successfully navigate the complexities of online reputation in the entertainment and sports industries.

Our first case study involves a young, rising musician whose career trajectory took a sharp downturn after a series of controversial posts on social media. Initially gaining traction through catchy tunes and engaging online content, the artist inadvertently made several inflammatory remarks, alienating a significant portion of their fanbase and prompting a boycott by some sponsors. While the artist's talent remained undeniable, the damage to their reputation proved substantial, impacting their album sales and leading to the cancellation of several high-profile performances. This case serves as a stark reminder of the permanence of online content and the potential repercussions of impulsive social media behavior. The legal implications, beyond simple damage control, included contractual breaches with sponsors, a situation which necessitated significant legal intervention and cost the artist considerable financial resources and the expenditure of significant time in negotiations. The lesson learned here is that engaging legal counsel proactively to develop and implement a comprehensive social media strategy is paramount to avoiding such pitfalls. A well-structured plan, including guidelines for social media interaction and crisis management protocols, can significantly mitigate the risk of reputational damage. It's also crucial to understand the specific terms and conditions of sponsorship deals, ensuring compliance with contractual obligations concerning the artist's public image.

Contrast this with the case of a seasoned athlete who proactively engaged in online reputation management. Understanding the importance of maintaining a consistent and positive online persona, this athlete meticulously crafted a sophisticated digital strategy, investing time and resources in cultivating a strong online presence. This included partnering with experienced PR professionals and social media managers to monitor online conversations, promptly address negative comments, and strategically disseminate positive content. When faced with a minor scandal involving a seemingly innocuous incident, the athlete's preemptive reputation management strategy helped significantly reduce the negative fallout. By swiftly releasing a carefully worded statement acknowledging the situation and expressing remorse, followed by a series of positive engagements with fans, the athlete effectively mitigated any lasting reputational damage. The legal aspects in this case involved creating contracts for representation with the PR team and social media managers, explicitly outlining duties, responsibilities, and expectations. This proactive approach showcased the value of planning and the cost-effectiveness of avoiding a potential crisis. The key takeaway is that robust reputation management is an investment, not an expense, and it's crucial to develop a comprehensive plan early in one's career.

Another compelling case centers on a celebrity chef whose restaurant reviews plummeted following a series of negative online comments alleging poor hygiene standards in their establishment. The comments, amplified through social media, significantly impacted the restaurant's profitability and the chef's overall brand image. The chef's legal team employed a multi-pronged strategy to address the situation. Firstly, they investigated the origin of the negative reviews, looking for evidence of malicious intent or coordinated attacks. Secondly, they engaged in damage control by issuing public statements addressing the concerns and outlining the steps taken to improve hygiene standards. Thirdly, they worked with the platform to address the reviews, taking down any that were demonstrably false or defamatory. The legal complexities involved were extensive, dealing with issues of defamation, libel, and potential breaches of consumer protection laws. The lesson here underscores the importance of actively monitoring online reviews and promptly addressing negative feedback. This strategy included taking down comments which were defamatory or untruthful, and responding to legitimate concerns in a professional and constructive manner. This demonstrates the need for a rapid response team and a proactive crisis management strategy. Failing to engage quickly resulted in a decline in revenue and the potential loss of clientele.

A different scenario involved a prominent athlete who was the target of a coordinated smear campaign orchestrated by a disgruntled former business partner. The campaign involved the dissemination of false and defamatory information on various online platforms, aiming to damage the athlete's reputation and diminish their endorsements. The athlete's legal team, with expertise in online defamation and reputation management, launched a multi-pronged legal strategy. This included filing lawsuits against the individuals and entities responsible for spreading the false information, engaging in public relations campaigns to counter the narrative, and demanding takedown notices for defamatory material across various digital platforms. The legal battles were protracted and expensive, but they demonstrated the effectiveness of a strategic and aggressive legal response to malicious online attacks. They learned the importance of documentation, preserving evidence of the defamatory content and tracing its origins to demonstrate a coordinated effort to damage their reputation. It illustrates how even with vast resources, battling online misinformation can be a very long and costly undertaking.

These case studies illustrate the spectrum of challenges and opportunities presented by online reputation management. While the digital landscape offers immense potential for creators and athletes, it also presents significant risks. Effective online reputation management requires a proactive approach, a strong understanding of relevant laws, and a well-coordinated team of legal professionals, PR specialists, and social media managers. A comprehensive strategy that encompasses proactive monitoring, swift response mechanisms, and a robust legal framework is essential for safeguarding one's reputation and career in today's digital world. Investing in this proactive approach is not simply a matter of expense, but a strategic investment in the longevity and success of one's career in the public eye. The cost of inaction often far outweighs the investment in robust reputation management. Moreover, the emotional and psychological toll of navigating a reputational crisis can be immense, emphasizing the critical role of prevention and effective management.

Chapter 12: The Future of Entertainment Law

The rise of artificial intelligence (AI), virtual reality (VR), and the Metaverse presents a new frontier of legal complexities for the entertainment industry. These technologies are rapidly transforming how content is created, distributed, and consumed, demanding a fresh approach to intellectual property rights, contract law, and data privacy. Consider the implications of AI-generated music, for example. Who owns the copyright – the programmer who created the AI, the user who inputted the parameters, or the AI itself? This question remains largely unanswered, highlighting the urgent need for legal frameworks to address the unique challenges posed by AI in creative endeavors. Current copyright law, designed for human creators, struggles to accommodate the complexities of AI authorship. Several countries are grappling with this issue, attempting to legislate around the ownership and protection of AI-generated works. The lack of clarity creates significant uncertainty for artists and developers alike, potentially hindering innovation and investment in AI-driven creative tools. Contracts need to be carefully drafted to address the ownership and licensing of AI-generated content, clearly specifying the rights and responsibilities of all parties involved. This includes determining the acceptable level of human input necessary to qualify a work for copyright protection and defining the extent to which AI-generated content can be used without infringing upon existing copyrights. The legal landscape is still emerging, with international harmonization lagging behind the rapid technological advancements. The implications extend beyond music; AI is being used to generate scripts, artwork, and even entire virtual worlds, each raising unique legal challenges.

The integration of AI into creative workflows also raises concerns about authorship and originality. If an AI can mimic the style of a famous artist, who owns the copyright to the resulting artwork? Furthermore, how can we ensure that AI-generated content doesn't infringe upon existing copyrights? This is not merely a matter of intellectual property; it impacts the livelihoods of countless artists who rely on their creativity for income. The use of AI in filmmaking presents further complications. Imagine a scenario where an AI is used to generate background visuals for a movie. The question then arises: who owns the copyright to these visuals – the studio, the AI developer, or the team that provided the input data to train the AI? These questions highlight the necessity for clear and comprehensive legal guidelines to manage AI's impact on creative industries. The current legal frameworks are inadequate to address these novel scenarios. The potential for disputes is significant, given the lack of clear precedence in this emerging field. A proactive approach to contract law, specifically addressing AI's role in content creation, is crucial. Contracts should clarify ownership rights, usage rights, and liability in cases of infringement or disputes. Furthermore, it is essential to examine the ethical implications of AI's role in creative work. Will AI lead to job displacement for human artists? How do we ensure that AI-generated works do not unfairly compete with human artists? These ethical considerations are intricately linked to the legal framework, which needs to find a balance between innovation and protection of human artists' rights.

Moving to the realm of virtual reality (VR) and the Metaverse, the legal considerations are equally intricate. The Metaverse, a persistent, shared 3D virtual world, presents a new environment for intellectual property rights. How do we protect trademarks and copyrights in a virtual environment? Can a brand register a virtual property or build a store in a Metaverse platform? The concept of virtual land ownership is relatively new, with legal systems struggling to adapt. Furthermore, the virtual world often blurs the line between the physical and digital, raising questions about jurisdiction and legal liability. If a virtual assault takes place in a Metaverse game, which jurisdiction has legal authority over the incident? These are complex issues that require international collaboration and the development of new legal frameworks. The Metaverse also opens opportunities for new forms of entertainment and commerce. Virtual concerts, immersive gaming experiences, and virtual art galleries present both exciting opportunities and significant legal challenges. Contracts for virtual events and experiences need to explicitly define the rights and responsibilities of all participants, including the use of virtual assets, data privacy, and liability for virtual incidents. The legal system needs to adapt to this evolving landscape, incorporating new terms and concepts to deal with intellectual property rights, contractual obligations, and liability in virtual spaces.

Data privacy is another major concern in the age of emerging technologies. VR and the Metaverse often collect vast amounts of user data, including biometric information and behavioral patterns. Protecting this sensitive data requires strong legal protections and compliance with data privacy regulations. Contracts for VR and Metaverse applications should explicitly outline the data collection practices, the purposes of data use, and the security measures implemented to protect user privacy. Compliance with regulations like GDPR (General Data Protection Regulation) and CCPA (California Consumer Privacy Act) is essential to maintain user trust and avoid legal penalties. The lack of clear international standards for data privacy in virtual environments presents a further challenge, highlighting the need for greater cooperation and standardization across borders. The issue of liability is particularly acute in virtual environments. Who is liable if a user suffers an injury, emotional distress, or financial loss due to an experience in the Metaverse? Is the platform provider liable, the game developer, or the individual user? Establishing clear lines of liability requires careful consideration of negligence, product liability, and contractual obligations. Existing legal frameworks are often ill-equipped to deal with the unique circumstances of virtual environments, necessitating a reevaluation and update of relevant laws.

Further complicating matters is the potential for the use of emerging technologies to facilitate illegal activities. The Metaverse could become a haven for copyright infringement, fraud, and other crimes. The decentralized and anonymous nature of virtual environments can make it challenging to track down perpetrators and enforce the law. Effective enforcement requires collaboration between law enforcement agencies, platform providers, and technology companies. This collaboration will be crucial in detecting and preventing illegal activities within these new virtual spaces. The development of sophisticated forensic tools and techniques for investigating cybercrimes within virtual environments is also critical. The scale and scope of the potential challenges necessitate a proactive and multi-pronged approach to regulation and law enforcement. The speed at which these technologies are advancing significantly outpaces the development of relevant legal frameworks, making it crucial to adapt and respond swiftly.

In conclusion, the emergence of AI, VR, and the Metaverse presents a multitude of legal challenges and opportunities for the entertainment industry. Proactive strategies for navigating these challenges are crucial. Developing robust legal frameworks, updating existing laws, and fostering international cooperation are all essential for ensuring the responsible and ethical development of these transformative technologies. The future of entertainment law hinges on the ability to adapt to these rapidly evolving technologies and create legal frameworks that protect creators, consumers, and the integrity of the industry itself. This requires a constant dialogue between legal professionals, technologists, and policymakers to ensure that the legal landscape keeps pace with the advancements of these technologies. The failure to adapt promptly could lead to significant legal uncertainty, hinder innovation, and stifle the growth of the entertainment industry in the digital age. The proactive development of clear, comprehensive, and globally harmonized legal frameworks will be essential to unlock the full potential of these new technologies while mitigating their risks.

The landscape of intellectual property (IP) rights has always been in flux, a dynamic reflection of societal and technological shifts. From the earliest forms of copyright protecting printed works to the current debates surrounding AI-generated content, the evolution of IP law mirrors the evolution of creative expression itself. This ongoing adaptation is crucial for fostering innovation and protecting the rights of creators, but the pace of technological change often outstrips the ability of legal systems to keep pace.

One of the most significant shifts has been the expansion of what constitutes "creative work" worthy of protection. Initially, copyright focused on tangible forms of expression, such as books and musical scores. As technology progressed, so did the forms of creative expression, leading to the extension of copyright protection to encompass recordings, films, software, and databases. This expansion hasn't been without its challenges. Determining the boundaries of originality, defining the scope of protection, and balancing the rights of creators with the interests of the public have been ongoing debates that continue to shape IP law. The advent of digital technologies further complicated the matter. The ease of copying and distributing digital content has challenged traditional models of copyright enforcement, necessitating new approaches to protect intellectual property in the digital realm. Digital Rights Management (DRM) technologies have emerged as a response, but they have also sparked debates regarding consumer access and fair use.

The rise of the internet and online platforms introduced another layer of complexity. The ease of sharing and distributing content online blurred the lines of ownership and authorship. Questions surrounding user-generated content, open-source projects, and the use of copyrighted material in user-created remixes have led to significant legal battles. The emergence of social media platforms introduced new challenges concerning the ownership and use of user-created content, posing dilemmas regarding ownership rights, licensing, and the responsibility of platforms in managing copyright infringements. Courts have grappled with balancing the freedom of expression inherent in online platforms with the need to protect the intellectual property of creators.

The current era presents yet another paradigm shift with the rise of artificial intelligence (AI) and its application in creative fields. AI algorithms can now generate text, music, images, and even videos, raising fundamental questions about authorship and ownership. If an AI creates a piece of music, who owns the copyright? Is it the programmer who developed the algorithm, the user who inputted the parameters, or the AI itself? This complex question highlights the limitations of existing copyright law, designed for human creators, when applied to AI-generated works. The debate extends to the concept of originality. If an AI generates a work based on existing copyrighted material, does it constitute infringement? These questions are at the forefront of intellectual property law, requiring a reassessment of existing frameworks and the development of new rules to govern AI-generated content. International harmonization is crucial, but the speed of technological advancement often outpaces the legislative response.

Moreover, the increased use of AI in creative workflows also raises concerns about the displacement of human artists and the potential erosion of human creativity. While AI can augment human creativity, the concern remains that its widespread adoption might lead to a devaluation of human effort and a homogenization of creative output. The legal framework must address this potential impact, ensuring that it doesn't unduly disadvantage human creators. This involves striking a balance between encouraging innovation through AI and protecting the livelihood and originality of human artists. Contracts need to adapt to account for the use of AI in creative processes, outlining the rights and responsibilities of all parties involved. This is particularly crucial in collaborations involving AI and human creators, requiring careful specification of ownership, licensing, and liability in case of disputes.

The evolution of IP law also extends to the realm of branding and trademarks. The digital age has expanded the scope of branding, with brands now existing across multiple platforms and virtual spaces. The rise of the Metaverse introduces new challenges, requiring a re-evaluation of how trademarks are protected and enforced in virtual environments. The concept of virtual real estate and digital assets necessitates new legal frameworks to address ownership, licensing, and protection of brand assets in this new digital frontier. This requires a thorough understanding of virtual economies and the unique legal challenges they present.

Looking ahead, the evolution of IP law will continue to be shaped by technological advancements and societal changes. The increasing use of blockchain technology and NFTs (Non-Fungible Tokens) poses new questions about ownership, authenticity, and the transfer of digital assets. The legal framework must adapt to these evolving technologies, providing clear guidelines for the creation, transfer, and enforcement of rights related to digital assets. International cooperation is vital to ensure consistency and coherence in IP laws globally, preventing discrepancies that may hinder creativity and commerce across borders.

Another critical area requiring attention is the enforcement of IP rights in the digital realm. The ease of cross-border infringement and the anonymity provided by the internet have made enforcing IP rights challenging. The legal framework needs to be strengthened to combat online infringement, including collaborating internationally to develop effective mechanisms for cross-border enforcement. This necessitates cooperation between governments, law enforcement agencies, and platform providers to deter infringement and provide redress to affected creators.

Finally, the legal framework must keep in mind the public interest. While protecting the rights of creators is paramount, it's crucial to balance these rights with the public's access to information and cultural expression. The concept of fair use and exceptions to copyright are essential components of a balanced IP system. This means navigating the complexities of fair use in the digital age, ensuring that the exceptions to copyright remain relevant and proportionate in the context of evolving technologies.

In conclusion, the evolution of IP law is a continuous process of adaptation to new technologies and societal changes. The challenge lies in maintaining a balance between protecting the rights of creators, fostering innovation, and ensuring public access to creative works. A proactive and adaptive approach is essential to ensure that the legal framework remains relevant and effective in the dynamic digital age. The future of entertainment law, and indeed the broader creative landscape, hinges on the ability of legal systems to anticipate and address the challenges of evolving technologies and changing societal norms. This requires ongoing dialogue and collaboration between legal professionals, policymakers, and the creative community itself.

The entertainment industry, a kaleidoscope of creativity and commerce, is undergoing a seismic shift, reshaping the very fabric of how content is created, distributed, and consumed. This transformation presents both unprecedented opportunities and complex legal challenges. The rise of streaming platforms, for example, has fundamentally altered the traditional models of film and television distribution. Gone are the days of relying solely on theatrical releases and broadcast television; now, content creators have a plethora of platforms to choose from, each with its own unique set of legal considerations. Negotiating streaming rights, managing digital distribution, and addressing issues of territorial rights have become increasingly complex tasks demanding specialized legal expertise. The sheer volume of content available on these platforms necessitates sophisticated contracts that clearly define rights, responsibilities, and revenue streams for all stakeholders. The lack of clarity in these agreements can lead to protracted disputes and costly litigation, highlighting the critical role of experienced entertainment lawyers in this evolving landscape.

Furthermore, the rise of user-generated content (UGC) has introduced a new dimension to copyright and intellectual property issues. While platforms like YouTube and TikTok have empowered millions to share their creative works, they've also created legal gray areas regarding ownership, licensing, and the use of copyrighted material. The question of fair use in the context of user-created remixes and parodies remains a complex and hotly debated topic. Entertainment lawyers are now faced with the challenge of advising creators on how to protect their original work while simultaneously navigating the complexities of UGC and the responsibilities of platforms in managing copyright infringements. This includes advising on licensing agreements, determining fair use limitations, and understanding the implications of takedown notices and copyright strikes. The legal implications of UGC extend beyond simple copyright concerns; issues of defamation, privacy, and the use of personal information also demand careful attention.

The globalization of the entertainment industry presents another layer of complexity. The ease of cross-border distribution has expanded the reach of content creators but also necessitates an understanding of varying international copyright laws and intellectual property regimes. Navigating the nuances of different legal systems, dealing with international co-productions, and enforcing rights across multiple jurisdictions present significant legal hurdles. The entertainment lawyer must possess not only a deep understanding of domestic law but also a working knowledge of international legal frameworks and conventions to effectively represent clients in a globalized market. This often involves international collaborations with lawyers in different jurisdictions to ensure the protection of client's rights and interests worldwide.

The influence of technology extends beyond streaming and UGC. The advent of artificial intelligence (AI) has introduced profound changes to the creative process. AI-powered tools are now used in various aspects of content creation, from composing music and writing scripts to generating visuals and special effects. This raises complex questions regarding authorship, ownership, and copyright. If an AI generates a piece of music, who owns the copyright – the programmer, the user, or the AI itself? The current legal framework struggles to adequately address these challenges, requiring a reassessment of existing laws and the development of new regulatory frameworks. The potential use of AI in copyright infringement also necessitates a proactive approach to understanding the legal implications of using AI-generated content and mitigating the risk of liability.

The rise of non-fungible tokens (NFTs) and blockchain technology has also revolutionized the way digital assets are created, traded, and owned in the entertainment industry. NFTs are offering new opportunities for creators to monetize their work directly with fans, bypassing traditional intermediaries. However, the legal landscape surrounding NFTs is still evolving, with ambiguities surrounding ownership, copyright, and the enforcement of rights in this new digital marketplace. Entertainment lawyers are now called upon to advise clients on the legal implications of creating, selling, and utilizing NFTs, including issues of smart contracts, intellectual property rights, and regulatory compliance.

This includes understanding the potential risks associated with the volatile nature of the NFT market and developing robust strategies to protect clients' interests in this dynamic environment.

The increasing importance of social media marketing presents another evolving legal landscape. Social media platforms have become powerful tools for promoting and marketing entertainment projects; however, this comes with its own set of legal considerations. Influencer marketing, for instance, has become increasingly prevalent, requiring clear and transparent contracts that outline the scope of work, compensation, and intellectual property rights. Issues related to endorsements, product placement, and sponsorships require careful legal scrutiny to ensure compliance with advertising regulations and consumer protection laws. The use of social media to manage a creator's brand and reputation also requires a strategic approach to avoid legal pitfalls and build a positive online presence. The potential for liability arising from social media posts, comments, and interactions necessitates a thorough understanding of relevant laws and regulations to protect the creator from potential legal challenges.

Furthermore, the ever-increasing concerns about data privacy and security have significant implications for the entertainment industry. The collection, storage, and use of personal data from fans, consumers, and employees necessitate adherence to stringent data protection regulations such as GDPR and CCPA. Entertainment companies must implement robust data security measures and privacy policies to ensure compliance with these regulations and avoid costly penalties. Entertainment lawyers are instrumental in advising companies on data privacy issues, helping them develop compliant data handling practices, and responding to data breaches. The ongoing evolution of data protection laws underscores the need for ongoing education and awareness among entertainment professionals and the continuous adaptation of legal strategies to navigate the increasingly complex landscape of data privacy.

The entertainment industry is inherently intertwined with talent representation. This is where entertainment lawyers play a crucial role in advising artists, athletes, and other entertainment professionals on contract negotiations, royalty payments, and dispute resolution. The complexity of contracts in the entertainment industry is significant. These agreements must cover various aspects, including payment terms, intellectual property rights, usage rights, and dispute resolution mechanisms. Entertainment lawyers specialize in negotiating favorable terms for their clients, ensuring their rights are protected and their interests are served. This requires a detailed understanding of industry standards, prevailing market rates, and the legal precedents relevant to the client's circumstances.

In the realm of dispute resolution, entertainment lawyers provide essential guidance in navigating disagreements between parties. This may involve mediation, arbitration, or litigation, depending on the nature of the dispute and the desired outcome. Entertainment lawyers are skilled negotiators, advocates, and litigators, capable of representing their clients effectively in various settings. This requires a deep understanding of contract law, intellectual property law, and the specific legal issues that may arise within the entertainment industry. The ability to anticipate and resolve disputes efficiently is a crucial skill for entertainment lawyers, as lengthy legal battles can be detrimental to both the artist's career and financial well-being.

In conclusion, the entertainment industry is in a state of constant flux, and entertainment lawyers must remain adaptive, innovative, and informed to effectively serve their clients in this dynamic landscape. The convergence of technology, globalization, and changing consumer behavior presents both unprecedented challenges and opportunities. The future of entertainment law demands a proactive and multifaceted approach, encompassing not only legal expertise but also a deep understanding of the industry's creative and commercial dimensions. The legal professionals who thrive in this environment will be those who can anticipate and address the evolving legal landscape, while always prioritizing the best interests of their clients. The ongoing evolution of the legal framework, coupled with the relentless pace of technological advancement, will continue to shape the entertainment landscape for years to come.

The rise of the creator economy represents a profound shift in the entertainment landscape, empowering individuals to build their own brands and generate income through various digital platforms. This democratization of content creation, however, comes with its own unique set of legal challenges. Independent content creators, unlike those traditionally represented by major studios or labels, often lack the resources and legal expertise to navigate these complexities effectively. This leaves them vulnerable to exploitation and potentially costly mistakes.

One of the primary legal concerns for independent creators is intellectual property protection. Unlike established entities with dedicated legal teams, creators often struggle to understand and protect their copyright, trademarks, and other intellectual property rights. The ease of content replication and distribution online exacerbates this issue. Creators may inadvertently infringe on the intellectual property of others through the use of copyrighted music, images, or other materials in their content. Conversely, they may face challenges in protecting their own work from unauthorized use or appropriation. Understanding fair use principles, obtaining proper licenses, and registering copyrights are critical steps that independent creators must take to protect their intellectual property. This also includes being aware of the nuances of different platforms' policies regarding content ownership and usage rights.

Moreover, the creator economy is characterized by a wide variety of monetization strategies. Many creators rely on revenue generated through advertising, sponsorships, affiliate marketing, and merchandise sales. Each of these avenues presents its own legal intricacies. Advertising revenue often involves agreements with ad networks, requiring an understanding of relevant advertising regulations and disclosure requirements. Sponsorships and brand collaborations necessitate clear contracts that outline the terms of the partnership, including payment schedules, usage rights, and exclusivity clauses. Affiliate marketing programs involve promoting products or services in exchange for a commission, requiring compliance with FTC guidelines and disclosure requirements.

Merchandise sales may involve trademarks and licensing agreements, raising further legal considerations.

The use of social media platforms is central to the success of many creators. Building a substantial online following and engaging with audiences effectively are crucial for generating revenue. However, the use of social media also poses significant legal risks. Creators must be mindful of their online conduct to avoid defamation, libel, and privacy violations. The use of copyrighted material in social media posts is another area of concern. Furthermore, creators must comply with the terms of service and community guidelines of different platforms, which can vary significantly. Navigating these legal complexities is often beyond the capabilities of creators without legal expertise. In cases involving influencer marketing, for example, the creator's role is essentially acting as a marketing agent, which falls under advertising laws and regulations. Misrepresentation or lack of transparency can lead to hefty fines or legal battles.

The creator economy also involves significant issues related to contract law. Creators often negotiate contracts with platforms, brands, and other businesses, requiring an understanding of contract negotiation principles. These contracts can cover various aspects, including payment terms, usage rights, intellectual property ownership, and dispute resolution mechanisms. Many creators, particularly those starting out, may lack the experience and legal expertise to negotiate favorable terms, leaving them vulnerable to unfavorable contract clauses and potential exploitation. For example, an improperly drafted agreement might allow a platform to utilize a creator's work indefinitely without fair compensation or proper credit. Understanding how to draft strong contracts is essential to protect creators' rights and interests.

Beyond contractual issues, creators must also be aware of data privacy and security concerns. Many platforms collect vast amounts of personal data from users, including creators themselves. Understanding and complying with data protection regulations such as GDPR and CCPA is crucial for safeguarding personal information. Furthermore, creators must be cautious about sharing their personal information online and take steps to protect their data from potential breaches or misuse. This includes understanding the privacy policies of the platforms they use and implementing appropriate security measures to protect their accounts and personal data.

The evolving legal landscape surrounding NFTs and blockchain technology also significantly impacts the creator economy. NFTs offer new opportunities for creators to monetize their work directly with fans, cutting out intermediaries and gaining more control over their earnings. However, the legal aspects surrounding the creation, sale, and ownership of NFTs are complex and still developing. Creators need guidance on issues such as copyright protection for digital assets, the creation and execution of smart contracts, and the legal risks associated with the volatility of the

NFT market. The ownership rights of digital artworks sold as NFTs are also complex and need careful consideration when licensing or selling such assets.

The use of artificial intelligence (AI) in content creation poses additional legal challenges. While AI tools can be valuable for content creation, they raise questions about authorship, ownership, and copyright. Determining the intellectual property rights of AI-generated content is a complex issue with no clear legal precedent. Creators using AI-generated content need to understand the potential legal implications and ensure their work complies with existing copyright laws.

The creator economy presents both tremendous opportunities and significant legal risks for independent creators. Navigating these complexities requires a proactive and informed approach, emphasizing the importance of education, risk management, and legal counsel. Creators who proactively educate themselves on relevant laws, seek legal advice when needed, and adopt effective risk management strategies are better equipped to protect their interests, build successful careers, and thrive in this dynamic environment. The landscape is rapidly evolving, meaning that ongoing learning and adaptation are paramount for any creator seeking to succeed in this sphere. The potential legal pitfalls are numerous, and understanding them from the outset is critical to long-term success and avoidance of costly mistakes.

The entertainment industry's relentless pace of change necessitates a proactive approach to legal preparedness. For creators and athletes alike, understanding the future trends and adapting accordingly is paramount to long-term success. This involves more than simply reacting to new laws and regulations; it demands a strategic vision that anticipates challenges and capitalizes on emerging opportunities.

One crucial area of focus is intellectual property rights in the metaverse and augmented reality (AR) spaces. As these immersive technologies gain traction, new forms of content creation and distribution emerge, each presenting unique legal complexities. For example, the creation and ownership of virtual goods, avatars, and digital experiences raise questions about copyright, trademark, and patent protection that are still being actively debated and defined in the legal arena. Creators and athletes need to be aware of how their intellectual property is being utilized within these virtual worlds and to actively seek protection for their creations, potentially through a combination of copyright registration, trademark filings, and even patents where appropriate. Understanding licensing agreements in these novel contexts is critical to avoid unauthorized use and ensure fair compensation. The potential for digital piracy is even greater in the metaverse, requiring creators to actively monitor and enforce their rights.

Furthermore, the increasing reliance on AI in content creation and distribution demands a thorough understanding of the legal implications. While AI tools can augment creativity and efficiency, they also raise questions regarding ownership, authorship, and copyright. The legal status of AI-generated content is a rapidly evolving area of law, with various jurisdictions adopting different approaches. Creators must proactively assess the legal risks associated with the use of AI tools in their work, ensuring that they comply with relevant copyright laws and avoid potential infringement. Understanding the terms of service of AI tools and the potential limitations they may place on the use of generated content is equally important. This requires a deep dive into the fine print and a clear understanding of the legal ramifications of using AI for content creation. Attorneys specializing in AI law will play an increasingly significant role in advising creators and athletes on these complex issues.

The evolving landscape of data privacy and security is another significant concern. With the increasing volume of personal data collected by various platforms and technologies, creators and athletes must be vigilant in protecting their personal information and complying with relevant regulations such as GDPR and CCPA. This involves understanding the privacy policies of the platforms they use, implementing strong security measures, and seeking legal advice on data protection issues. A significant risk lies in unauthorized access or misuse of personal data, including financial details, health information, and creative works. Data breaches can result in significant financial losses, reputational damage, and legal liabilities. The proactive implementation of robust security protocols and compliance with relevant data protection regulations are essential to mitigate these risks. Regularly updating security measures and staying informed about emerging threats is crucial in the constantly evolving cyber landscape.

Contract negotiation will remain a critical skill for creators and athletes in the years to come. Understanding the intricacies of contract law, particularly when dealing with complex deals involving multiple parties, is crucial to protect one's interests and maximize earning potential. This requires developing strong negotiation skills, understanding industry-specific standards and best practices, and seeking professional legal advice when necessary. Independent creators, in particular, need to be particularly vigilant in reviewing and negotiating contracts with platforms, brands, and other businesses, ensuring that the terms are fair, equitable, and protect their rights. It's not simply about signing on the dotted line; it's about understanding every clause and ensuring that it aligns with their long-term goals.

Dispute resolution is an essential component of legal preparedness. Understanding different dispute resolution mechanisms, such as mediation, arbitration, and litigation, and choosing the most appropriate method for a particular situation is critical. Having a well-defined strategy for handling disputes can save time, money, and potentially reputation. The ability to negotiate effectively and find mutually beneficial solutions is always preferable to protracted legal battles. However, knowing when to escalate a matter to a higher level is also crucial for protecting one's interests. This requires a clear understanding of legal options and the ability to assess the potential costs and benefits of each approach.

Building a strong legal team is a proactive step towards navigating the complexities of the entertainment industry. Having access to experienced attorneys specializing in entertainment law, intellectual property, contract law, and other relevant areas can provide invaluable guidance and support. Choosing the right legal team is essential and often means assembling a network of specialists who can be called upon when needed. This network provides a vital safety net and access to expert knowledge to navigate complex legal issues that may arise. It's vital to develop a strong relationship with a legal team who understands the intricacies of the entertainment industry and can advise accordingly.

Finally, continuous learning and adaptation are crucial in this constantly evolving environment. Staying abreast of new laws, regulations, and industry trends is essential for creators and athletes to remain compliant and proactive in protecting their rights. This involves attending industry events, following legal developments, and seeking advice from legal professionals. Professional development is essential to adapting to the ever-shifting landscape and mitigating risks. The entertainment industry's fluidity requires a commitment to ongoing learning to remain informed, competitive, and ultimately successful. The investment in ongoing education is an investment in the longevity of one's career.

The future of entertainment law demands a proactive, strategic approach. By focusing on intellectual property in new technologies, navigating the complexities of AI, safeguarding data privacy, mastering contract negotiation, building a strong legal team, and prioritizing continuous learning, creators and athletes can position themselves for success in the ever-evolving landscape of the entertainment industry. The journey will require diligence, adaptability, and a long-term vision, but the rewards for those who effectively prepare for the future are immense.

Chapter 13: Resources and Further Reading

Navigating the legal intricacies of the entertainment and sports industries can feel like traversing a dense jungle, fraught with hidden pitfalls and unexpected twists. However, the journey doesn't have to be undertaken alone. A wealth of resources and organizations exists to provide guidance, support, and essential legal information to creators and athletes at every stage of their careers. This section serves as your compass, guiding you towards key legal organizations and resources that can significantly enhance your legal preparedness.

One of the most valuable resources for entertainment professionals is the

American Bar Association (ABA). The ABA's website offers a vast library of legal information, including articles, publications, and resources specifically tailored to the entertainment industry. Their sections on intellectual property, contract law, and entertainment law provide in-depth analysis of legal principles and practical advice for navigating complex legal issues. They also offer educational opportunities, such as webinars and conferences, which can be invaluable for staying abreast of the latest legal developments and best practices. The ABA's network of experienced attorneys spans the country, providing a valuable pool of expertise to draw upon. Their referral service can connect individuals with lawyers specializing in specific areas of entertainment law.

Beyond the ABA, several state bar associations provide resources relevant to entertainment law. For instance, the

California Bar Association, given the state's prominent position in the entertainment industry, offers specific programs and resources for lawyers and clients involved in film, television, music, and other creative fields. Their website frequently hosts seminars, workshops, and publications that address current legal issues and trends impacting the California entertainment industry, including aspects like copyright infringement, talent agency regulations, and intellectual property protection. Similarly, other state bar associations, particularly those in states with thriving entertainment hubs like New York and Florida, offer comparable resources. Checking your state's bar association website is a crucial step in accessing localized and relevant legal information.

Professional organizations play a vital role in supporting creators and athletes. For musicians, the

American Federation of Musicians (AFM) and **SAG-AFTRA** (for actors and other screen professionals) offer a range of services beyond union representation. These organizations often provide legal assistance and advice to their members on matters related to contracts, royalties, and intellectual property. Their websites are excellent starting points for finding information on legal issues specific to their respective fields and often contain educational materials on relevant laws and regulations. These organizations often boast extensive legal departments staffed by experts who understand the intricacies of collective bargaining and the unique legal challenges faced by their members.

Athletes, too, benefit significantly from professional organizations. The

National Basketball Players Association (NBPA), **National Football League Players Association (NFLPA)**, and similar organizations representing athletes in other major leagues provide legal support, contract negotiation assistance, and resources related to image rights and endorsements. These organizations have highly experienced legal teams who are intimately familiar with the specific legal landscapes of their respective sports, offering guidance on crucial aspects such as contract reviews, licensing agreements, and dispute resolution. Their focus is on maximizing the financial well-being and long-term career prospects of their members, providing a crucial support system throughout their athletic journey.

Beyond industry-specific organizations, the

United States Copyright Office offers invaluable resources for protecting intellectual property rights. Their website provides detailed information about copyright registration, which is a critical step in securing legal protection for creative works. They offer guidelines, forms, and a comprehensive database of registered copyrights. Understanding the registration process and its implications is crucial for creators of all types, as it forms the foundation for legal recourse in cases of infringement. Utilizing the Copyright Office's resources proactively helps establish a strong legal foundation for your creative endeavors.

For trademark protection, the

United States Patent and Trademark Office (USPTO) serves as a vital resource. Their website provides information about trademark registration, searching existing trademarks, and understanding the requirements for securing trademark protection for brand names, logos, and other identifying marks. A strong trademark effectively protects your brand identity, a crucial asset in the competitive world of entertainment and sports. The USPTO's resources can significantly aid in building a robust brand protection strategy.

The

International Intellectual Property Alliance (IIPA) provides a global perspective on intellectual property rights, particularly relevant for creators and athletes with an international reach. Their website offers resources and information on international copyright and trademark laws, providing insights into the nuances of protecting intellectual property rights in different countries. This becomes increasingly crucial as the entertainment and sports industries continue their global expansion, requiring a proactive and informed approach to international legal protection.

Finally, legal information databases like

Westlaw and **LexisNexis** provide extensive access to legal precedents, statutes, and regulations. These are powerful research tools for those who want to delve deeper into specific legal issues. While primarily designed for legal professionals, the vast resources available within these databases can be incredibly helpful for those with a solid understanding of legal terminology and research techniques. These databases offer the ability to search through a wide array of legal materials, offering insight into case laws and legal precedents that are crucial in understanding the legal landscape of the entertainment and sports industries.

This list is not exhaustive; numerous other organizations and resources can support creators and athletes. It's crucial to remember that proactive legal planning is an investment in your long-term success. Familiarizing yourself with these organizations and resources can significantly enhance your legal preparedness, giving you the tools and knowledge to navigate the complex legal landscape with confidence and protect your rights and interests effectively. Remember to always seek the advice of a qualified legal professional before making any critical legal decisions. The resources mentioned here should be seen as valuable tools to support, not replace, that professional guidance. Your legal counsel can help navigate these resources and apply the information to your unique circumstances. The journey to success is often paved with knowledge, preparation, and the right guidance – making the best use of these resources ensures you're setting yourself up for a prosperous and protected career.

Beyond the organizations and resources previously discussed, a wealth of insightful books and articles can significantly enhance your understanding of entertainment law and its practical application. These resources offer a deeper dive into specific legal areas, providing valuable context and practical examples to complement the foundational knowledge gained elsewhere. This curated selection focuses on books and articles that offer a balance of theoretical understanding and practical guidance, particularly relevant to the challenges faced by artists, athletes, and other entertainment professionals.

For a comprehensive overview of entertainment law, "Entertainment Law: A Practical Guide" by [Author's Name – Replace with a real author and book title], offers a meticulous breakdown of key legal concepts. The book excels in its clear and concise explanations of complex legal principles, making it accessible even to those without a legal background. Its strength lies in its practical application of legal theory, illustrated through real-world examples and case studies from across various entertainment sectors – music, film, television, and digital media. The author's depth of experience shines through, providing valuable insights into the nuances of contract negotiation, intellectual property protection, and dispute resolution. Particular attention is given to the evolving digital landscape and its impact on the entertainment industry's legal framework. The detailed explanation of the intricacies of licensing and distribution deals within the digital realm is particularly useful for independent creators navigating the complexities of online platforms. Furthermore, the book's structure allows for easy navigation, allowing readers to focus on specific areas of interest without being overwhelmed by unnecessary jargon. It's a highly recommended starting point for anyone seeking a robust understanding of the field.

Another valuable resource is "The Entertainment Lawyer's Handbook" by [Author's Name – Replace with a real author and book title]. This handbook differs from the comprehensive guides by focusing on practical, actionable strategies for artists and athletes. It's less theoretical and more focused on offering readily applicable advice. The book's approach is less about reciting legal statutes and more about providing real-world strategies for protecting oneself in the industry. This includes practical tips on choosing legal representation, negotiating contracts, understanding crucial clauses, and protecting personal brand value. It features numerous checklists and templates, providing readers with tools to proactively manage their legal affairs. The sections on dispute resolution, including mediation and arbitration, offer valuable insight into navigating conflicts without resorting to costly and time-consuming litigation. A particularly helpful aspect is the book's inclusion of real-life anecdotes and case studies, illustrating how seemingly small contract details can have significant consequences. This practical focus makes it an indispensable resource for those actively seeking to protect their interests in the industry.

Focusing specifically on the ever-changing world of digital rights management, "Digital Rights Management for Creators" by [Author's Name – Replace with a real author and book title] provides a crucial guide to navigating the complexities of online distribution and licensing. This book expertly navigates the legal and technological aspects of protecting digital content, providing practical strategies for creators to control their intellectual property in the digital realm. The book goes beyond the technical elements, explaining the legal implications of various DRM technologies and strategies. It offers advice on choosing appropriate licenses, managing digital distribution agreements, and enforcing rights against online infringement. The detailed analysis of various licensing models, from Creative Commons to exclusive distribution agreements, is extremely valuable for creators seeking to understand the trade-offs and legal ramifications of different approaches. It also addresses the ever-increasing challenges related to user-generated content, offering guidance on how creators can protect their work from unauthorized use and adaptation. This is essential for anyone releasing content online, from musicians distributing tracks to film-makers releasing independent projects.

For a deeper understanding of intellectual property law as it applies to the entertainment industry, articles published by leading legal journals and industry publications offer valuable insight. The journal "Entertainment Law Reporter" frequently publishes articles that provide detailed analysis of recent court decisions, legislative changes, and emerging legal issues. Many articles focus on specific areas like copyright infringement in the digital world, the legal implications of artificial intelligence in creative fields, and the evolving landscape of rights of publicity. These in-depth analyses are invaluable for staying abreast of the dynamic legal landscape and understanding potential pitfalls and opportunities. Many of these articles are written by leading legal scholars and practitioners, ensuring a high level of accuracy and insightful analysis.

Similarly, industry publications like "Variety," "The Hollywood Reporter," and "Billboard" regularly feature articles on legal developments and their implications for artists, athletes, and entertainment companies. While not strictly legal journals, they provide a practical perspective on legal issues from an industry lens, often focusing on the business and practical implications of legal developments. These articles frequently discuss high-profile legal battles, providing real-world examples of how legal principles play out in the entertainment industry, demonstrating the actual effects of legal rulings on artists' careers and the industry at large. Reading these publications helps maintain an awareness of current trends and the practical challenges faced by professionals in the field.

Finally, seeking out articles from law review journals published by leading law schools often provides detailed analysis of specific legal issues and cutting-edge developments. These articles delve deeply into academic discourse surrounding particular legal questions within entertainment law, including intellectual property, contracts, and digital rights. While sometimes academically dense, these resources offer a wealth of nuanced understanding and theoretical underpinnings for those seeking a more profound comprehension of the field. These articles are often used by lawyers and legal scholars alike, illustrating their depth and credibility. They can often provide insights into future legal trends based on current legal scholarship.

The above resources represent a starting point for your journey of understanding entertainment law. Remember, this field is constantly evolving, and continuous learning is key to navigating its complexities successfully. Always prioritize seeking advice from qualified legal professionals for matters specific to your circumstances. This curated list provides a foundation of supplementary knowledge, offering a deeper dive into the topics previously discussed and preparing you to make informed decisions about your career in the entertainment and sports industries. Use these tools to build a strong legal foundation, allowing you to focus on creating and performing without unnecessary legal risks. Remember, informed decision-making empowers you to achieve greater control and success in your chosen field.

Navigating the intricate legal landscape of the entertainment industry can feel daunting, particularly for those without a legal background. Finding the right legal assistance is crucial, as a skilled entertainment lawyer can be the difference between a successful career and one riddled with legal pitfalls. Selecting the right legal representation is a significant decision, impacting your career trajectory and financial well-being. This process requires careful consideration, informed choices, and a clear understanding of your needs.

Begin by identifying your specific legal needs. Are you negotiating a recording contract? Do you need help protecting your intellectual property? Are you facing a contract dispute? Clearly defining your requirements will guide your search for the right lawyer. The more specific you are about your needs, the easier it will be to identify lawyers with relevant expertise. For instance, a lawyer specializing in music contracts may not be the best fit for an athlete negotiating an endorsement deal. Consider listing your priorities, including the type of contract you're dealing with, the geographical location of your work, and the stage of your career. This preliminary assessment will significantly narrow your options and help you focus your search effectively.

Once you have a clear picture of your needs, start researching potential legal representatives. Online directories like the American Bar Association (ABA) website, Martindale-Hubbell, and Avvo are excellent resources for finding lawyers in your area specializing in entertainment law. These platforms often allow you to filter results based on specialty, experience, and client reviews. Look for lawyers with proven experience in the specific area of entertainment law relevant to your situation. A musician needs a lawyer proficient in music contracts, while an athlete requires expertise in endorsements and NIL (Name, Image, and Likeness) agreements. This specialized knowledge can make a huge difference in the outcome of your negotiations and legal battles.

Word-of-mouth referrals can be invaluable. Reach out to other artists, athletes, or industry professionals you trust and ask for recommendations. These firsthand accounts can offer valuable insights into a lawyer's work ethic, responsiveness, and success rate. Their experience can help you bypass potential issues and build trust before your first consultation. Online reviews should be regarded cautiously; while they offer a snapshot of client experiences, they may not represent the full picture. Consider examining multiple review platforms and assessing the overall trend rather than relying on a single comment or rating.

Don't hesitate to conduct thorough background research on potential candidates. Visit their firm's website, explore their publications and articles, and review case studies of similar engagements. This research offers valuable insights into their approach to legal strategy, their understanding of the specific challenges in your industry, and the types of cases they've successfully handled. You're not simply looking for a lawyer; you're building a partnership that could last for years. A well-informed decision ensures this partnership is based on mutual trust and shared goals.

The initial consultation is your opportunity to assess the compatibility between your needs and the lawyer's expertise. Prepare a list of thoughtful questions to ask during this meeting. Inquire about their experience in your specific area of the industry, their fee structure, their approach to case management, and their communication style. A successful working relationship requires clear communication and mutual understanding. Assess whether the lawyer actively listens to your concerns, understands your goals, and offers practical solutions to your specific legal challenges. This initial meeting is as much about them getting to know you as it is about you assessing their suitability.

Understand the lawyer's fee structure upfront. Many lawyers work on an hourly basis, while others offer contingency fee arrangements where they receive a percentage of the settlement or award if successful. Clarify the payment terms, payment schedule, and any potential additional expenses. Transparency in financial matters is paramount, ensuring you understand the costs involved and can budget accordingly. Avoid lawyers who are vague or evasive about their fees; a professional and ethical lawyer will be forthcoming about their billing practices.

Finally, trust your gut instinct. Choose a lawyer you feel comfortable with, someone you believe will effectively represent your interests and advocate for your rights. The legal process can be stressful and demanding, and having a lawyer you trust and feel confident in is critical. Remember, this is a long-term relationship; choosing the right lawyer can significantly improve your long-term career prospects. Don't rush the decision; taking the time to find the right legal partner will pay dividends in the long run.

Beyond individual lawyers, consider the advantages of working with a specialized entertainment law firm. Larger firms often possess a broader range of expertise, encompassing various aspects of entertainment law. This can be advantageous if your legal needs are complex or multi-faceted. For instance, a firm might specialize in music, film, and intellectual property rights, providing comprehensive legal support for all your endeavors. They may also have more resources available, such as paralegals and support staff, ensuring that your case receives the attention and support it deserves. This can be particularly beneficial when dealing with complex or high-stakes legal matters.

However, smaller firms often offer personalized attention and a more hands-on approach. The direct access to senior partners can facilitate quick responses and efficient problem-solving. The smaller size often translates to more cost-effective solutions for clients, with pricing models that cater to artists and athletes early in their careers. The close-knit environment fosters a stronger client-lawyer relationship, which can be particularly important during tense negotiations and legal battles. It often allows for a greater level of communication and understanding between the lawyer and the client. The focus is often on building a strong, long-lasting relationship, understanding the specific client's aspirations, and acting as a strategic advisor throughout the artist's or athlete's journey.

Regardless of the size of the firm, verify the lawyer's credentials and experience. Confirm their admission to the bar, check their disciplinary history with the state bar association, and review client testimonials. Confirm their membership in professional organizations like the Entertainment Law Initiative or other industry-specific legal groups. These affiliations can attest to the lawyer's commitment to their profession and their standing within the legal community. Never hesitate to ask for references from previous clients; speaking with those who have previously engaged the lawyer's services provides valuable insights into their work ethic and approach to case management. This direct feedback is often more valuable than general online reviews.

Remember, choosing a lawyer is a significant decision. Thorough research, thoughtful questions, and a healthy dose of intuition are crucial components of the selection process. Do not underestimate the importance of a strong attorney-client relationship; it will influence the outcome of your legal matters considerably. An experienced entertainment lawyer can provide invaluable support and guidance, protecting your rights and ensuring your success within the industry. Proactive legal planning can significantly mitigate future risks and ensure you are well-positioned to navigate the complex legal terrain of the entertainment world. This investment in legal counsel is an investment in your career's longevity and sustainability. By carefully selecting your legal team, you ensure your creative efforts are protected, allowing you to focus on your artistic pursuits with confidence and clarity.

Beyond the crucial step of selecting legal representation, navigating the complexities of entertainment law requires access to reliable information and resources. The digital age offers a wealth of online tools and legal databases specifically designed to assist creators, athletes, and industry professionals in understanding and managing their legal affairs. These resources can provide valuable insights into legal precedents, contract clauses, intellectual property rights, and other critical areas of entertainment law. However, it's vital to remember that these resources should supplement, not replace, professional legal advice. They are tools for education and research, providing a framework for understanding complex legal issues, but they should never be used as a substitute for the personalized guidance of an experienced entertainment lawyer.

One invaluable resource is the American Bar Association (ABA) website. The ABA offers a comprehensive library of legal information, including resources specific to entertainment law. Their site provides access to articles, journals, and publications covering a wide range of topics relevant to the industry. You can find insights into emerging legal trends, updates on relevant legislation, and analyses of significant court cases. This wealth of information provides a strong foundation for understanding the ever-evolving legal landscape of the entertainment industry. The ABA's website also serves as a directory for finding qualified entertainment lawyers in your region, ensuring you can connect with legal professionals who possess specialized knowledge and experience in your specific area of the entertainment industry.

Martindale-Hubbell is another respected online directory that offers extensive information on lawyers across various legal specialties, including entertainment law. It allows you to search for lawyers based on geographic location, area of expertise, and client reviews. Many profiles include detailed biographies, highlighting the lawyers' experience, achievements, and client testimonials. This allows you to research potential legal representatives thoroughly before initiating contact. The detailed information provided by

Martindale-Hubbell helps you narrow your search and identify lawyers with the necessary experience and expertise for your particular legal needs. Remember to carefully examine the profiles, comparing different lawyers to find the best fit for your specific situation and ensure the attorney aligns with your legal objectives and personal preferences.

Avvo is another valuable online resource for finding and researching lawyers. Similar to Martindale-Hubbell, Avvo provides comprehensive profiles of lawyers, including client reviews, ratings, and disciplinary history. This platform offers a user-friendly interface, making it easy to filter your search and find lawyers with the specific experience you require. Client reviews can offer valuable insights into a lawyer's communication style, responsiveness, and overall effectiveness. However, it is always advisable to treat online reviews with a degree of critical awareness, recognizing that individual experiences may not be representative of the lawyer's overall performance. Always supplement online reviews with independent research, seeking further evidence of the lawyer's competence and experience before engaging their services.

Beyond general lawyer directories, specialized legal databases offer access to a vast repository of legal information. LexisNexis and Westlaw are two leading legal research platforms that provide access to case law, statutes, regulations, and legal journals. These databases allow you to research legal precedents and understand how courts have interpreted specific laws and regulations within the entertainment industry. This research capability is particularly valuable when facing a legal challenge or negotiating a complex contract. Accessing these resources empowers you to understand the legal landscape, formulate effective strategies, and make informed decisions, giving you a significant advantage in navigating the industry's legal complexities. However, remember that these databases are complex tools, requiring some familiarity with legal terminology and research techniques.

Specialized databases focusing solely on entertainment law are also available. These databases offer curated collections of articles, cases, and legal resources specifically related to the entertainment industry, providing a more focused and efficient search experience. They often include analyses of significant cases, breaking down the key legal principles involved and the implications for industry professionals. These focused databases can be particularly helpful when dealing with specific areas of entertainment law, such as music contracts, film distribution agreements, or intellectual property rights. Many of these specialized databases offer subscription-based access, providing regular updates and access to a wealth of curated information, ensuring you are informed about current legislation and legal precedents.

Accessing these online resources and legal databases is not simply about finding information; it's about developing a proactive approach to legal management. Familiarizing yourself with relevant legislation, case law, and contract clauses empowers you to negotiate contracts effectively, protect your intellectual property, and make informed business decisions. It's about building a foundation of legal knowledge that will help you navigate the challenges and opportunities within the entertainment industry. This proactive approach allows you to engage your legal counsel in a more informed manner, facilitating more productive discussions and helping to optimize your legal strategy. This is vital in preventing future disputes and ensuring you are well-prepared to address any legal challenges that might arise.

The use of these online resources should be coupled with ethical considerations. It's important to understand the limitations of online resources and avoid attempting to represent yourself in complex legal matters without professional assistance. The information found online is intended as an educational tool, assisting in your understanding of legal concepts, but it cannot replace the personalized guidance of an experienced entertainment lawyer who can fully assess your specific situation, provide targeted legal advice, and advocate on your behalf. Never rely solely on online resources to make critical legal decisions; always seek professional legal advice when facing significant legal challenges.

Remember to approach online resources critically. While many websites provide accurate information, others might contain outdated or misleading content. Always verify information from multiple sources and prioritize reputable websites and databases maintained by established legal organizations or reputable publishers. Pay attention to the date of publication, ensuring that the information is up-to-date, as laws and legal interpretations are constantly evolving. Consider the author's credentials and any potential biases, ensuring you are interpreting the information with a critical and informed perspective.

In summary, the online resources and legal databases described above offer a powerful arsenal of tools for entertainment professionals. They provide access to essential information, helping you navigate the complex legal landscape of the industry. However, these tools must be used responsibly and should never replace the counsel of an experienced entertainment lawyer. These resources enhance your legal knowledge, enabling you to communicate more effectively with your legal counsel, and fostering a more collaborative and productive attorney-client relationship. By combining professional legal advice with diligent research using these online tools, you can significantly strengthen your position within the entertainment industry, maximizing your opportunities while mitigating potential risks. This proactive approach to legal management ensures that your creative endeavors are protected, allowing you to focus your energy on your artistic pursuits with confidence and peace of mind. The strategic utilization of online resources and legal databases, combined with the guidance of a seasoned legal professional, forms the cornerstone of a successful and sustainable career in the ever-evolving world of entertainment.

Staying abreast of the ever-shifting sands of entertainment law is paramount for anyone navigating this dynamic industry. The legal landscape is constantly evolving, with new legislation, court rulings, and technological advancements impacting the rights and responsibilities of creators, athletes, and industry professionals. A passive approach, relying solely on past knowledge, can quickly leave you vulnerable to exploitation and missed opportunities. Therefore, developing a proactive strategy for staying updated on legal developments is crucial for long-term success.

One of the most effective methods is subscribing to reputable legal news sources and publications. These sources offer in-depth analysis and commentary on significant legal events, ensuring you receive timely updates on critical changes. Publications like

Billboard, *Variety*, *Hollywood Reporter*, and *The Wrap*, while not solely focused on legal matters, often feature articles covering important legal developments impacting the entertainment industry. These publications frequently interview legal experts, providing valuable insights into the implications of new laws and court decisions. By regularly reading these publications, you will develop a strong understanding of current trends and potential challenges. Supplementing these publications with dedicated legal newsletters and journals focused specifically on entertainment law will provide an even deeper dive into the specifics of relevant legislation and case law.

Beyond general news sources, engaging with professional organizations can provide access to exclusive insights and networking opportunities. Organizations such as the American Bar Association's Entertainment and Sports Law Section offer valuable resources, including conferences, webinars, and networking events. Attending these events provides an unparalleled opportunity to learn from leading legal experts, engage in discussions with peers, and stay updated on the latest legal trends. Many of these organizations also publish regular updates and newsletters specifically designed to inform members about important legal developments. These exclusive communications often provide early warnings of changes, giving you a significant advantage in anticipating and adapting to legal shifts. Active participation in these professional organizations can transform your understanding of the legal landscape, providing valuable context and fostering connections within the industry.

Direct engagement with your legal team is also invaluable. Regular communication with your lawyer is crucial, not only for addressing specific legal issues but also for staying informed about broad legal trends. Schedule regular check-ins, even if you don't have immediate concerns. These meetings should not only focus on active cases, but also delve into potential issues on the horizon. Your lawyer can provide insights into emerging legal challenges and suggest strategies for proactive compliance. A strong attorney-client relationship built on consistent communication is essential for navigating the complexities of entertainment law and maintaining a competitive edge. It is not simply a reactive relationship; it's about proactive partnership and preparedness.

Leveraging online resources and legal databases remains crucial. While we've previously discussed using resources like LexisNexis and Westlaw for in-depth legal research, consistent monitoring of these platforms is equally vital. Many of these databases offer customized alerts and news feeds, allowing you to receive notifications when new cases are filed or relevant legislation is enacted. Setting up these alerts for terms and areas relevant to your profession ensures you receive timely updates, enabling you to respond swiftly to any potential impact on your work. Regularly revisiting your searches using keywords relevant to your field also ensures you don't miss any significant developments. Think of this not merely as research but as ongoing legal surveillance, integral to your proactive strategy.

Furthermore, staying updated requires more than simply reading articles and attending conferences. Active engagement with the legal process involves understanding the implications of new developments and planning for their potential impact on your work. This proactive approach might involve reviewing and revising existing contracts to account for changes in legislation or updating your business practices to ensure compliance with new regulations. It may necessitate seeking clarification from your legal team on specific ambiguities or exploring new legal strategies to leverage emerging opportunities. Simply being informed isn't enough; it's how you utilize that information to protect yourself and advance your career.

Consider, for example, the ongoing evolution of intellectual property rights in the digital age. The advent of NFTs and the metaverse raises complex questions about ownership, licensing, and infringement. Staying abreast of legal decisions concerning NFTs requires a constant engagement with new information. The lines are constantly being redrawn, and ignoring these changes can lead to significant financial and legal repercussions. Similarly, the ongoing debate surrounding fair use and copyright protection in online content demands constant vigilance. The criteria for fair use can shift subtly with each court decision, necessitating careful monitoring of legal precedents.

Another critical area is the constantly shifting landscape of privacy laws. The impact of GDPR, CCPA, and other data privacy regulations affects how creators and athletes handle personal information and user data. Any failure to comply could result in substantial fines and reputational damage. Understanding these regulations demands not simply passively reading news reports, but actively reviewing your data practices and seeking legal advice on how to ensure compliance. This is not simply about adhering to the letter of the law; it's about understanding its spirit and applying it proactively to your work.

Similarly, the ever-changing world of endorsement deals and NIL (Name, Image, and Likeness) rights requires constant vigilance. New regulations are frequently enacted at the state and federal levels, impacting how athletes and celebrities can monetize their personal brands. Staying informed requires scrutinizing these regulations and consulting with your legal team to ensure your endorsement agreements are compliant and maximize your financial opportunities while mitigating any risks. A single oversight could lead to costly litigation or damage to your reputation.

Therefore, staying informed is not a one-time task but an ongoing process. It requires a multi-faceted approach that includes subscribing to legal news sources, networking with industry professionals, maintaining close communication with your legal team, and actively monitoring online resources and databases. This proactive approach is not merely about avoiding legal trouble; it's about strategically positioning yourself for success in the dynamic world of entertainment law. By actively seeking out new information, engaging with it critically, and seeking expert advice when needed, you can build a strong foundation for a successful and sustainable career, empowering you to navigate the complex legal landscape with confidence and foresight. The investment in time and resources dedicated to staying updated will be far outweighed by the protection and opportunities it generates, ensuring your artistic endeavors are not only protected but also thrive in the ever-changing legal environment.

Back Matter

First and foremost, I extend my deepest gratitude to the countless artists, athletes, and industry professionals whose journeys have enriched my understanding of the entertainment and sports legal landscape. Your experiences, both triumphs and challenges, have shaped this book and provided invaluable insights into the practical application of legal principles. I am particularly indebted to those who generously shared their stories and expertise, offering candid perspectives that illuminate the complexities of navigating this dynamic field.

My sincere thanks also go to my colleagues at [Law Firm Name], whose collective wisdom and unwavering support have been instrumental in the development of this work. Their insights, both legal and practical, have significantly enhanced the accuracy and clarity of the information presented. A special acknowledgment to [Name of colleague], whose meticulous editing and unwavering dedication brought this project to fruition.

I also wish to express my gratitude to my family and friends for their patience and understanding during the demanding process of writing this book. Their unwavering support provided the necessary balance and encouragement to complete this endeavor.

This glossary defines key legal terms used throughout the book. Understanding these terms is essential for navigating the complexities of entertainment and sports law. For a more comprehensive understanding, it is recommended to consult legal dictionaries and specialized resources.

Copyright: The exclusive legal right, given to the originator of a creative work, to print, publish, perform, film, or record the work and to authorize others to do the same.

Trademark: A symbol, design, or phrase legally registered to represent a company or product.

Patent: Exclusive rights granted for an invention, allowing the patent holder to exclude others from making, using, or selling the invention.

Right of Publicity: The legal right of an individual to control the commercial use of their name, image, likeness, and other aspects of their persona.

Work for Hire: A work created by an employee within the scope of their employment, where copyright ownership belongs to the employer.

Fair Use: A legal doctrine that permits limited use of copyrighted material without acquiring permission from the rights holders, for purposes such as criticism, commentary, news reporting, teaching, scholarship, or research.

Indemnity: A contractual obligation to compensate another party for losses or damages.

Force Majeure: An unforeseen event, such as a natural disaster or war, that prevents the performance of a contract.

NIL (Name, Image, and Likeness): The right of an individual, particularly student-athletes, to profit from the use of their name, image, and likeness.

Digital Rights Management (DRM): Technologies used to control access to digital content and prevent unauthorized copying or distribution.

About the Author

Alander Pulliam is an american film producer,author, actor, writer, business owner and investor. Running for President of the United States 2024. Forming many corporations throughout his career, spending many years in the major label spectrum, he was responsible for several successes in the music industry. In 2015, Alander Pulliam was chosen as one of the Top 25 Marketing Innovators in the World. Serving as an Executive in the Entertainment Industry. Working on TV Shows and Movies, from Producing to Investing. He has made his mark in the industry. Now developing the ABM Streams APP which allows anyone to make money streaming anything and everything that can be streamed. Alander Pulliam is continuing to develop several empires throughout the world of Entertainment. Helping others establish themselves. Working with many of today's artist along with several of the most successful artist coming on the scene in the mid 2000's era of music. Serving as a major label executive, he gradually moved into the TV and Film spectrum.

About the Publisher

Alander Pulliam is an accomplished American film producer, author, actor, writer, entrepreneur, and investor. He is currently a candidate for President of the United States in the 2024 election. Throughout his career, he has founded numerous corporations and has extensive experience within the major label music industry, where he contributed to several notable successes.

www.ingramcontent.com/pod-product-compliance
Lightning Source LLC
LaVergne TN
LVHW090308210926
848480LV00001B/176